Abigail E. Weeks
Memorial Library
Union College

presented to the Students
by

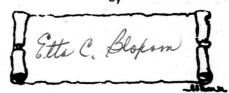

Etta C. Blossom

IN
HAWTHORNE'S
SHADOW

IN

HAWTHORNE'S SHADOW

AMERICAN ROMANCE FROM MELVILLE TO MAILER

Samuel Chase Coale

THE UNIVERSITY PRESS OF KENTUCKY

Copyright © 1985 by The University Press of Kentucky

Scholarly publisher for the Commonwealth,
serving Bellarmine College, Berea College, Centre
College of Kentucky, Eastern Kentucky University,
The Filson Club, Georgetown College, Kentucky
Historical Society, Kentucky State University,
Morehead State University, Murray State University,
Northern Kentucky University, Transylvania University,
University of Kentucky, University of Louisville,
and Western Kentucky University.

Editorial and Sales Offices: Lexington, Kentucky 40506-0024

Library of Congress Cataloging in Publication Data

Coale, Samuel.
    In Hawthorne's shadow.

    Bibliography: p.
    Includes index.
    1. American fiction—History and criticism.
2. Hawthorne, Nathaniel, 1804-1864—Influence.
3. Romanticism—United States. I. Title.
PS374.H35C6 1985   813'.009'145   84-25792
ISBN 0-8131-1545-0

CONTENTS

To Gray and Sammy—
"A Flood of Sunshine"

PREFACE

HOW does one become obsessed or at the very least fascinated with certain writers and certain fictions? For me it began with a game of cards in my grandmother's green-gabled house in New Haven when I was a child. The game was "Authors," and I remember gazing fixedly at a certain dark and solemn face with dark mustache and darker eyes, staring back at me from the face of the card. Beneath the face was written, "Nathaniel Hawthorne, author of *The Scarlet Letter*." I tried to imagine how a letter that you would mail could possibly be scarlet, unless of course it was written in blood. I never forgot that brooding face.

A native New Englander, I began picking up bits and pieces about Hawthorne and his work through school. When I first read *The Scarlet Letter* (as a junior in high school?) I found it cumbersome, fascinating, and grim—and loved it. At Trinity College in Hartford, Paul Smith led me through its grim corridors again. But it was Hyatt Waggoner at Brown University, where I arrived in 1965 as a naive and petrified graduate student (I'd applied to other graduate and law schools, attended a law class, hated it, spotted the Brown American Civilization flier pinned to the wall outside the men's room in the bowels of the Trinity English Department, and applied) who confirmed Hawthorne's mastery of style and the dark vision, which I already believed in. The darkness seems to be always with me: Halloween superstitions, autumn nights in Vermont towns, decaying New England seaports, lofty old houses. Hyatt Waggoner convinced me of the interpenetration of literature and life, of the personal commitment one must make to both in order to make each worthwhile.

That's the most of it. I've been writing this book, in my head at least, for years: bits and pieces here and there, articles on Kosinski, Frost, Faulkner played off against the unrelenting shadow of our first great American romancer. And if Hawthorne was that, then certainly some of his ideas and his literary form could be extended down to our own day, like the shadow of the past, into contemporary American fiction, however furtive, however fugitive. Conversations with writers as disperate as John

Cheever and Anthony Burgess contributed to my pursuit, along with hints from John Gardner and Updike's 1979 address at the American Academy of Arts and Letters.

I hope to show that American romance is far more than a mere disguise for traditional allegory, as some critics of the term have suggested, that it embodies most of the great cultural and moral questions of American society. Romance also reveals the conflicts between the American notions of history and myth that continue to plague us. In any case it has been both delightful and despairing work—Manichean to the end! And even now the writing hasn't eradicated that dark face on that dark card of more than thirty years ago. It continues to burn red hot, and I'll pursue it still.

Without the time to write, nothing could be written. Therefore I'm very grateful for my Fellowship for College Teachers, 1981-1982, from the National Endowment for the Humanities, along with my spring sabbatical from Wheaton College in 1984 and the Andrew W. Mellon Grant Fellowship for the Wheaton College Faculty Development Program, administered by Wheaton, for September through December 1981.

Without the boost of such editors as James Dean Young, Arlin Turner, Robert G. Collins, Robert A. Morace, and Kathryn Van Spanckeren, who were responsible for the publication of articles on Joan Didion, William Styron, Harold Frederic and Nathaniel Hawthorne, John Cheever, and John Gardner, I might not have been able to sustain the "long haul" of getting this book written. I want to thank them, their journals, and their publishers (which include *Critique: Studies in Modern Fiction*, *American Literature*, G. K. Hall, and Southern Illinois University Press) for permission to reprint in revised form those earlier articles. And I would also like to thank *Essays in Literature* and *The Nathaniel Hawthorne Journal* for publishing my articles on *The Marble Faun* and Hawthorne's *American Notebooks*.

Neal Smith and Tom Woodson at Ohio State University were both helpful and generous when I flew to Columbus to examine Hawthorne's letters in June 1982. Every morning in that third-floor office hidden away in the Ohio State University Library, they would help me sort out notes, addenda, references, and biographical information. At all times they were enthusiastic and a delight to be with.

Without the speedy and forever cheerful typing of Alice Peterson at

Wheaton, none of this would ever have seen the light of day but would have remained forever in Hawthorne's shadow. She transferred all my paragraphs and chapters and footnotes onto the computer as quickly as I supplied them from my ancient portable typewriter—not even electric!— at home.

And I should mention Gray Coale, who helped insulate me from the rest of the world so that my own obsessions and ideas could both fester and flower. And at day's end, as I staggered out of my study, she would engineer sweet reunions between us, son Sam, Mavro the black lab, and Tanqueray. Such devotion cannot go unrewarded. And when I returned from a jaunt in India with Trinity Square Repertory Company, Gray presented me with a complete new study, designed by friend Bob Pierce. Now there's a vote of confidence!

And one final sweeping "thank you" to so many of my friends with whom I talked and debated, to whom I wrote and sent bits and pieces of ideas and plans: to Hyatt Waggoner, who suggested what I should do in arranging the final manuscript (as always his prophecies proved correct); to poet-playwright Jim Schevill, critic Robert Morace, poet Craig Challender; to George Hunt, who invited me to speak on Cheever and Hawthorne at LeMoyne College in Syracuse and to talk again with Cheever during his reading and visit there; to Curtis Dahl, Ed Briggs, Toni Oliviero, and Dick Pearce at Wheaton; to members of USIA, who allowed me to travel to Poland, Czechoslovakia, Pakistan, and Sweden to try out my ideas and thoughts; to Maurice Dolbier, literary editor of the *Providence Journal*, who helped me immensely, in writing book reviews, to change my style from the stolid gray prose of graduate school to the livelier, more fluid writing (I hope) of personal commitment and enthusiasm; to the students I met in Poland and Czechoslovakia, to Andrzej and Iva and Jurek; to all these and more, I am forever grateful, and if I have forgotten anyone—and I'm certain I have over the many years of this project—I hope their encouragement and interest in this book will remain undaunted.

The shadow lingers, but I hope I've grappled with a vital part of it and its long reaches. That has given me the most pleasure.

ONE

Hawthorne's Shadow

"THERE is a fund of evil in every human heart, which may remain latent, perhaps through the whole of life; but circumstances may arouse it to activity."[1] The vision of that heart of darkness, which Nathaniel Hawthorne described in 1836, would never change in his subsequent fiction. It lies at the base of all his speculations and explorations from seventeenth-century Boston to nineteenth-century Rome, from ancient house to pastoral masquerade, from darker forests to poisoned gardens. And that evil heart was born within a grim, imprisoning world: "The world is so sad and solemn, that things meant in jest are liable, by an overpowering influence, to become dreadful earnest; gaily dressed fantasies turning to ghostly and black-clad images of themselves."[2] Overpowering influences assaulted Hawthorne from within and from without, and conjured up that shadow that haunts his fiction and his journals.

The radical dualism in Hawthorne's mind—that essential vision of the separateness and mysterious doubling of all things—where did it spring from? Psychological analyses build upon the absent father, the reclusive mother, the New England temperament. The Puritans, fled to a wilderness where the devil's initiates lurked behind every tree, created their Calvinistic world free from European social circumferences that might have tempered their rigid outlook. New England winters confronted New England summers, a vivid contrast that Henry Adams thought helped to mold his own attitudes. Lévi Straus, in reducing all myths to binomial formulations, viewed the human brain as divided in half, a dualism directly related to the physiological functions of the mind. And Cartesian vortices split a world in two, turning the mind's landscape into a crossroads of metaphysical battles between realities, entirely questioning the single mind's relation to the external world. "America is . . . one of the countries where the precepts of Descartes are least studied and are best applied," Alexis de Tocqueville noted.[3] And even the novel, our distinctly modern art form, reveals this dualism at its very core. As William Barrett suggests, "It shows the deepest traits of the Cartesian epoch: Its history is a long tug-of-war between the subjective and objective poles of experience."[4] From these and other sources may spring the radical dualism in Hawthorne's vision. And from Hawthorne springs much of the vision of a continuing American tradition in the novel.

Hawthorne's haunted mind viewed a physically visible world as dark and inscrutable. His mind, attracted to cemeteries, crypts, caverns, and dark forests, displayed "a passive sensibility, but no active strength; when the imagination is a mirror, imparting vividness to all ideas, without the power of selecting or controlling them," one becomes a kind of victim to a hypnagogic state, seduced and arrested by dark phantoms. To Hawthorne, the world of matter remained impenetrable, a place of inert material devoid of moral or religious values. As Harold Bloom described nature from Wordsworth's perspective, that world remained "the hard phenomenal otherness that opposes itself to all we have made and marred."[5] Hawthorne's notebooks attest over and over again to this shock of recognition in that one repeated emblematic scene: the single soul—Hawthorne—confronting dark matter, at once attracted and repelled and always oppressed by it.

The appearances of a dark world led Hawthorne on to darker thoughts. He responded to such mystery, to "the rude contact of some actual circumstance," in a manner that threatened whatever moral values he wished to uphold. Such a physical space was not to be trusted; it vitiated any moral imagination and conjured up images of an imprisoning gothic past or a nihilistic, all-too-mortal future. And yet the moral imagination he did possess spawned only thin allegories, an other-worldliness that struck him as purely mental and ultimately as threatening as the world of matter. Facts seemed too substantial; he felt himself at the mercy of them; the darker, the more obeisant. Values and moral judgments seemed too insubstantial; he felt imprisoned in a fantastic world that left him in ethereal straits, isolated and remote.

Calculatedly, painstakingly he sought a solution, a middle ground, the "neutral territory" of his tales and romances. He found it in "The Custom-House," "somewhere between the real world and fairy-land, where the Actual and the Imaginary may meet, and each imbue itself with the nature of the other." Mirrors, reflections, the surfaces of streams and puddles supplied him with the images of the place he needed. His letters, notebooks, and fiction constantly conjure up his mind's favored landscape, at once trying to resolve the age-old clash between fact and value, and creating the form and fabric of his romances. His would be an inner world to explore, projected onto the screen of the outer world that he had himself sufficiently distanced and shaded so as to strike a balance he rarely achieved.

The battle between mind and matter, moral imagination and dark void, spirit and substance provides the basic pattern of Hawthorne's fiction. At times spirit can transform substance; human sympathies or the recognition of mutual guilts and needs can override the gloom of the dark world. At other times substance easily overrides spirit, and men and women are doomed to past curses and deeds, present isolation, Puritan superstitions, and a will-less spiritual torpor that paralyzes their actions. Still, in other instances substance may be able to transform the spirit, as if good were being resurrected out of evil, and characters seem "enriched by poverty, developed by sorrow," as the knowledge of death mysteriously contributes to the growth of love. Each of these confrontations, however, appears in nearly all the romances, leaving the reader—and Hawthorne—as uneasy and as uncertain as if none of them had ever actually happened. And the landscape of "reality" hovers elusively between light and shadow, revealed and obscured, veil leading on only to other veils.

In "Graves and Goblins" Hawthorne's narrator is a ghost who describes the "essence" of his vision as distinctly ghostly and his "conceptions," written in language and therefore tainted and untrue, as "earth-clogged," "gross," and "heavy." He feels as though his own "ethereal spirit" is barely perceptible, "glimmering along the dull train of words." The "earth-dulled soul" plots its wary course but knows only ultimate defeat in the world and the word that imprison it. Such an outlook suggests the Manichean shape of Hawthorne's shadow.

Hawthorne was no heretic in the sense of practicing some kind of fire-worship or arcane rites, but a Manichean sensibility, "a deep urge to flee the world,"[6] does inform the vision that propels him. It suggests the "overpowering influences" on his self and his art. Many critics have detected this strain in American literature, as described for instance by Leo Marx: "Our writers, instead of being concerned with social verisimilitude, with manners and customs, have fashioned their own kind of melodramatic, Manichean, all-questioning fable, romance, or idyll, in which they carry us, in a bold leap, beyond everyday social experience into an abstract realm of morality and metaphysics."[7] Richard Chase, Daniel

Hoffman, Lionel Trilling, Michael Bell, William Shurr, to mention only a few, would agree wholeheartedly with this general assessment. The historical background also shadows much of Hawthorne's vision. As Hoffman maintains, "Puritanism was perhaps as close to the Manichean as any Christian sect has come; the Power of Evil was acknowledged with the same fervor as the Power of Light. Indeed, it was a faith more pessimistic than that of the ancient dualists, for it made no provision for the goodness of man."[8] In fact, Hawthorne was mesmerized by "that Manichean pre-possession with the dark side of man's nature which [he] presents as the special sin of the Puritans."[9] Perhaps that fascination with man's dark side suggests that "gothic quest for renewed contact with the numinous, the supernatural, the occult forces in the universe" which may lead ultimately "into the moral self."[10] In any case, Hawthorne's Manichean vision provides the basis for his description of the American romance, and that description, in his prefaces and elsewhere, provides the best introduction to, if not the ultimate source of, American romance as we know and understand it. Hawthorne's very theory of the romance as "radically dualistic in its separation of fancy and reason, imagination and actuality"[11] is itself a major indication of his Manichean outlook.

To the Manichean mind the world remains a prison, created in a demonic cosmos by someone other than God, some Demiurge or evil Jehovah sprung from the hosts of darkness. In that prison man languishes, a prisoner of his own flesh and desires. He often seems possessed by others, by some dark fate not of his making, and whatever spirit lingers and flickers within him, it can only view itself as violently separated from all that surrounds it. The senses lie; the darkness of the world entraps; language kills. The only hope of rescue is in some "gnosis," some wisdom buried deep within the cosmos that resides in the spirit and seeks deliverance. Most Manicheans, in contrast to Christians, took delight in their own subversive allegories, in which the snake in Eden and the mark of Cain symbolized their heroes, the outcasts from the Christian God's and the Jewish Jehovah's infernal constructs. Historians suggest that Manicheism failed as a religion because it was too passive and too antisocial, judgments one could easily make about Hawthorne's art and person.

Hawthorne looked out upon a dark, imprisoning world. He also looked within to a soul imprisoned and isolated. The world oppressed the self, which in turn oppressed the soul, the inner spirit. The ultimate horror, however, was the perception of an inner soul and an outer world both of which were dark and impenetrable, separated only by the shifting veils of the self's "personality," which was shaped by both inner and outer spheres but which remained too tenuous to grasp. Veils appear throughout Hawthorne's fiction—the veils of outer roles, language, conceptual imaginings, images, names. But what remains is the sense that the dark soul and the dark world can obliterate each other. There can be no rescue except in that "neutral territory" where ghosts prowl and veils can be dropped and lifted at will. That notion of irreconcilable conflict, of insoluble contradiction and polarization at the center of things, underlies Hawthorne's Manichean vision. And as Daniel Schneider makes clear, "The warring symbols of the Manicheans tie man firmly to actual contradictions in his experience . . . his ineluctable bondage to the conditions of the corporeal world and to recognize that the ideal must never masquerade as the final truth."[12]

Hawthorne's is no Manichean mandate. He does not force a character to choose, in the old heresy's way, between ascetic withdrawal and a kind of demonic libertinism, although Hawthorne is drawn irrevocably to each in his psychological alternations between withdrawal and the intellectual "libertinism" of Paul Pry. His darker heroines' physical yearnings suggest libertinism of another order. Rather, Hawthorne sees the world, both inner and outer, as Manichean mystery, that place of irreconcilable conflict beyond the kind of paradox that generates notions of Emersonian compensation. Opposition breeds further opposition; contradiction spawns further contradiction. What Emerson called the bipolarity of unity becomes in Hawthorne's view a unity of ultimate bipolarities, or as Richard Chase described it, a "unity *in* disunity."[13] Hawthorne radicalized the dualisms implicit in Christianity beyond the Christian faith in accommodation and union, just as the century around him, imbued with its vision of rampant materialism, sought refuge in veils of sentimentality or nihilistic prophecies. Perhaps a fellow writer, John Updike, has grasped this perspective most gracefully:

> From Christianity Hawthorne accepted the dualism, and made it more radical still. Orthodox doctrine bridges matter and spirit with a scandalous Incarnation, Jesus Christ. In Hawthorne, matter verges upon being evil; virtue, upon being insubstantial. . . . The haunted is a degenerate form of the sacred. . . . The axis of Earth-flesh-blood

versus Heaven-mind-spirit with a little rotation becomes that of
the world versus the self. In this opposition the self fights submergence. . . . *The Blithedale Romance* . . . in its smallest details conveys Hawthorne's instinctive tenet that matter and spirit are inevitably at war.[14]

The publisher Evert A. Duyckinck summed it up best in a letter to his
wife on August 9, 1850: "Hawthorne is a fine *ghost* in a case of *iron*"[15]
(italics mine).

'We need not review the history of romanticism," Wylie Sypher asserts,
"to show how Schopenhauer spoke for all the romantics by reaffirming
the self against the *res extensa*, asserting that the world is *my* idea of the
world, a creation of my own will and idea."[16] And in this self Hawthorne, in his preface to *The Snow Image*, identified his Manichean landscape and the source of his theory of psychological romance, "burrow-
ing . . . into the depths of our common nature" at the expense of "external habits": "These things hide the man, instead of displaying him."

The essential experience of the Manichean soul, despite Hawthorne's
momentary enchantments, is his central isolation and his disconnection
from all others. The psyche lies at the heart of the investigation, the center
of the cosmic drama. Society (as Hawthorne pointed out in his preface
to *The House of the Seven Gables*) and social manners are the subjects for
the novelist. To call oneself a romancer is to proclaim the psychic territory of one's exploits. Truth reveals a Manichean battleground deep
within the soul, and as such it cannot help but subvert the more public
notions of American progress, enlightenment, "E Pluribus Unum," and
godlike self-reliance. Such a realm experiences guilts of all kind, and sins
in its guilt. The past haunts and devours, for it reveals what the battlefield in the soul already recognizes: that doom as unending contradiction
and conflict will not cease. From such a dark well, "the truth of the
human heart" can be known and the nature of man's motives and desires
be foretold.

Polarized selves in Hawthorne's tales and romances symbolize the psychic and moral forces in battle. Each character suggests one particular
psychological facet, state, or condition. No wonder allegory appealed to
Hawthorne. He used it to reflect and refract the Manichean vision, because
of both allegory's own Manichean postures and the compulsive, obsessive
psychologies of characters caught up in their allegorical pursuits. The

observer, the artist, the materialist, the lover battle it out amidst the dark shadows and fragile lights. Idyllic and demonic states square off in a dreamlike world which Faulkner described as reflecting "the human heart in conflict with itself."

The upshot of the experiment? Not the usual successful rescue of most traditional romances, with St. George surviving his perilous journey, overcoming a dark night of the soul, slaying the evil dragon, and carrying off the innocent maiden in heroic triumph. Hawthorne describes failed rescues, further recognitions of infinite separations, from paralysis to abandonment to death. The most we can expect is the dark equilibrium of *The Scarlet Letter*, so perfectly embodied that every ray of light casts its complementing shadow, but with each opposite shadowed by a "dark necessity." The worst reveals the mechanistic sexual jealousies of *The Blithedale Romance*, the skull beneath the skin, and the shrill, unresolved duel between Hilda and the abyss of Rome in *The Marble Faun*. An ultimate aloneness, anathema to traditional romance, haunts the Manichean mysteries of Hawthorne's romances.

Perhaps the only "reconciliation" that can occur in Hawthorne's fictional world is that between Hawthorne's vision of isolation—his "public" image as a secret shadow behind the veils of prefaces—and the reader's acknowledgment of and immersion in it. Our own self-consciousness is invaded by Hawthorne's consciousness of the separate self, as if the text were one more dark veil we should slip through to find ourselves in the poisoned garden of Hawthorne's psyche and our own. And perhaps such a blasted union confirms once again Hawthorne's Manichean sensibility, for we have only exchanged one prison for another, and find ourselves as darkly entrapped in a demonic cosmos as we may have suspected before.

"All things swim and glitter," Emerson wrote in "Experience" (1844). "Our life is not so much threatened as our perception. Ghostlike we glide through nature, and should not know our place again." In "Alice Doane's Appeal" (1835) Hawthorne not only recognizes the truth of Emerson's statement, which is so close to his own perception of things, but self-consciously reveals the various forms and techniques of his romance in the process. Writing in his notebooks in 1835 about a writer writing a tale, Hawthorne suggested, "It might shadow forth his own fate—he having made himself one of the personages."[17] The statement seems appropriate to Alice's appeal.

If Hawthorne started out in "Alice Doane's Appeal" "to make one's

own reflection in a mirror the subject of the story,"[18] that process of
doubling and the polarization of the self, he certainly succeeded. Incest,
fratricide, parricide, and the romancer's art itself reflect one another as
mirror images of "a hateful sympathy in our secret souls." The "lonely
sufficiency to each other" between Alice and Leonard Doane; the recognition of similarities that Doane discovers in the mysterious Walter Brome,
"like joint possessors of an individual nature, which could not become
wholly the property of one, unless by the extinction of the other"; the
eerie similarities between Doane's murder of Brome and the death of his
(their) father, as he shudders "with a deeper sense of some unutterable
crime"; the recognition of twin brothers, an acknowledged cunning device
of the wizard whom the reader is meant to discover as the perpetrator
of the entire dark scenario ("all the incidents were results of the machinations of the wizard"); the similarities between the wizard's plot and the
narrator's in his attempt to set the nerves of his two lady listeners trembling on top of Gallows Hill; the gathering of ghosts in the graveyard
"swept . . . into one indistinguishable cloud together"—all are implicated
in that "hateful sympathy." As Sharon Cameron suggests, "No one is
innocent. Any single action—indeed, any single being—has its counter-
part in an antithetical being, or an antithetical feeling and action."[19]
Each individual soul is swept up into the enveloping drama of the past,
of conflicting guilts, of patterns of separation and murder so bloodthirstily
conjured up that none can escape. And when "the wanderers from old
witch times" head back to town, the narrator recognizes that such a stain
can never be eradicated from any of us, "while the human heart has one
infirmity that may result in crime." "There is a fund of evil in every
human heart . . . circumstances may arouse it to activity."

In order to subvert the daylit world and undermine its habitual sway
over us, the romancer carefully creates his remoter setting, his "neutral
territory" where his Manichean mysteries may proceed. Whether it be
a theatre, a daydream, or a fairy precinct, the intent is the same: a shadowy
place where emanations of a dark past and darker moods, of isolation
and ghostlike happenings can enjoy complete sovereignty. "This haunted
height" of Gallows Hill provides such a setting here. There is even a
physical curse on the land, the wood-wax which smothers the hill and
prevents grass from growing. Ghosts in graveyards are transformed with
"fiendish lineaments"; "indistinctness" conjures up further "horror,"
as the narrator "plunged into my imagination for a blacker horror, and

a deeper woe, and pictured the scaffold—." The "murdered man" wears "a look of evil" in death. Ice reflects, congeals, kills. And after the splendid description of "a frigid glory," the narrator reveals his romancer's art: "By this fantastic piece of description, and more in the same style, I intended to throw a ghostly glimmer round the reader, so that his imagination might view the town through a medium that should take off its every day aspect, and make it a proper theatre for so wild a scene as the final one." Here indeed is the medium, the theatre, for Hawthorne's art, whether it be found in seventeenth-century Boston, in an ancient house with seven gables, in a remote pastoral retreat, or in the sordid, deathlike air of Rome. It is the touchstone of the American romance, this "fantastic" setting which the romancer must first create before peopling it with his "villains" and "viler wretches." One thinks of similar scenes which begin Cheever's novels, Oates's *Bellefleur*, Faulkner's *Absalom, Absalom!*, the mysterious Sambuco in Styron's *Set This House on Fire*, or the dark interior of the pyramid of Khufu in Mailer's *Ancient Evenings*.

Hawthorne relies on "historic influence" and the "shadowy past" of the "witchcraft delusion" to provide his "daydream and yet a fact" with ballast, a kind of anchoring in the real demonic circumstances of the past. Historical creatures parade in his graveyard: Cotton Mather appears on horseback, "the one blood-thirsty man, in whom were concentrated those vices of spirit and errors of opinion, that sufficed to madden the whole surrounding multitude." History lends a kind of credence that outright allegory and surrender to the hypnagogic state cannot. It lends that "authenticity of outline" to the "license to invent" that Hawthorne describes so well in "The Custom-House." And it also reveals Hawthorne's holding to the "real world" of fact and incident, one he could not shake and that he needed to ground his "neutral territory" upon a solid foundation, however much he also needed to undermine and transform it into his Manichean morality play.

The romancer, to lure the reader into his dark art, must create a spell. Faulkner's winding sentences, Cheever's dark corners, Oates's breathless prose, and Didion's chantlike style of incantation work toward that end. In "Alice Doane's Appeal" the narrator struggles to hold the ladies' attention, conjuring up images of the town long ago, the "veil of deep forest," that time when the "prince of hell held sway." When the ladies begin to laugh, the narrator keeps "an awful solemnity of visage, being indeed a little piqued," and goes on to call up a vision of Gallows Hill in his romancer's medium to set their nerves trembling once and for all: "I called back hoar antiquity, and bade my companions imagine an ancient multitude of people." The setting and time of day provide the necessary ambience: "Twilight over the landscape was congenial to the obscurity of time," as if the day were acting the romancer's role and giving the narrator the necessary distance and chiaroscuro "to realize and faintly communicate, the deep, unutterable loathing and horror." He presses on to the scaffold, knowing he has them in his wizard's clutches, for "I had reached the seldom trodden places of their hearts, and found the well-spring of their tears," that place where Mather, the dead, the past, and thoughts of murder and revenge congregate forever.

Melancholy provides the appropriate mood of the spell, just as the lengthening sentences acquire a hypnotic, lulling quality, as "we threw, in imagination a veil of deep forest over the land." Roofs and spires in the imagined ancient village appear "peaked," "projecting," "pointing," the repeated consonant adding to the incantation, just as the repetition of the name "Pyncheon" in the first paragraph of *The House of the Seven Gables* acquires a similar chantlike intensity. The lengthening string of clauses draws out the enveloping veil of the romancer's medium, a technique Faulkner would make entirely his own and bring to its ultimate spell-binding authority. And over all that "atmospheric medium" of "strange enchantment," the play of light and shadow illuminates and obscures the players and the play, emphasizing again the Manichean polarities in Hawthorne's art and his mingling the marvelous with the strange tale to bring out its chillier, gothic presences.

Throughout the tale the narrator remains visible as he makes connections, speculates, signifies, ties up loose ends, offers undigested shards of exposition to move, in this case, from set piece to set piece, from "frigid glory" to Doane's belabored conversations with the wizard. We see the narrator brooding on the matter at hand, much in the manner we imagine Hawthorne doing. We watch him exploring his own materials as Cheever and Updike do, as Joan Didion does in her latest novel, *Democracy*. Here too we recognize both the separation between narrator and tale and his/her hypnotic fascination with it. The narrator calls back and summons his "ghostly glimmer" to achieve the romancer's medium he wants. Other tales our narrator tells us he burned, but not this one, since he admits to being "driven by stronger external motives, and a more passionate impulse within." What do Doane and Brome—twin sounds as well as twin brothers—tell us about the narrator, about ourselves? The narrator's own dark heart, a wizard's curse, fascinates us as much as the tale in which it is reflected.

The structure of most American romances reveals episodic tableaux, the kind of emblematic episodes that present the self in extremis—of the characters, of the narrator—and that illuminate the crux of the Manichean matter. The scaffold epiphanies of *The Scarlet Letter*, in which the characters are revealed from different angles and different perspectives as the narrative surrounds and transforms them, foreshadow these symbolic scenes. Cheever's art is built almost entirely of these emblematic epiphanies; Faulkner's art whirls around two or three great tableaux in *The Sound and the Fury*, in *Light in August*. The Manichean clashes in John Gardner's *The Sunlight Dialogues* (the title itself betrays the Manichean mysteries within) are writ large and stand out as clearly as Hawthorne's characters on the scaffold. And Didion's fictions surround epiphanic moments the reader tries to unravel and discover.

The fragments of "Alice Doane's Appeal" are carefully arranged. Exposition fills in between such stark scenes as the discovery of the murdered man in the snow, Doane's dream of his father's death, that splendidly chilling "frigid glory" of a world made romantic wizard's medium, transformed into ice, death, the lineaments of a dream, all "in their frozen hearts" shivering "at each other's presence." The seeming separation between present selves and the Puritan past, between men and women, victim and victimizer, the dead and the living, trembles as fragment leads on to fragment, implicating everyone in Alice's appeal to absolve her "from every stain," and releasing no one, until all these Manichean polarities are transformed into the raging conflicts within every single heart. In three early scenes the murdered man's face is slowly revealed by the stranger who discovers him, Leonard Doane, in his confession to the wizard, and by the narrator who finally identifies the corpse exactly.[20] And when that face becomes a twin's, the horror is complete. Identity implicates all of us.

Slowly, explicitly (and the explicitness of the tale, which suits our purposes of description here as an example of the romancer's art, relegates it to a minor niche in Hawthorne's work) Hawthorne moves from the outer world of Gallows Hill to the inner world of the self and finally into the ultimate interior of the human heart and soul, plunging us back into the present with his wish for a monument in "dark, funereal stone" to stand as the ultimate emblem of this dark quest. The setting inspires the melancholy mood which in turn feeds the narrator's imagination. That imagination produces his vision of "old witch times," and within that the strange tale itself can begin. When "the past had done all it could," we are left enclosed in the myriad reflections and polarizations of the tale and in that one human heart forever capable of crime.

Hawthorne laments the fact that no "lettered stone of later days" has been set on the hill "to assist the imagination in appealing to the heart." No scarlet letter has been discovered that will burn with symbolic heat into the observer's soul. Hawthorne seeks some hieroglyphic remembrance, at the same time recognizing that his own tale may be "too shadowy for language to portray." In his earlier notebooks he thought of words as "darksome veil[s] of mystery," as "poor rags and tatters of Babel" that are used solely "for purposes of explanation . . . for explaining outward acts and all sorts of external things, leaving the soul's life and action to explain itself in its own way." The Manichean clash between language as expression and as evasion haunts every American romancer, and the "dark, funereal stone" at the end of "Alice Doane's Appeal" corresponds to John Irwin's descriptions of hieroglyphics that remain indecipherable, the dead letters on the wall of a tomb.[21] Hawthorne's "gnosis" of the separate self and the human heart as dungeon and tomb would strike Melville as that "power of blackness" that he too strove to unleash and explore. As the narrator of "Graves and Goblins" fears, his vision, "heavy with the burthen of mortal language, that crushes all the finer intelligences of the soul," may reflect one more Manichean conflict between earthly alphabets and that ghostly glimmering of personal perception that cannot be resolved. Language provides not insight but one more "dark, funereal" veil. "Who has not been conscious of mysteries within his mind, mysteries of truth and reality, which will not wear the chains of language?"

One other aspect of the romancer's art is, of course, his use of allegory to convey spiritual and psychic states or conditions in insoluble conflict with one another. In many tales and romances the author sets up a clash between those characters who remain absolute in their allegorical faiths and those whose allegorical speculations rest solely on their shifting moods. The first are static and literally take Manichean sides. One thinks of Hilda in *The Marble Faun*, of Gardner's Sunlight Man, many of Updike's ministers, Mailer's demonic magi, and O'Connor's mad prophets. The second suggest forerunners to modern ambiguity, to the more fluid dreamlike states found in contemporary American fiction: the ambiguities of Hester, Zenobia and Miriam, Faulkner's beseiged and obsessed narrators, Didion's women, Cheever's suburban souls.

Several critics see Hawthorne himself as a writer torn between the use of allegory in its didactic, traditional way, based on Puritan typology, which constricts and petrifies much of his fictional manner, on the one hand, and on the other, in its broader, more psychological sense in which separate characters allegorize one another, based on the mood and idea of the particular moment, which can easily shift and change direction and which channels his fictional form into the fluid, more ambiguous processes of a dream. It seems to me, however, that the clash of allegorical stances in Hawthorne's fiction reflects the Manichean conflicts in his vision, and that F.O. Matthiessen's description of Hawthorne's "device of multiple choices" is in effect not merely a device but at the core of his Manichean landscape.[22] Both kinds of allegory are at work in confrontation with one another in his fiction, as they essentially were in his own mind. And he employs both of them to capture the essential contradictions and polarities of that fiction.

In Hawthorne's best tales, such as "My Kinsman, Major Molineux," "Young Goodman Brown," "Rappaccini's Daughter," and "Roger Malvin's Burial," to mention only a few, a "male monist," a believer in definite allegorical truths, confronts a world of Manichean mystery, of ambiguity and irreconcilable conflict. The "clashing monistic imperatives"[23] that he experiences he must resolve in an either/or manner, and the tale pursues his usually failed initiation into that world where he thinks specific resolutions must succeed. It is not surprising that many of these determined young men—and old—strew the landscape with the female victims of their allegorical pursuits: Beatrice Rappaccini, Georgiana, Esther in "Ethan Brand." Hawthorne skillfully plays off the male's sense of allegorical rightness with his own acknowledgment of ambiguity and duplicity.

Isolated individuals fall prey to their own obsessions, usually embodied in an object—a ribbon, a birthmark, a veil, a letter—and pass into that darker realm of possession in which the object itself appears to harbor strange powers that have taken over the individual's entire heart and mind. The self then enters that strange hypnagogic state in which it both projects its obsessions upon the world and causes them to create havoc, or is itself possessed by that very world it has created and is reduced to a mere function of it. That gothic "no-man's-land" between mind and matter, where meditation and water are not only wedded but mysteriously interpenetrate one another, provides the darkest heart of the American romance. Self-reflection, demonic doubling, narcissistic hypnosis, and cyclical patterns which repeat all of these create a claustrophobic circle of self that dissolves into a kind of "black hole," a place where several meanings or none at all battle it out on into an unrelenting Manichean maze. And the romancer himself—Hawthorne, Rappaccini, the Reverend Hooper—reproduces that Manichean dreamscape in his art, his poisoned garden, the dark world blocked from his veiled eyes, turns the self into an emblem of that world, and imprisons himself there, surrendered to its "gnosis," its demonically insoluble contradictions.

The romantic form has been described by many critics in many ways: as that dialectic between enchantment and disenchantment by Edgar Dryden; as Richard Brodhead's "actualization of fantasies" in a world far from the ordinary world of the novel; as allegory and dream; as Flannery O'Connor's "action of grace" in the devil's territory of social determinism; as John Lynen's moments on the scaffold of both the present and the eternal; as Patricia Carlson's "monistic dualism"; and as Joel Porte's stylized spell conjured up with guilt at its center to be transformed into some semblance of communion.[24] Implicit or explicit in these and other theories lie Hawthorne's Manichean tenets, the Manichean mystery lying between spirit and flesh, mind and matter, bounded by ghostly glimmerings, transpiring in remote settings, leaning toward incantation and the play of light and shadow, toward allegorical clashes, scaffold epiphanies, and historical shadows. Hawthorne's explanation of the romance, his descriptions of his own techniques and the forms he chose to use, laid the groundwork for the American romance that was to follow. If he did not create it out of whole cloth, he did discuss it in a deliberate fashion that both explained and excused the methods necessary to his art. As Joel Porte asserts, "Without Hawthorne there could be no firm theory of American romance."[25]

At Bowdoin College Hawthorne would have discovered an early "recipe" for his psychological romances in Horace Walpole's preface to the second edition of *The Castle of Otranto*. For Walpole, imagination and fancy initiate the action of ancient romance; the rules of nature and of psychological probability underlie modern romance. He wished "to blend the two kinds of romance, the ancient and the modern," thereby combining "the boundless realms of invention" with "a strict adherence to common life . . . in short, to make [the characters] think, speak, and act, as it might be supposed mere men and women would do in extraordinary positions."[26] Walpole's remarks clearly foreshadow Hawthorne's own descriptions of romance.

Hawthorne admired Charles Brockden Brown's fiction[27] and certainly must have been drawn to the various themes and techniques there that so many critics view as forerunners of his own. The Manichean clash between head and heart, between reason and emotion; the "fascination with second selves" and the consequent use of doubles and doubling in the narrative;[28] the "fascination of evil itself"[29] in a character such as Carwin in *Wieland*, himself an ancestor of Hawthorne's intellectual and scientific villains; "the problem of perception"[30] which has consistently haunted the best American romancers; and the murky elusive pursuit of man's hidden motives and his own psychological compulsions: these themes in Brown must have attracted Hawthorne at an early age. The often rhetorical, hypnagogic style with its alternative suggestions and redoublings also must have resonated in Hawthorne's mind, as well as Brown's conscious use of "the Gothic mode as a vehicle for psychological themes,"[31] a new twist to gothic fiction which heralded America's transformation of the form from the addled and clumsy ghosts of *Otranto* to the demons in Rosa Coldfield's imagination in *Absalom, Absalom!* and the incestuous ghosts in John Gardner's *Mickelsson's Ghosts*. Ultimately, as Donald A. Ringe makes clear, Brown "turned a limited kind of fiction—at once both sensational and aridly rationalistic—into an interesting vehicle for testing significant ideas."[32] Hawthorne would have delighted in that, and Brown certainly pointed him in the right direction in terms of creating and exploring an American brand of romance. Hawthorne's "neutral territory" barely survived his own Manichean mysteries, since he succeeded in achieving it in book-length form only once in all its dark glory.

Only in *The Scarlet Letter* did Hawthorne achieve that dark equilibrium, that study in essential unresolved opposites, that his Manichean vision embodied. Darkness wins, as if the consistent dualism of the romance were itself a demonic apparition. Ambiguities, doubts, the melancholy mood brooding in a gloomy iron world haunt the world of the book. Each image reveals its double-edged shadow, as if Hawthorne were perched at the apex of a great "A" and seeing everything double, like the legs of that "A." The "good" light of sunshine opposes the "bad" light of passion; a "good" darkness of fertility and growth suggests also the "bad" darkness of the forest and sexuality; the prison's iron door stands for order and structure, but for inhumanity and inflexibility, too. Public selves hide private sins, as public allegory affirms and denies personal passions. Hawthorne never loosens this stringent counterpoint, knowing finally that everything exists "only by contrast" and that "sweet moral blossoms" cast shadows that suggest blacker flowers of passion.

At the center stands and shimmers the scarlet "A," both a historically authentic object from the past, at least as created in "The Custom-House," and as a letter of language, the world and the word together, symbolizing social outrage and repression as well as personal passion and artistic expression. It remains a constant, though its meanings shift and change. The Puritans view it as a social stigma for adultery; to Hester it represents herself as unrepentant artist; the townspeople shift its significance from adultery to angel to able, as their view of Hester changes. The "A" represents Dimmesdale's secret shame, and to Hawthorne, for whom it burns as hot a "mystic symbol" as it does for Hester, it stands for his romance, his own design, his own artistic consciousness. The "A" suggests allegory, that actual phenomenon of human psychology and imagination in which the world and the word are nearly one, separate but equal. We allegorize the world, proclaim these signs as "realities," and then act accordingly. "In Adam's Fall, We Sinned All," proclaimed the New England Primer, thus suggesting that history itself can be seen as an allegory of the fall of man. And even America begins with an "A," that new Eden we named ourselves, using the inherited language of time past and thereby tainting the new world with perceptions and names from the old. America, once named, is no longer Eden.

All these "A's" lead to moral and allegorical contradictions. They undermine the rigid authoritarian structure of the Puritans, but the self is not thereby left free and feckless, saddled as it is, as Hawthorne was, with conflicting, irresolvable opposites. The essence of his art reflects Hester's embroidery on her badge of shame, the tendrils and curlicues that suggest infinite speculations and unending meanings. The multiplicity of meanings creates a gesture of ultimate freedom, but at the same time, as seen in Hawthorne's romance, it really suggests ultimate dread. Attempts are made to "relieve the darkening close," but it is the darkness that triumphs, the ultimate uncertainty of Manichean oppositions that lead on to further dualisms and battling polarities. A consistent gloom, the weight of sin, the tragic burden of self-doubt and querulous irresolutions produce that vision of a frail and fractured humanity which lurks at the heart of Hawthorne's romances and tales and which in the later ones eventually triumphs over any possibility of equilibrium.

Like the men in Hawthorne's great tales, Dimmesdale and Chillingworth transform themselves into "dark necessities," reducing their humanity to false confession and single-minded revenge. The women shift and grow, first seen as allegorical emblems of society—the passionate adulteress, the child of sin—then viewed in a more "socialized" manner as able human beings, as bastard become full-grown woman. Surely this is Hawthorne's vision of himself, almost as if Manichean matters were male obsessions, a cold product of Cartesian will and reason. Yet ambiguities cluster around even this stab at the dark.

The House of the Seven Gables constitutes Hawthorne's inversion of *The Scarlet Letter*. Romantic rescue will succeed here; Holgrave and Phoebe will wed, break the curse of Pyncheon and Maule, and the evil Judge will die. Hawthorne makes the latter apparent in his all too gleeful celebration of Judge Pyncheon's death. Domestic sentimentalities and the detail of the Dutch realist painters will combine to transform the "dark necessities" of *The Scarlet Letter* into cheerful resolutions.

It doesn't work, of course. Hepzibah and Clifford are far more believable as full-bodied and multidimensional characters than the flatter, one-dimensional Phoebe and Holgrave. The dark house triumphs over all of them in Hawthorne's evocation of the past, of hidden deeds, hidden chambers, ghostly processions, the angles of a gothic vision. Manichean contrasts he sets up to override, but they remain demonically present either from Clifford's arched window or in the organ grinder's grim assessment of a world controlled by the cyclical regularities of fate. As much as Hawthorne tries to dodge, blur, and muddy the stark dualisms of his tale, he cannot. Yes, "life is made up of marble and mud," and the "poetic insight is the gift of discerning in this sphere of strangely mingled elements, the beauty and the majesty" of things, but these strange elements are mysteriously "*compelled* to assume a garb so sordid" (italics mine). The compulsion remains Manichean and can also too easily assume the "iron countenance of fate" that dogs every Hawthornian device here. The Pyncheon Elm continues to whisper "unintelligible prophecies," darker intimations that *The House of the Seven Gables* can try to evade but cannot conceal. The families' feud, ruined flesh and ruined spirit, the past itself viewed inconsistently as aura, picturesque effect and fixed destiny remain unresolved.

One gets the feeling that after *The Scarlet Letter* Hawthorne's vision of the world as a dark, impenetrable place that undermines all else—ideas, hopes, reconciliations, even equilibrium—grew to haunt and overwhelm him. It was always there in his notebooks, his letters, hinted at in his prefaces. And his faith in his "neutral territory" seemed to evaporate, as if it had been only the most tenuous of beliefs.

The world of *The Blithedale Romance* subverts romance itself, turning everything into masquerade and veil, except for the hard realities of greed and lust, the machinations of Westervelt, whose vision of the world as a place of slaves and masters is never adequately challenged. Westervelt reflects Coverdale's demonic "Other," for both realize the brutalities of existence, however different their techniques and expression, and the iron hardness of America in mid-century. Coverdale pries and Westervelt manipulates; the would-be poet reflects only the sentimental mask of the outright patron of power and possession. As the magician controls the Veiled Lady, so Coverdale manipulates his would-be art, Hollingsworth manipulates Zenobia and Priscilla, Zenobia manipulates Priscilla. A world of vampirish wills undermines any pretensions to romance as a way of seeing, as a self-embodied imaginative vision.

The veils are stripped away from Coverdale the man, Coverdale the romancer, the idea of Blithedale itself, and the self-delusions of the other characters, and we stand unillusioned surveying the machinations of plot, as if the utmost Manichean faith were complete: the material world taints everything, the spirit is confined within and reduced to a twitch or a shiver, and a demonic cosmos, of which Westervelt (western world) is the chief disciple, remains a dark and ominous place. The sentimental and the demonic reflect one another, Manichean opposites as flip sides of the same dark coin. The moral vacuum swallows the whole, as the dark river swallows Zenobia, and the splendid tense equilibrium of *The Scarlet Letter*—the dark balance between the moral/aesthetic and the social/personal—shatters. Hawthorne has accomplished Ethan Brand's sin: "He was now a cold observer . . . converting men and women to be his puppets."

The Marble Faun attempts a remarkable leap of faith. If inversion marks the intentions of *The House of the Seven Gables* and subversion those of *The Blithedale Romance*, conversion seems to be the key here: out of darkness, light. Out of murder and betrayal, growth and rebirth. Darkest sin can educate and raise us up. But the Manichean mandate derails that impulse. Hawthorne's Rome kills. Like the darkness of fact itself, it paralyzes the romance, interrupts the narrative, spawns images of corruption, graves, the weight of the past, the abyss. And Hilda, shrill conventional Puritan that she is, cowers in her tower, withholds her sympathies from friends in need, upbraids Kenyon, and rejects possible conversion. The dead and the dove battle to a draw, so wide apart that no reconciliation is possible. Rome swallows the book, as Hilda tries to maintain her self-righteous posturing on its very edge. Such virulent opposites paralyze the text; we get static set pieces, gaping holes in the plot, ruminations on art and morality. It suggests Melville's paralysis in *The Confidence-Man* and Norman Mailer's gargantuan paralytic feat in *Ancient Evenings*.

The symbolic ambiguities of Beatrice Cenci and Cleopatra battle the allegorical certainties of Guido's Archangel and Praxiteles' Faun. Catholic humanities confront Puritan rigidities. Hawthorne's own picturesque aesthetic clashes with the allegorical aesthetic, the first built upon suggestive contrasts, the second demanding that one choose sunshine and transcend the gloom. The Manichean mixture of good and evil, irreducibly in conflict at the core of existence, produces complicated theories, symbolized in the Laocoon, of lost innocence and fortunate falls. The puritanical Hilda, in cahoots with Hawthorne's other intimations, demands that one choose between good and evil, or all else will be lost. This fascinating book lurches between allegorical descriptions and the recurring surfaces of a mythic dream, and each remains totally at odds with the other.

The riddle of the soul's growth remains the dark heart of Hawthorne's last published romance. Is it a loss or a gain? Does it even occur? Is a moral phase initiated or does one just move into another, deadlier phase? Is it a "mysterious process" or is it only "half imagined"? The riddle reflects Hawthorne's Manichean mysteries, and from such a polarized perspective no amount of allegory can resolve it.

The Marble Faun records no sudden "conversion" on Hawthorne's part to some gloomier, more melancholy vision. That was with him from the start. And slowly, book by book, that black inscrutable world caught up with him and reduced his entire romantic art to masquerade and subterfuge. Are we usually aware in actual experience of the dualisms between thought and sensation? Doesn't actual experience produce, however fleetingly, the sense of the oneness of things, the complete fullness of life, however grim or gleeful? And isn't after all the Manichean vision an intellectual concept, a way of describing the forces of evil in the world that a belief in a single God cannot do, unless that God shares Westervelt's plots and Rome's corruption? Perhaps. But for Hawthorne experience did create that separation of himself from the world, of himself from himself, as if alienation were a key ingredient in the entire development of the American romance.[33] And that vision produced the Manichean lineaments of his art and his life, an abstract reasonable notion, which he perhaps both lived and derided. As Michael Bell puts it, "The idea that abstract notions violate life is itself, after all, an abstract notion. An anti-allegorical allegory is still an allegory—self-reflexive but not expressive."[34] And allegory, itself a Manichean notion to some degree, haunted Hawthorne's art in all its many phases and discrepancies. If there was a fall in Hawthorne, it was never fortunate but existed from man's beginnings, a Manichean tenet of faith that he may not have believed utterly but which he constantly reproduced in his dark romances.

The darkness that overtook Hawthorne's later romances foreshadows similar patterns in the works of other American romancers—in Melville and Mailer, in Updike and Oates. Others work feverishly to resist such a demise, as in Cheever's last short novel and Gardner's almost willful wrenching of his material to transform Peter Mickelsson from doomed philosopher to loving human being. McCullers's art broke up as she approached the realm of fact, particularly in her last novel, *Clock Without Hands*, and in *The Reivers* Faulkner deliberately avoided his Doomsday Book and recreated a past rich in nostalgia and delight. Hawthorne anticipated all of them, and founded and articulated the American romance that they would wrestle with.

Hawthorne's last romances go nowhere. Fixated on strange objects—giant spiders, ancestral footsteps, magic elixirs, and, in *The Dolliver Romance*, the "enormous serpent, twining round a wooden post" that "looked like a kind of manichean idol"—he stalks them relentlessly, but they cast no moral shadow, no suggestion of possible significance that he can use to make the sense of his manuscript cohere. And the outright fumblings, the expressions of meaninglessness and unfocused ramblings, are painful to read: "I do not at present see in the least how this is to be wrought out." "The utmost pains must be taken with this incident to give it an air of reality; or else it must be quite removed out of the sphere of reality by an intensified atmosphere of Romance." "If I could but write one central scene . . . I have not yet struck the true key-note of this Romance." He is left with only threads "in the wild web of madness," feverish dreams, and asides to deepen this, explore that, recreate something else. And too often he throws up his hands: "Can nothing be done with this?" "Nonsense! No!" Idea and image no longer reflect one another; the "A" has been split in two. His material seems as intractable as the world of fact that haunted and betrayed him. Here is Manichean revenge with a vengeance, the romancer doomed to matter without the glimmer of spirit to transform it.

The ironies of the romance form as created by Hawthorne fuel further Manichean dilemmas. He originally created his "neutral territory" to evade or transcend that very Manichean world of impenetrable imprisoning matter which he experienced and perceived. And yet the romance he created reflected entirely that world and all its dualistic antagonisms, in effect reproducing the very Manichean world he had attempted to surmount. This irony, I think, embodies the great American theme of escape from and submission to that world of fact that appears again and again in the fantastic, overwrought romances of great American writers. Others since Hawthorne have grappled with the self-same Manichean polarities, discovering fleeting reconciliations but more often starker, irreconcilable contradictions. From Melville to Didion this pattern reasserts itself over and over again. Hawthorne stands at the forefront of that tradition in fiction. The shadow he cast from his own dark vision of himself and of his country continues into our own day, into our own age, when Manichean heresies may have become the reigning religions of contemporary times. The "evil in every human heart" and the "sad and solemn" world continue to haunt us, for Hawthorne's "black-clad images" conjure up Manichean visions in the American psyche that will not scare.

TWO

Melville to Mailer:
Manichean Manacles

WHETHER or not Nathaniel Hawthorne cast the shadow of an Apollo-nian icon upon the adoring young author Herman Melville, as Edwin Miller suggests, the facts do seem to indicate that Melville, struggling with his great book on whaling, "in effect rewrote the entire book after his meeting with Hawthorne. The manuscript, supposedly finished in August 1850, was not completed until September 1851."[1] Melville him-self acknowledged as much: "I feel that the Godhead is broken up like the bread at the Supper, and that we are the pieces . . . . Once you hugged the ugly Socrates because you saw the flame in the mouth, and heard the rushing of the demon—the familiar—and recognized the sand; for you have heard it in your own solitudes."[2] We don't know whether or how in Hawthorne's letters to Melville the older man greeted the younger one at the beginning of a great career, but to Melville in his review of *Mosses from an Old Manse*, the implication is clear. In Melville's eyes the older man impregnated the younger, bringing his long simmer-ing to a rapid boil: "Hawthorne was . . . a presence, perhaps a kind of shrine against which he tossed his ideas while his novel was broiling in hell-fire."[3] The perceptive Sophia watched "this growing man dash his tumultuous waves of thought up against Mr. Hawthorne's great, genial, comprehending silences."[4] In fact Melville's growing fascination with the terrors of a "dumb blankness" may also have come from his wooing of the veiled Salem recluse. The line of succession, however webbed and delicate, had begun.

Hawthorne's Manichean vision reaches its apogee in the nineteenth-century romance in Melville's *Moby-Dick*. The scaffold epiphanies, the rhetorical spell of language, the "neutral territory" of a whaler on metaphysical seas, the polarities of Ahab and Ishmael, Melville's own labyrinthine speculations on fate and fantasy, sign and symbol, the weighted shadow of the past—all these attributes of Hawthorne's romance appear in that great book. Melville's romance plunges beyond Hawthorne's "calmer" and more balanced dialectics between self and society, the individual and the often sentimental commitments of his age to home and hearth, and strikes out for bolder territory in the darker seas of Ahab's monomaniacal quest. So complete is Melville's vision, so total in its scope and power, and so great a place does that romance occupy in all of American literature, it is no wonder that it continues to reverberate in much contemporary fiction. In this regard comparisons between the fiction of Melville and Mailer require no great leap of faith but reveal a recognizable link between the American romance of the 1850s and those of the 1960s and 1970s.

In the next chapter we will see what became of Hawthorne's romance during the rise of realism in the 1870s and 1880s, how his Manichean allegorical vision surfaced in the naturalism of the last decade of the nineteenth century. After Melville, Hawthorne's shadow hovers at the edge of literary debate rather than in the center, even though the Manichean vision and allegorical structure do surface in the elaborate realistic novels of Henry James and often in a more muted manner in the bland fictions of William Dean Howells. In any case, with the "romantic revival" implicit in the rise of naturalism—Frank Norris argued very explicitly for American naturalism's incorporating "the sensationalism and depth of romanticism,"[5] as we shall see—and with the polarities implicit in the haunted minds of many modernist writers in the early part of the twentieth century, the links between Melville and Mailer in the tradition of American romance become readily apparent.

Over a century later, Lieutenant Hearns in Norman Mailer's *The Naked and the Dead* (1948) would write a college thesis on "A Study of the Cosmic Urge of Herman Melville." Mailer himself would eventually build a writer's career on cosmic urges, a fact which threatened and has perhaps paralyzed his fictional technique in much the same way it paralyzed Melville's. Cosmic urge and fictional form would fight it out to a draw until both seemed to evaporate in the shrill, ponderous impenetrabilities of *Pierre*, *The Confidence-Man*, and *Ancient Evenings*. "Un livre immense sur les sentiers d'Herman Melville," proclaimed French critic Alain Bosquet in *Le Figaro* about the French translation of *Ancient Evenings*. "Sentiers," certainly, but also the paralysis of pyramidical silences and emptied tombs.

Manichean visions tormented both writers. "Matter in end will never abate / His ancient brutal claim," Melville insisted in one of his poems as he grappled with the contraries of existence, the "Descartian vortices," the clash of demonic opposites that frighteningly spilled over into a universe of such appalling blankness and silence that the only possible truth was to recognize that "the invisible spheres were formed in fright." Calvinism shadowed forth "an extreme development of Persian sacrifice," since "most of the mythologists read by Melville tended to conceive of the periodic avatars of these conflicting principles in Manichean terms, comparing them most often to Ormuzd and Ahriman of the Zoroastrians and Osiris and Typhon of the Egyptians."[6] As Kingsley Widmer suggests, "Melville's art in *Benito Cereno* testifies to our enslaving Manicheanism . . . its crucifyingly destructive powers of darkness."[7] An annihilating blankness, ostensibly dissolving all opposites and reducing the contraries to that "colorless, all-color of atheism from which we shrink," still threatens all consciousness like some primal, terrifying void, perhaps the most threatening Manichean universe in all of American literature.

"Mailer's Manichean mills"[8] come as no surprise. "God . . . is not all-powerful; He exists as a warring element in a divided universe, and we are part of—perhaps the most important part—of His great expression," Mailer asserts.[9] These "mills" nearly overwhelm his fiction, his nonfiction, his interviews, his entire perception of things. Survival of the fittest underscores his pervasive metaphor of war, and his rigidly Manichean categories—self and society, instinct and consciousness, sex and stasis, the primitive and the civilized—permeate that constant battle. Conflict is vision. His bipolarities supply the tenuous unity of his outlook on mid-century America. But as Richard Poirier suggests about these "deadening acts of cosmic division . . . Mailer often creates divisions in his material so simplistically extreme as to allow him an unearned rest, exonerated, in the middle of it all, freed of choice or even temptation."[10]

Joyce Carol Oates views Melville's *The Confidence-Man* as revealing a "surface display of negation . . . a dualistic universe of irreconcilable forces . . . a perhaps feigned Manichean dualism" which degenerates all too quickly into a "final nihilism."[11] Likewise she suggests that Mailer's "energetic Manichaeanism forbids a higher art. Initiation . . . brings the protagonist not to newer visions . . . but to a dead end, a full stop."[12] In both instances, in Melville's and Mailer's later fiction, Manichean dualism seems to have produced a paralysis, either one of tensionless similitude in which life degenerates into an enervated and repetitious masquerade, or one in which Manichean polarities freeze and produce nothing but dark, blank stasis within Egyptian walls. The Manichean vision itself may not be responsible for such "full stops"—there are so many other factors involved in Melville's and Mailer's struggles with fiction—but it is a strong and suspect symptom of "the power of blackness" driven in upon itself.

William Barrett's understanding of Descartes' thought and strategy underlies both Melville's and Mailer's concept of the self: "The will in its freedom chooses to go against nature and natural impulse in order to conquer nature and its secrets."[13] Mailer's "man-centered revival of Manicheism"[14] parallels Melville's belief in the sovereignty of the self, however ultimately inscrutable. Neither writer, however, could abide the notion of an autonomous self that can understand the universe completely, foresee enlightened progress in all things, act as simplistically as Davy Crockett advised—"Be sure you're right, then go ahead!"—and forever view a mysterious but ultimately benevolent deity as some kind of long-suffering but knowledgeable father or judge. For each of them, Manichean dualities involve the individual self in a constant "ontological morality play,"[15] spawning unresolvable antitheses and dialectical energies that cease only in death. Barry Leeds's description of Mailer's "existential" heroes could easily fit Melville's with its emphasis on facing up to immediate dangers, confronting the ambiguities of death, existing without roots in a kind of self-selecting exile, and setting out "on an uncharted journey into the rebellious imperatives of the self."[16]

Despite Mailer's existential epithets involving Being and Dread, despite his witch's broth of Freud, Marx, Reich, and Kierkegaard, an essential romantic anarchism lies at the center of his characters and his vision of them. He is really in the process of shoring up "with his ontological fragments the ruins of romanticism,"[17] mining the same territory that frightened Melville. Melville's nihilism, as described by Widmer, reflects a darker romanticism in its fundamental attempt "to overcome or to repudiate the past on behalf of an unknown and unknowable but hoped-for future."[18] In the ruins of Calvinism Melville discovered darker foundations.

Both writers at their best write as romancers, not as novelists in

Hawthorne's sense of the opposed terms. Mailer's description of the novel in *The Armies of the Night* sounds strangely like Hawthorne's of the romance: "The novel must replace history at precisely that point where experience is sufficiently emotional, spiritual, psychical, moral, existential, or supernatural to expose the fact that the historian in pursuing the experience would be obliged to quit the clearly demarcated limits of historic inquiry." And so Mailer "will now unashamedly enter that world of *strange lights and intuitive speculation* which is the novel" (italics mine). And Melville, who declared himself a romancer, took the same distinct path, releasing himself from the more-or-less confines of the historical "facts" of living among the cannibals and striking out for other territories, requiring "only that play of freedom & invention accorded only to the Romancer & poet."

Both romancers employ allegory and rhetoric to polarize their vision of the world around them and to strike out beyond that polarization in the heroic images and metaphors of their prose. Ahab in *Moby-Dick* and Rojack in *An American Dream* create a world of Manichean certainties and at the same time reach for rhetoric and perceptions that will transcend the very categories they have created. Ahab's death and Rojack's escape may reveal just how much language can imprison or free us, according to both authors.

Other similarities tease us. Both Melville and Mailer absorb the cultural crises of their country into their own personal crises. The elusive uncertainty of their characters' sovereign selves reflects the same uncertain "truisms" of their country's idea of democracy, the individual, notions of progress, and faith in a rational, knowable will. Each invents fictional characters who play roles and shift shapes as easily as they change clothes. Voices, roles, and selves shimmer and shatter in the masquerades aboard the *Fidele* and in the reincarnated posturings of Menenhetet I. Ascetic withdrawals and libertine lusts for power and for flesh mesmerize both the creator of the white whale and that of the white Negro. Cosmic urges flail at them both.

Startling similarities and dissimilarities occur in Melville's and Mailer's use of and reliance upon ancient Egyptian myths and images. From one perspective Mailer's *Ancient Evenings* strikes me as the culminating apotheosis of Egyptian undercurrents and symbol-mongering in American literature. This immense and stolid book, whether intentionally or not, builds upon Melville's own wrestlings with indecipherable hieroglyphics, empty tombs, dead letters, and Manichean mysteries. The "vast, undefiled, incomprehensible, awful" pyramids that Melville described in his visit to the Holy Land haunt Mailer as well, and both men seem to be, in Melville's words, "oppressed by the massiveness and mystery" of them. The Manichean sensibility seems to have led them both back to the epic struggles of Osiris and Seth to confront some heroic but doomed psychological struggle within themselves and their culture, a spirit that, for them both, seems to have eventually partaken, in Melville's words, of "barrenness."

Ahab and Ishmael at first divide up the Manichean territories of *Moby-Dick* between the obsessed demonic romantic who acts and the skeptical humanist who reflects. Ishmael's constant reflections produce "a veritable anatomy of allegory,"[19] as he projects and posits, suggests and broods on the wedding of mind and matter, of meditation and water. Verbal dexterity rescues him from succumbing entirely to Ahab's quest, as he constantly invents, discovers, deciphers, and distrusts his own hypotheses and mental charts. Every choice proves faulty and deluded, despite his human contact with others, since "there is no quality in this world that is not what it is merely by contrast." His sense of the contraries, that Manichean-Gordian knot of insoluble contradiction at the center of things, leads him to recognize "the image of the ungraspable phantom of life," to know that "this is the key to it all," and to realize that it can never be grasped or contained. "Meditation and water are wedded for ever," but in their related separateness lies that phantom of a mystery that no man can ever hope to solve.

On the other hand, Ahab espouses his own understanding of the Manichean mystery of the universe and transforms it into Manichean mandate. The gnostic vision conjures up a world of matter that is inherently evil. Visible objects remain mere masks, blank walls. Beyond them hovers some "Demiurge," creator of the universe, that "still reasoning thing" of "inscrutable malice" which directs the vengeful necessities of life. Ahab's acting looses the operating forces of evil. Action strips the mask and, be the whale agent or principle, the battle of wills is engaged. Zoroastrian dualisms fuel Ahab's rage, and in his recognition of fire as an evil light to worship and the sun as the good light to avoid, we see the same hellish and inevitable dichotomies that underlie the entire construct and vision of Hawthorne's *The Scarlet Letter*.[20]

Ahab, of course, projects his own self upon an ultimately inscrutable universe, as personal mandate replaces impersonal mystery. If the presence of objects suggests only the absence of their "essences," of that "still reasoning thing" behind and beyond them, then objects take on the very nature of language. The presence of words indicates in part the absence of the objects described, as hieroglyphics on a tomb suggest only the absence of life within. In Ahab's obsessive view, both visible objects and language remain mere masks; the world and the word dissolve into one vast void, peopled only by Ahab's self-projections and rage. "Holding to no radical otherness and affirming itself as the only great noun, the self collapses into an immense vacancy."[21] And Ahab fills that vacancy with the dark stalking shadow, masquerading as a white whale, of his own demonically romantic ego.

Ahab's second choice, that there is "nought behind," he overrides. In fact this is probably Melville's position, akin to Ishmael's sense of the ungraspable phantom of mystery, tinged ultimately with that appalling, self-annihilating whiteness that threatens consciousness itself, a "dumb blankness" that no dualism can tolerate. In any case Ahab chooses the "orthodox" Manichean route and serves Fedallah's prophecies.

It seems to me that both Ahab and Ishmael believe in a radical dualism, however distinct from one another. Ahab acts irrationally from a "rational" belief in some "still reasoning thing" beyond the masks of his existence. His Manichean vision may be a product of Cartesian reason, a projection of the will choosing to go against nature in order to subdue and conquer it. His scheme of things produces not only the "ungodly, god-like" self but also the "irrational, rational" man. It is action he demands, and the very notion of action against something must posit an opponent, a combatant.

Ishmael, on the other hand, choosing reflection in place of action (though he too experiences "a wild, mystical, sympathetical feeling" within which "Ahab's feud seemed mine"), submits to his notion of the contraries, of the mysterious unfathomable "wedding" of opposites. If Ahab's vision stems from his own "monomaniac incarnation," his own personification of evil, Ishmael's sense of evil derives from that appalling whiteness that lurks at the dumb blank center of the universe beyond such personal vendettas.

In any case, both Ahab's "inscrutable malice" and Ishmael's "dumb blankness" remain demonic and ultimately threatening to human existence. There may not be a vengeful Demiurge within, but there is the suggestion of a charnel-house. Visible absence and demonic presence both carry demonic attributes. A Manichean malignity, whether dumb or determined, lurks at the appallingly vacant or vengeful center of things. "Though in many of its aspects this visible world *seems* formed in love, the invisible spheres *were* formed in fright" (italics mine). Whether terror lies in us or in "it," it is still terror, and a demonic Manichean presence, though perceived as a silent absence, threatens both mind and matter and the very mysterious wedding they have undergone. "Wonder ye then at the fiery hunt?" Light alone, with no medium of language or consciousness to "contain" it, may reduce all matter to a "blank tinge," but whether Ahab defines that as conspiracy or Ishmael as Nature's painting like the harlot, the charnel-house yawns beyond the white veil, and a vast shudder of evil and demonic divinity, however silent and unseeing, causes the web of the universe to tremble.

Melville uses Egyptian images in *Moby-Dick*, among a vast array of other mythological images and ideas, to suggest the ultimate indecipherability and inscrutability of man and the world around him. Egypt suggested "an unfathomable antiquity and a religious awe"[22] for Melville, as H. Bruce Franklin has suggested. Franklin goes on to document fully Melville's use of the Osiris-Seth/Typhon myth in his tale of Ahab's quest for the white whale, viewing *Moby-Dick* as an "Egyptian myth incarnate."[23] In several instances Melville's comments on hieroglyphics involve their ultimate indecipherability: "Champollion deciphered the wrinkled granite hieroglyphics. But there is no Champollion to decipher the Egypt of every man's and every being's face. Physiognomy, like every other human science, is but a passing fable." The surface of the Sperm Whale reveals certain marks that appear to be "hieroglyphical; that is, if you call these mysterious cyphers on the walls of the pyramids hieroglyphics, then that is the proper word to use in the present connexion." And these suggest "old Indian characters chiselled on the famous hieroglyphic palisades on the banks of the Upper Mississippi." And "like those mystic rocks, too, the mystic-marked whale remains undecipherable." Queequeg's tattoos and the carved lid of his coffin may contain in hieroglyphic form "a complete theory of the heavens and the earth, and a mystical treatise on the art of attaining truth; so that Queequeg in his proper person was a riddle to unfold," but that riddle remains "unsolved to the last." The Sperm Whale moves only in "his pyramidical silence," even though or because his head suggests "the sphynx." Egyptian images suggest age and awe but also the indecipherable and the silent. The pyramid as a "death motif"[24] will haunt Melville's later fiction.

"Cunning duplicates" in the mind between nature and the soul challenge Ahab and fuel his rage, but even he acknowledges that these are "beyond utterance." Linked analogies lead only to pyramidical silences, the dead letters on the walls of tombs, and Leviathan sheds "older blood than the Pharoah's," a primordial link that leads back only into inscrutable darkness.

Much of *Moby-Dick* remains both "undecipherable" and "inscrutable," to repeat two of Melville's favorite adjectives, but it is the inscrutability of things that shadows Pierre's doomed footsteps. At least a written sign, however enigmatic and indecipherable, is a sign, a consciously human emblem meant to be decoded and understood. Inscrutability suggests only ultimate mystery beyond any possible attempts at decoding or deciphering. In *Pierre* we move from the mysterious writings on the wall of the pyramid, a human action of some comprehensible if not understandable design, to the dark depths of the pyramid itself, where only vacancy yawns and swallows our hero.

"Explain this darkness, exorcise this devil, ye cannot," Pierre laments. Like Hawthorne in *The Marble Faun*, Pierre seems determined to erect an idealistic quest upon an inscrutable riddle, allegorical certainties upon ultimate ambiguities, and he goes on to mask it in the social charade of a wedding. Isabel turns his pastoral world upside down, and Manichean opposites breed so many Manichean opposites that they cancel one another out in their self-lacerating manner and leave Pierre stranded amid "sphinxlike shapes" in the empty sarcophagus of his being: "He felt that what he had always before considered the solid land of veritable reality, was now being audaciously encroached upon by bannered armies of hooded phantoms, disembarking in his soul, as from flotillas of spectre-boats." If Isabel at first feels "that all good, harmless men and women were human beings, placed at cross-purposes, in a world of snakes and lightnings," Pierre comes to see at his feet "the soft ground-lightnings, snake-like, playing in and out among the blades of grass," and when he kisses her passionately at last, "they changed; they coiled together."

Inscrutability haunts everything. God, Pierre's Terror Stone, Isabel's glances, the dark face in Pierre's dark incestuous fantasies, Plotinus— everything remains "palpable to the senses, but inscrutable to the soul." Everything partakes of trance, dream, spell, as Isabel herself suggests the fluidity of things, of sex, the sea, music, death. Hawthorne's hypnagogic state eradicates a world, as if Pierre, like young Goodman Brown, were slowly strangled by the inscrutable intermixture of noble ideals and his sexual, fantastical phantoms. And against this quivering inscrutability Melville hurls language drunkenly. If Nature provides a cunning alphabet only, so will he in his overwrought, babbling prose, full of gothic doom, mountain passes, forest ghosts, dark phantom faces, and gagging peach-juice. At one point he describes Pierre "dabbling in the vomit of his loathed identity," a queasy line which suggests Mailer at his overripe worst. It seems to foreshadow Mailer's own inscrutabilities and manic wrestlings with language yet to come.

Vice and virtue tremble and fall in one upon the other; the Bad will tend the Good. Blonde Lucy and dark Isabel collapse in death, as Pierre in the moment before his own suicide recognizes his own essential neuterness, the "dumb blankness" of his being. We "have arrived at the Pole, to whose barrenness only it points, there, the needle indifferently respects all points of the horizon alike"; at ultimate silences that suggest the voice of God and undermine any prophet's attempts to interpret it; at "the heart of man; descending into which is as descending a spiral stair in a shaft, without any end, and where that endlessness is only concealed by the spiralness of the stair, and the blackness of the shaft." Incest is all. And Melville has forewarned us in the cunning alphabet of the first page of this crazed romance, in the pastoral masquerade of which are lodged the words "mystery," "silence," "repose," "trance," all of it "dreamily." None of these states threatens yet, but they are already there waiting to strike like the snake in the grass.

The Egyptian images embody *Pierre*'s inscrutabilities and frame them in shadows of death. Pierre's Memnon Stone in the woods suggests Memnon's noble self-sacrifice at Troy and a primordial "egg" of womblike resonances. But the rock also suggests Pierre's Terror Stone, as menacing, silent, inscrutable, and tomblike as death itself. Do the hieroglyphics etched on its face translate into "Solomon the Wise"? Hardly. Manichean terrors jostle for position beneath that massive headstone, and both Memnon Stone and Terror Stone dissolve in a "haze of ambiguities . . . lost among our drifting sands."

At the center of the pyramid lies an empty sarcophagus that, like the soul of man, appalls by its vacancy: "By vast pains we mine into the pyramid; by horrible gropings we come to the central room; with joy we espy the sarcophagus; but we lift the lid—and no body is there!—

appallingly vacant as vast is the soul of a man!'' Manichean opposites
lead on to Manichean opposites, insoluble contradictions, the inscrutability
of stone, "the world being nothing but superinduced superfices.'' Vacancy
confronts vacancy, with no attempt or desire to hold Hawthornian veils
in place. Bainard Cowan has suggested in his history of allegory that "the
body is the realm of process. To transfer writing onto it is to replace
the finished inscription of the stone tablets with a project wherein the
truth of the allegory will have to be worked out in living.''[25] If this is
so, then Melville has opted for a cunning alphabet of dead letters on dead
stone only. If the Christian sense of allegory involves the "turning away
from a petrified text to embrace a body and to reinscribe the text on the
body," that body being Christ's,[26] then Melville reads Christianity as
one more dead letter, one more indecipherable hieroglyphic on the wall
of a still-Manichean universe, embodied/disembodied in a pervasive, incestuous, descending silence, a demon of "dumb blankness." Pierre resembles the naked, castrated Enceladus, fallen from his "fame-column,'' entombed in the Mount of Titans, where Memnon and Terror resemble
one another and nothing "delectable" remains.

Hawthorne clung to his Manichean opposites, however addled and
threatened by Westervelt's machinations and the abyss of Rome. He sought
recourse in Phoebe, the wan Priscilla, the shrill Hilda, even as his fiction
dethroned and undermined them. He would not surrender veils, however
fragile and ethereal. Melville's Pierre sacrifices himself to the demonic
silences beyond the veils, recognizing the vacancy in the tomb. From the
perspective of the Christian faithful, the vanished body suggests Christ's
resurrection and deliverance, but in the lacerating Manichean ambiguities
of his text, Melville found only emptiness. On this Egyptian rock he built
his vision, and his style, mutilated and ravaged, fell apart.

To explore Melville's later fiction is to watch the Egyptian images take
hold, freeze, and finally evaporate. Miller describes accurately, I think,
the landscape of the short stories: "Melville depicts with almost frightening
consistency a wasteland in which nothing grows and no one matures.
The characters . . . are frozen . . . in infantile responses or flee from
life.''[27] The "dead-wall reveries" of Bartleby lead to the Tombs, where
"the Egyptian character of the masonry weighed upon me with its gloom,''
and to revelations of "the Dead Letter Office at Washington." The letters reflect Melville's own: "On errands of life, these letters speed to
death." The attorney-narrator marvels at the "soft imprisoned turf," which

suggests to him "the heart of the eternal pyramids, it seemed," but we know better. Atufal, harbinger of death in "Benito Cereno," resembles "one of those sculptured porters of black marble guarding the porches of Egyptian tombs," and the aged sailor trying to warn Delano of the true nature of life aboard the *San Dominick* "looked like an Egyptian priest making Gordian knots for the temple of Ammon." Manichean opposites in the tale suggest another ultimately demonic universe, in which "darkness takes on superlative powers, transcendent and tempting, which pervade and master all. Melville's imagination, in other works as well as here, often seems trapped within the Manichean-Christian madness."[28]

By the time we reach *The Confidence-Man: His Masquerade*, fiction is dead. The series of dialogues in mind-numbing double talk reveals a Manichean vision turned to dust, a "pic-nic *en costume*" filled with flat exposition, explanation, and exhortation. The river barber's sign of "No Trust" contrasts with the fair stranger's placards about charity, just as in the last chapter the cosmopolitan and the cynical juvenile peddler match wits and dupe the solitary old man. The placid surface obviously hides all kinds of ideas blasphemous to nineteenth-century middle-class faiths, but the self-canceling, enervated prose kills the demonic game on contact: "The interview offered such a contrast to the scene around, that the merchant, though not used to be very indiscreet, yet, being not entirely inhumane, remained not entirely unmoved." Huh? What sort of demonic laughter is this? "A sort of laugh more like a groan than a laugh; and yet, somehow, it seemed intended for a laugh." The Manichean mystery swallows itself, as if the contraries in smothering spawned contraries evaporate into a lifeless, bottomless trance. Truman, Ringman, Goodman, Noble: "The devil . . . appears to have understood man better even than the Being who made him." Of course in gnostic circles the Devil made him: another unfleshed irony to uncover.

Fiction itself collapses. Terror may be the Indian-hater's epitaph and the motivating force within *Moby-Dick*, but here we get stale asides about original characters, odd characters, the nature of fiction, the nature of vengeance. *The Confidence-Man* is torpid, not terrifying. The ancient Egyptians might call Noble something, but Mark Winsome is too addled to spit it out. For him, "death, though in a worm, is majestic; while life, though in a king, is contemptible." Contempt smothers this book. The Devil has never looked so dull, and the final Manichean depiction of a "horned altar, from which flames rose, alternate with the figure of a robed man, his head encircled by a halo," dissolves in the extinguishing of the solar lamp. It may be fun to decipher the hieroglyphics of *The Confidence-Man*, but to read them is to succumb to the torpor of the tomb, of Manichean vision become the bare outlines of a vision etched in cold stone.

Norman Mailer's cosmic urge complements Melville's, at least in his urge to dive deep if not in the actual fictional realization of it. As Alfred Kazin suggests, Mailer lays strong claim to "knowledge from within, romanticism as propaganda"[29] in his ongoing, omnivorous desire to explore and explain contemporary America, himself, our deepest lusts, in all the rhetorical and metaphorical sweep that he can muster. "That nightmare of entropy turned Manichean which seems to obsess American writers,"[30] as Tony Tanner puts it, continues to fascinate and hold Mailer spellbound in all his works. No "dumb blankness" here, but a polarized dialectic of opposites that startles at the heart of things. It is his "dialectical conception of existence with a lust for power, a dark, romantic, and yet undeniably dynamic view of existence,"[31] as conjured up in his famous and overexposed essay, "The White Negro" (1958), that haunts Mailer relentlessly. And it takes over his vision of America in *The Armies of the Night*: "Whole crisis of Christianity in America that the military heroes were on one side, and the unnamed saints on the other! Let the bugle blow. The death of America rides in on the smog." As Jack Abbott, a murderer and one-time Mailer protégé, once expressed it in a letter to me, "Christians are no longer aware of it but they embrace that Manichean heresy in their religious outlook *today* (*en masse*) and do not even know it."[32] And as Richard Poirier, one of Mailer's most astute critics, sees it: "All is imagined only in oppositions, unable even to imagine one side of the opposition without proposing that it has yet another opposition within itself . . . within each side [of a dialectical opposition] a sense of internal embattlement."[33]

The Manichean vision grew slowly in Mailer's fiction and did not achieve its final eruption until the advent of *Advertisements for Myself* (1959), though we see it smoldering in his early fiction. War and individual survival lie at the root of *The Naked and the Dead* (1948) and are both products of a naturalistic literary tradition and the spiritual essence of writers such as Stephen Crane and Ernest Hemingway. Man may contain both beast and seer, as Mailer has suggested, but the beast tends to get the upper hand, even as Mailer tries to unite them in a dynamic dialectic that will

lead to further Manichean prophecies. The villain emerges as some kind
of totalitarian unit—the state, the army, the party, women, whatever—
but the universe remains bestial, not spiritual, a place in which man's
furious motions can only hope to suggest the remote possibilities of
free will.[34] Again the scriptural account in "The White Negro":
"Movement is always to be preferred to inaction. In motion a man has
a chance. . . . For life is a contest between people in which the victor
generally recuperates quickly and the loser takes long to mend, a perpetual
competition of colliding explorers." No free-market American Puritan
would disagree.

Although the windy political speeches and long tedious dialogues destroy
Barbary Shore (1951) as a work of fiction, yet that novel reflects Mailer's
growing Manichean consciousness in its battle between capitalism and
Marxism, its unassimilated parts of political allegory and psychological
symbolism. John Stark has pointed out the similarities between *Barbary
Shore* and *The Blithedale Romance*, however simplistically.[35] The two
Hollingsworths emerge as tempters; Lovett and Coverdale as sensitive
young men; Guinivere's Zenobia contrasts with Lannie's Priscilla; McLeod
shares Westervelt's machinations and conspiracies. The political allegory
strikes truer notes, I think, as the characters are parcelled out in terms
of Bolshevism, Trotskyism, capitalism, with the much-abused Guinivere
representing the masses, wooed from all sides. But Lovett's hypnagogic
state, which runs through the book like a constant motif—"And while
I was asleep or perhaps even waking, almost certainly a fantasy and yet
I could not disprove it existed"—and signals the stirrings of the romantic imagination, too easily undermines the Marxist pretensions to history
as a determined, realistically defined clash of class interests. The novel
shifts from politics to psyche too erratically, or, as Stark suggests, "Mailer's
work is a battleground on which thematic and technical opposites
struggle."[36] It is as if Mailer's own attitudes were so decidedly
Manichean that he cannot coordinate them, but they are visible here. And
Hawthorne's shadow, however ethereal, does hover round the novel.

The moral darkness of Desert D'Or in *The Deer Park* (1955) suggests
a kind of Jamesian exploration of private fantasy and public form, an uncertain look at the complexities of impulse and desire that lead or should
lead to an unselfish heart: "The essence of spirit, he thought to himself,
was to choose the thing which did not better one's position but made
it more perilous. That was why the world he knew was poor, for it in-

sisted morality and caution were identical." Sex, the will to power, the
"monster in the human heart," the artist's wrestling with the world
and his work involve the desire "to explore the totality of the All, if
indeed there be an All and not an expanding mystery," that the quiet
brooding prose only smothers and avoids. Marion Faye's sense of God
and the Devil and the last-minute ruminations on "Sex as Time, and
Time as the connection of new circuits" suggest Manichean themes and
Mailerian images to come but leave them virtually unexplored and flat.
The querulous interactions between saints and lovers, O'Shaugnessy, Eitel,
Elena, and Lulu, dissipate as the book rambles on, but clear intimations
of future themes are here.

The "psychic crossroads of the mind," a kind of interior Cartesian
vortices, burst into Mailer's proclamation of a "nucleus of new imagination" in "The White Negro." Critics have championed this for years.
We get "energy, life, sex, force, the Yoga's *prana*, the Reichian's orgone,
Lawrence's 'blood,' Hemingway's 'good,' the Shavian life-force," all
rolled into one metaphoric mess. The overreaching metaphors excite Mailer
as the metaphysical method never can. We see language groping, breaking, stumbling over itself to try to express the inexpressible. It is this
romantic anarchism, step-child to personal survival in an unrelenting
Manichean war, that energizes and propels Mailer, not some finely tuned
philosophical system. George Schrader sees through the rhetoric to the
muddled middle: "It is not only a *dialectical* but a *contradictory* idea in
that rage and rebellion derive their force and meaning from civilized passion and can by no act of violence gain reentry into the innocence of
immediacy."[37] He is right, but the point is off center. It is the "gnostic
animism" of "the quest for the infinite . . . which is of course an infinite quest"[38] that fuels Mailer's vision. Or, as Jean Radford spells it
out, Mailer's "gifts lie primarily in his creative abilities with language
rather than in his naively systematizing kind of intelligence, and his neo-
primitivist world view."[39]

Why Are We in Vietnam? (1967) apotheosizes Mailer's barbaric yawp
in an obscenely funny *tour de force* of language and outrage. The book
is saturated with Mailer's Manichean faith, for God is "but a beast, some
beast of a giant jaw and cavernous mouth with a full cave's breath and
fangs," and all men are "killer brothers, owned by something, prince
of darkness, lord of light, they did not know." Mailer's "last moose
of the North" reveals his vision in emblematic certainty, where "sunlight

in the blood of its drying caught him, lit him, left him gilded red on one side," and "the full new moon now up before the sun was final and down silvering the other side of this King Moose." "D.J. could have wept for a secret was near, some mystery in the secret of things . . . some speechless electric gathering of woe, no peace in the North."

Impurities and savage ironies foul even the white Alaskan snowscape. American literature itself, with its celebration of nature as some kind of moral order and touchstone, shatters under D.J.'s assault. Corporate America infects everything. D.J.'s schizophrenic yowl, riddled with pop culture, outmoded gestures, rampant obscenity, and Texan exaggeration, reveals only ultimate disruptions, broken circuits, the buggered center of an impure but contemporary and all-too-knowing heart. Perhaps his obscene, spaced-out monologue may be a prelude to some kind of ultimate communion or collapse—"Don't get upset by the boys' last dialogue, they so full of love and adventure and in such a haste to get all the mixed glut and sludge out of their systems that they're heating up all the foul talk to get rid of it in a hurry like bad air going up the flue and so be ready to enjoy good air and nature"—but in fact it leads only to further Manichean recognitions, this time in Vietnam. Melville surfaces—"Herman Melville go hump Moby and wash his Dick"—and Mailer's preoccupations—"Love is dialectic, man, back and forth, hate and sweet . . . and corporation is DC, direct current, diehard charge, no dialectic man, just one-way street, they don't call it Washington D.C. for nothing"—but at the last the splendid voice shouts in a void. American dilemmas, macho myths, basic human realities are so intermixed and self-contradictory that D.J. swallows the very disrupted world he creates and finally leaves nothing but shadows.

The Manichean clashes between Western and Eastern voices, Mormon action and media reflection, angels and demons, devils and saints, buttress Mailer's huge "True Life Novel," *The Executioner's Song* (1979) and are sketchily reflected in Gary Gilmore's own proclamations about God and the Devil, reincarnation, karmic debts, and dark gulfs. And the romantic-mythic overtones Mailer seems determined to achieve surface in the very first paragraph with its elegiac rhythms, images of a clandestine crime when Gary was a child, and shadows of that first Edenic expulsion: "It was forbidden to climb in the orchard. . . . She climbed to the top and the limb with the good apples broke off."

But ultimately Mailer's calculated style and Gilmore himself work

against the book's wider pretensions. The style reflects "the same narrative style every hustler and psychopath would give you . . . we did this
and then, man, like we did that. Episodic and unstressed. Resolute
refusal . . . to attach value to any detail." The splintered narrative emphasizes the last lines of separate paragraphs as ironic understatements or satiric
"punch lines." The spaces, the "dumb blankness" between, disrupt the
flow of cause and effect, create ominous holes in the pattern that point
up uncertainties and doubt. And the hard, factual language with its veneer
of cinematic objectivity reflects Mailer's keen eye and calculated juxtapositions. But the fragments finally reflect the unreflective mindlessness of
the main characters and in deliberately stunting them drains them of more
complex human motives and despairs and often reduces them to soap-
opera types.

Gilmore suggests a kind of Joe Christmas, viewing his death in terms
of some ultimate apotheosis of the self, craving it as though self-destruction
and self-realization were one and the same thing. Mailer comments on
Gilmore's "twenty-seven poses . . . racist Gary and Country-and-Western
Gary, poetic Gary, artist manque Gary, macho Gary . . . Karma County
Gary, Texas Gary, and Gary the killer Irishman" and even suggests that
his self-hatred may stem from his desire or need to molest children: "There
was nobody in or out of prison whom hardcore convicts despised more
than child molesters." But finally Gilmore remains an undeveloped blank,
the surface of a documentary, not the soul of a novel. He remains, as
Frederick Karl puts it, "a dead spot. . . . A punk has no depth."[40] The
Manichean cosmic urge circles and often embraces him, but the media
circus overwhelms him and the target is lost. Better perhaps if the media
itself had become Mailer's ultimate focus. "The triviality of the man"[41]
will relinquish no cosmic secrets.

Which brings us finally to Mailer's *Moby-Dick*, *An American Dream*
(1965). Here is a romancer's territory, "the quest for apocalyptic struggle where clearly demarcated good and evil exist"[42] in all their Manichean ferocity. And the American romancer's roots reveal Mailer's traditional ties to Hawthorne and Melville. Stanley Gutman suggests that in
Hawthorne's fiction "fantasy, evil, and passion are often closely linked
to 'oracular' genius,"[43] although it is really Melville, as Richard Brodhead astutely points out, who "produces a figure Hawthorne never drew:
the heroic obsessive or the monomaniac as superior man."[44] Brodhead
believes, and quite rightly, that Melville redesigned *Moby-Dick* in

Hawthorne's shadow to include the figure of Ahab and his quest and that he "clearly noticed the conjunction of monomania and figure-making . . . a pathology whose action is the forging of metaphors,"[45] in Hawthorne's work. Rojack is Mailer's Ahab who pursues, in Peter Brooks's description of the melodramatic imagination, "the gothic quest for renewed contact with the numinous, the supernatural, the occult forces in the universe" that may eventually lead "into the moral self."[46] With the addition of Leo Braudy's description of Mailer's "hypotactic style . . . a style that is unsure of the meaning it searches for"[47] and that links Mailer to Hawthorne's and Faulkner's styles, the romantic territory of *An American Dream* is complete.

Melville's indecipherable silences and inscrutable masks parallel Rojack's "secret frightened romance with the phases of the moon." For him, "magic, dread, and the perception of death were the roots of motivation." Travelling in and out of his own hypnagogic consciousness—"My mind brought too much fever to each possibility. . . . There was a presence in the room like the command of a dead pharoah"—Rojack enters Ahab's world of inscrutable malice with hints of Ishmael's annihilating blankness. Objects and faces mask true intentions and "still reasoning thing[s]." That's "my wife," he proclaims over the bodies of Deborah and Cherry, caught in a world of relentless doubling that haunts the demonic landscape of American romance.

Rojack views himself as a Cain in the gnostic allegory that surrounds him. He matches the intensities of Ahab's Manichean pursuits and recognitions: "Yes, I had come to believe in grace and the lack of it, in the long finger of God and the swish of the Devil . . . which was a way of saying goodness was imprisoned by evil." Cherry's visions match his own, as do Barney Kelly's: "The Devil in such a scheme has to have an even chance to defeat the Lord, or there's no scheme to consider. . . . The only explanation is that God and the Devil are very attentive to the people at the summit." Rojack and Kelly, killer brothers, lovers of Ruta and Cherry and Deborah, stalk one another to the final confrontation.

Mailer, however, is far more imprisoned in his notion of society and civilization than Melville is. Kelly, whether agent or principle of evil, strikes us as more a social than a "natural" phenomenon. His evil consists of power, money, hidden conspiracies, dark politics, as his Manichean world involves too visibly the CIA, the FBI, and the police. Mailer's

Marxist prescriptions suggest that a decadent capitalist society is somehow vaguely at fault, the underlying evil of Rojack's battle with demons and angels. Civilization is accused by Rojack of having stolen that sense of dread which to the savage "was the natural result of any invasion of the supernatural . . . and the price we have paid is to accelerate our private sense of some enormous if not quite definable disaster which awaits us." Mailer's *Moby-Dick* carries with it the distinctly social prisons and conventions of the overwrought *Pierre*.

Blonde and dark maidens, demonic fathers, labyrinthine conspiracies haunt *An American Dream*, but as Roberts the policeman states, "I don't know how to put demons on a police report." The novel lacks Ishmael's reflective balance. However Manichean in its own right, New York often emerges more real than Rojack's fantasies. Does Rojack's mind contain idiocies or true instincts? And if he hungers to right himself, to exorcise this dark night of the soul, could he not exorcise the very Manichean vision that Mailer seems all too readily to cling to? "For I wanted to escape from that intelligence which let me know of murders in one direction and conceive of visits to Cherry from the other, I wanted to be free of magic, the tongue of the Devil, the dread of the Lord, I wanted to be *some sort of rational man* again, nailed tight to details, promiscuous, *reasonable*, blind to the reach of the seas. But *I could not move*." (italics mine.) Is this an Ishmaelian voice within the howls of Ahab? Or is it a confession of Manichean dialectic become static end? Does one move and in moving conjure up a Manichean world, as Ahab's actions seemed to call up that "still reasoning thing," and in standing still hope to eradicate that world? But if "movement is always to be preferred to inaction" and if "in motion a man has a chance," then is Mailer doomed to his Manichean wail without surcease? And does this avoid some kind of ultimate choice? "No, men were afraid of murder, but not from a terror of justice so much as the knowledge that a killer attracted the attention of the gods; then your mind was not your own."

Antisocial behavior creates the vision; civilization must be countermanded. A demonic Manichean act results in Manichean mysteries, but only then? "Mystery revolved about me now, and I did not know if it was hard precise mystery with a detailed solution, or a mystery fathered by the collision of larger mysteries." But Melville knew.

The ethics or morality of *Moby-Dick* suggests that the rational will, stretched to its zenith, self-destructs, and that human isolation is complete. This was Hawthorne's "lesson," and it was not lost on his avid disciple. The ungodly, godlike man dies of his own monomaniacal incarnation. Ishmael survives, mysteriously, by chance, but his reflections suggest a place for the human soul to abide, at least in considering alternate possibilities.

Mailer remains true to his initial vision of personal survival at all costs in a bestial, unending war. Society in all its manifestations remains the totalitarian "Other," and the hero's task is to defeat it and the vacancy, the dread, and the emptiness that invade him. Vampiric wills seek each other out either to dominate or to interpenetrate one another. Good sex may serve the latter purpose, but the former reveals the really gothic center of Mailer's landscape. Wills lock and thrash: "I traveled (eyes sealed) through some midnight of inner space, aware of nothing but my will, that casing of iron about my heart, and of her will anchored like a girdle of steel about her womb . . . our wills now met." Orgasmic sex can undermine the will and open Emersonian doors to a new consciousness, but this does not last. The "iron law of romance" for Mailer demands that "one took the vow to be brave . . . for I believed God was not love but courage. Love came only as a reward." In that Hemingwayesque resolution lies Mailer's Whitmanic efforts, the need to face up to the dread and conquer it. No Melvillian "dumb blankness" can upend him. The challenge must be met. Ahab can kill the whale and survive if he only plays his cards right. Rojack teeters on the parapet of his consciousness and heads off to Guatemala and Yucatan.

In *An American Dream* mood spawns metaphor. Rojack's trance triggers tropes that in the long run are meant to save him. Like some besieged poet he strives for "the elaborateness of immediacy rather than of development toward an idea,"[48] and thus images succeed images like Rojack's own "psychic particles" creating that scenario in his own mind: "I began to shudder; the picture I had given was real to me." Manichean metaphor grapples with a Manichean world too easily identified with power, money, bad sex, and paranoia. It is Pierre's quest with a renewed faith in the sheer, voluble spouting of it. The incarnation of language may be that one brave act that will save us, although it unquestionably mirrors the Manichean world Rojack is attempting to flee. What lies at the bottom of that exhilarating rush of images is a Nietzschean celebration of the will, in combination with a Whitmanic—or just plain manic?—faith in sex as salvation that may be, as Jean Radford suggests, the central idea of the twentieth century and certainly of much contemporary American fiction. For Mailer, "the romantic rather than existential positive in all his work is this triumphant assertion of the individual will against all odds and all comers."[49]

Melville explores the "dumb blankness" beyond Ahab's rigidly Manichean quest, and it remains terrifying, demonic, the product of sorcery, the dark ultimate of light. In its extraordinary brightness the world is reduced to mere masquerade in which Manichean mannequins parade as if embalmed in a mummy's windings. Mailer holds out the romantic hope, despite the repellent darkness and Manichean certainties, that "everything contained its possibility." Whatever jeweled city may shimmer in Rojack's mind is counteracted by the Las Vegases in the desert. However magic his sense of dread, the realistic city of the detective yarn remains unmolested, somehow sacrosanct beyond Manichean mysteries or itself a too solid stage for them. Social conventions again suggest Pierre's prisons, not Ahab's. Some kind of courageous synthesis might yet emerge from the melange of Freud, Marx, Reich, and Hemingway, but for the most part a moral muddle remains.

Despite the omnivorous Manichean polarities in *An American Dream*, as darkly romantic a nightmare as a contemporary American novelist has yet produced (with the possible exception of Pynchon's *Gravity's Rainbow*), and despite Mailer's provocative and evocative rhetoric, the center of the quest looms strangely hollow, not with Melville's terror but with Mailer's evasions of it. As Richard Poirier suggests, Mailer's cosmic divisions lead him only to "an unearned rest, exonerated, in the middle of it all, freed of choice or even temptation."[50] At the last, Mailer's novel may reveal more the symptoms of his contemporary era than a completed personal vision of it. Writing of the contemporary novelist, Flannery O'Connor may have seen through to the heart of the matter: "He may find in the end that instead of reflecting the image at the heart of things, he has only reflected our broken condition and, through it, the face of the devil we are possessed by. This is a modest achievement, but perhaps a necessary one."[51]

Walter Clemons titled his review of *Ancient Evenings* (1983), "A Novelist Builds a Pyramid,"[52] and for reasons different from his own, he was right on target. Mailer's conjuring up of the Egyptian Book of the Dead has produced a dead book, a necropolis of the spirit. Like a pyramid, the novel remains inert, immobile, massive, and ponderous. The humorless voice of exposition chants its every ritual, feast, and ceremony, tediously moving from set piece to set piece (some more successful than others, like the splendid recreation of the myth of Osiris, Isis, and Set in "The Book of the Gods") like some excruciatingly exquisite design on a well-overwrought burial urn.

Manichean vision saturates the work. "Crude thoughts and fierce forces" conjure up Thebes and Memphis, Amon and Ptah, the Divine Two-Lands of Ramses II, the powerful pharoah and the story-telling Magus, the high priest and brothel keeper, the killer brothers Osiris and Set. "The difference between a great truth and a dreadful lie might in the moment of greatest anguish weigh no more than a feather upon one's thoughts," but the book turns feathers into stone and embalms these truths seemingly forever.

Mailer's preoccupations—one would have to call them obsessions by now—involve the power and domination involved in sex, death, perpetual war, men and women. Ramses II's act of buggery upon Menenhetet I leads to Menenhetet's sexual revenge on Ramses' wife Nefertiti. Ramses accomplishes what D.J. and Tex Hyde did not. Despite Harold Bloom's description of buggery as a gnostic negative creation,[53] such vision strikes me as "gnostic gnonsense." The moment of death coincides with apocalyptic orgasm, when Meni in effect fathers himself in a fascinating but imminently circular process of reincarnation. He reappears after his first incarnation as a general for Ramses II, as a high priest, as a brothel keeper who becomes extremely wealthy, and again as a general, conjuring up his many lives in a battle of wills and often wits with the present pharoah, Ramses IX, Ptah-nem-hotep. His narrative reminiscences make up the bulk of the book.

Entry into Khufu's pyramid begins the long dark night of the soul, the descent into the tomb, entry into the Duad, land of the dead. Osiris's death, mutilation, and resurrection become political murder, fellatio, and endless wandering toward some unseen place. Mailer's reading of entrails reveals an imagination more fecal than fecund. Vision freezes into hieroglyphic image on a wall of stone.

The book fascinates, since Mailer's Egypt does become an icon of his Manichean outlook. Egyptians prayed for personal survival, not the merely spiritual immortality of the Christian faith.[54] Thus they mummified their corpses and made graven images of their gods. Personal survival—Mailer's ultimate message—meant that an image of presence, the mum-

mified corpse, had to be there to awake in the Duad. And that present
image the hieroglyphic symbolized. Such a view threatens the Christian
notion of vanished bodies, disembodied voices, God as a speaking absence,
and an alphabet of imageless letters, as Mailer's—and Melville's—visions
threaten the smug, bourgeois, capitalist concepts of autonomous selves,
enlightened and steady progress, and a knowable universe. But the danger
perhaps for a twentieth century's interpretation of such a lost faith is that
word will freeze into image and that a ponderous prose, seemingly secure
in the rigidity of its Egyptian vision, will produce only set pieces and
emblematic encounters, the static, descriptive, pictographic writing of
hieroglyphic signs on a tomb. Mailer in *Ancient Evenings* has realized Pierre's
quest and turned the world to stone. Enceladus and Menenhetet are blood
brothers, fellow ghosts entombed beneath the same mountain of rock.

Mailer chooses to quote Oscar Wilde's dictum that "to give an accurate description of what has never occurred is . . . the inalienable
privilege of any man of parts and culture." Perhaps. But Wilde suggests
mannerist art, that dreamscape of artifice and elaborate decor and ritual,
of "peacock phrases" and "languid air and rose aromas" that all too obviously fascinates Mailer here and congeals the usual turbulence of his
imagination and rhetoric. We watch a seemingly cold collector of exotic
scenes, sets, sensations as he produces a spiritually claustrophobic vacuum,
the result finally of his self-enclosed Manichean metaphysics. Meni I suggests to Meni II that "our Land of the Dead now belongs to them, and
the Greeks think no more of it than a picture that is seen on the wall
of a cave." Nor, sadly, does Mailer.

At one point Menenhetet pauses, "as if the difficulty of embarking
on such a long tale weighed upon him like a stone he was not yet ready
to bear." Can we detect an author's shock of recognition in this? Melville's
color white, perhaps "the most mysterious of hues," is reduced to "the
color of stone, for that is where the Gods take Their rest." It suggests
not pyramidical silences but final entombment. Time past and time present obliterate one another, as the Egyptian word for "eye" suggests both
"love" and "tomb" in a kind of deadening sameness at the heart of things.
Papyrus ("beneath the hands of men it becomes a field for scribes") becomes
a place where "they plant their messages. . . . All the plants of the papyrus
dwell in the clamor of all the writings." But stories "must gleam like
swords or be as beautiful as the flowers of the garden"; they must become
static objects to look at. And the Syrians' use of writing allows the com-

mon scribe the luxury of not supposing "that the words contain more than one message. . . . They have begun to copy our sacred letters and, in so doing, have polluted them."

Ancient Evenings is essentially an elaborate ghost story, the dead doubles, the Kas, of Menenhetet I and Menenhetet II communing within the dark walls of the pyramid. Meni I guides Meni II through his incarnations and the Land of the Dead. A dialogue of spectres is all that upholds Mailer's Manichean vision.

And he will not let it go: "And so I do not know if I will labor in greed forever among the demonic or serve some noble purpose I cannot name." Past and future intermingle, and dead hearts live in the final beautiful paragraph, but we are left "with lightning in the wounds of the Gods." Torpor replaces terror, as it did in Melville's *Pierre* and *The Confidence-Man*. The Manichean vision reaches its apotheosis in a kind of static evaporation. Melville got there first, to those "vast, undefiled, incomprehensible, awful" pyramids, and Mailer has followed in his footsteps. Hawthorne's veils are drawn away—both Melville and Mailer dive for their quarry—but the tomb is cold and empty, the word and the world turned to stone. Melville's cosmic urge becomes an ancient evening, and the dead letter of Manichean mystery in his and Mailer's hands wreaks its vengeance.

THREE

Harold Frederic:
Naturalism as
Romantic Snarl

THE MORE or less standard approach to the literary relationship between Hawthorne and the realist and naturalist writers of fiction in the 1890s has been described best by James W. Tuttleton, who suggests that the relationship must necessarily have been limited.[1] After all, Hawthorne's allegorical sensibilities, his interest in the deeper psychology of representative types of characters, prevented him from exploring the realistic details and social conventions which so fascinated the realists and naturalists. "He had a confessed 'weakness' for the romantic allegory," Tuttleton explains, and in preferring "fantasy to actuality," provided no great example for later writers.[2]

In decided contrast, Edwin H. Cady demonstrates that Hawthorne's reputation grew and prospered after his death in 1864 and that, with the posthumous publication of his notebooks and late unfinished romances, culminating in the twelve volumes of the Lathrop edition in 1884, "the first unquestionably major American fictional reputation" was born.[3] In fact, James and Howells used Hawthorne's texts in their own discussions of the merits of literary realism. *Life* magazine in 1887 used Hawthorne to castigate the new realists, praising the ideal elements in his art as opposed to the realists' coarser works.[4] And in 1883 English literature students at Yale were allowed to write their junior essays on "Hawthorne's Imagination," the only American author in their list of given topics.[5] So complete and powerful was the critical response to Hawthorne's works that "Hawthorne's example served steadily as an authorization and incitement to writers and inevitably as a critical touchstone."[6] Such was the posthumous influence of Hawthorne that Cady, having documented its authenticity, asserts that "a large and profitable study in itself would be that of the influence of Hawthorne on the American fiction writers of this extended generation."[7] Hawthorne's influence upon the realists was substantial: "Though a fragmentary literature on the subject exists, no one has yet truly elucidated the ways in which James and Howells, as features of their very rebellion against 'the Mage,' repeatedly created—and in psychological, moral, and even mystical as well as esthetic developments—significant variations upon themes by Hawthorne."[8] It would not be mere speculation, therefore, to suggest that Harold Frederic attempted to deal with similar variations.

Harold Frederic's *The Damnation of Theron Ware* has puzzled critics ever since its appearance on the best-seller list in 1896. Most have chosen to see it as yet another example of emerging American naturalism in the literary world. There are, indeed, reasons for this assumption, as we shall see, but Frederic was really trying to accomplish something else. Frederic himself, when asked about his "literary parentage," mentioned Emile Erchmann and Alexandre Chatrain, masters of historical and sentimental melodrama, *and* Nathaniel Hawthorne. If Hawthorne was indeed some sort of literary midwife or father figure for Frederic, then perhaps the naturalistic label which has stuck to him may be not only too simplistic but particularly misunderstood. As early as 1939 Charles Walcutt decided that "*Theron Ware*, to conclude, is not a naturalistic novel because its author could not eliminate ethical judgments and motivations in favor of materialistic ones."[9] While Walcutt's own definition of naturalism may be too simplistic, his early article, which briefly examines the psychological aspects of Frederic's masterpiece, points in the right direction.

Literary naturalism as a philosophy derives, in part, from Emile Zola's blend of the experimental method of science and the sociological notions derived from Darwin. To Darwin, environment was all; all organisms were shaped by it, man as one among them. Man existed as the sum of all his desires and instincts, the somewhat pitiful victim of a universe operating by blind and iron forces. Man's primitive yearnings for food and copulation propelled him through this field of forces into a perpetual void that he could never hope to comprehend.

The naturalistic vision in literature demanded a more accurate vision of sexual instinct in man's blind fumblings from womb to tomb, particularly if that could be observed in an urban slum, a railroad yard, or a meat-packing plant, or on a battlefront. The "smiling aspects" of William

Dean Howells's literary realism, with its attention to social and historical detail, dissolved in the face of more gruesome observations.

With the appearance of Frank Norris, Stephen Crane, and Frederic on the literary scene, Howells's smiling surface began to break up. As George Johnson suggests, these writers were in the process of "freeing the novel from the comprehensive, realistic rendering of life in society without losing solidity and density, while regaining the symbolic or mythic significance of the older tradition of Poe, Hawthorne, and Melville."[10] As Norris, Crane, and Frederic dug deeper below the cracked surface of social convention, they began to uncover wider social patterns, veritable new mythologies revealed in the mental processes of the mind. As a result, these writers began to abandon the objective techniques of the realist, the neoclassicist concern with the Standard Type draped in General Decorum, and opened up what they considered to be new symbolic patterns of experience. This focus upon primitive forces not only revealed a loss of confidence in the outward appearance of Western civilization but also uncovered new psychological and mythic patterns in those very forces that pointed toward new truths, eternally present beneath the flux of time and space. In turning from the abundant details of character in society to concentrate upon one soul or two, and in bending their visions inward, these writers approached the psychological and allegorical territory that had appeared in Hawthorne's fiction.

Frank Norris's definition of naturalism as "a fictional mode which illustrated some fundamental truth of life within a detailed presentation of the sensational and low"[11] strikes closer to what Harold Frederic was up to in his book. Norris viewed literary realism as a method of accuracy, a way of writing in which superficial details were carefully collected and displayed. Romanticism for him suggested digging "down deep into the red, living heart of things,"[12] searching for ultimate truth and revelation in a decidedly Hawthornesque manner. "Naturalism is a form of romanticism," he declared, "not an inner circle of realism."[13] Therefore, naturalism combined realism's accuracy with romanticism's revelation, transcending both in choosing any walk of life for its subject or theme, more often than not, low life. Frederic's appreciation of Hawthorne, then, according to Norris's definition of naturalism, should fit right into the mainstream of American naturalist fiction.

Briefly, what is *The Damnation of Theron Ware* about? First of all, there are at least two Theron Wares, perhaps reflecting the realistic character and the romantic prototype of Norris's definition of naturalism, an artistic problem I will consider below. The first is a product of Theron's American Protestant background, a totally vulnerable soul who has been reared on biblical teachings and deprived of any aesthetic fulfillment. Protestantism, or at least the fundamentalist Methodism of the novel, denies the spiritual validity of aesthetic and artistic concerns and feelings. In the words of Loren Pierce, " 'We walk here . . . in a meek and humble spirit, in the straight an' narrow way which leadeth unto life. We ain't gone traipsin' after strange gods, like some people that call themselves Methodists in other places. We stick by the Discipline an' the ways of our fathers in Israel. No newfangled notions can go down here. Your wife'd better take them flowers out of her bunnit afore next Sunday.' "[14] These impoverished yearnings become sublimated and demand occasional outbursts in camp or revival meetings, common to upper New York State, the "burned-over district" of the novel. Theron, therefore, is attracted to the voluptuous and vibrant spirit and display of the Irish Catholics in Octavius. To him they seem to transform secular and aesthetic feelings into sacred celebrations, and he is starved for such pomp and circumstance.

The other Theron complements the first. He is the American innocent, an almost allegorical figure in our literature, egocentric, prideful, and ignorant (in this case), convinced of his own confidence and imminent success. Frederic suffuses him "in a transfiguring halo of romance," reveals his "convictions that the South was the land of romance, of cavaliers and gallants and black eyes flashing behind mantillas and outspread fans." Theron believes that someday he will make a great pulpit orator, that he must "puzzle out and master all the principles which underlie this art, and all the tricks that adorn its superstructure," and that he can easily rise to "a lofty and rarefied atmosphere of spiritual exaltation." His romantic solipsism suggests the similar dilemmas of such characters as Young Goodman Brown, shrewd Robin, and Giovanni Guasconti.

Throughout the novel Theron confuses natural beauty with spiritual revelation. Aesthetically starved, he cannot judge any of what he sees and senses. His own curiosity, Frederic suggests, stems from his inner sexual and aesthetic desires, so that, in fact, that "innocent" curiosity is in itself already corrupt. Sexual instinct operates in the guise of intellectual enlightenment as it operates beneath the surface of much of the novel, and Theron cannot distinguish between the two. Even religion becomes a mere facade for sexual impulse, a pre-Freudian view that reveals the naturalistic heart of Frederic's novel. Throughout the book Frederic consistently muses "upon the curious way in which people's minds all unconsciously follow about where instincts and intuitions lead," and Dr. Ledsmar's disquisition on women and priests is not lost on Theron's consciousness. Sexual and oedipal tensions underscore the novel. Theron's proposed book on Abraham hopes to explore "the powerful range of possibilities in the son's revolt against the idolatry of his father, the image-maker, in the exodus from the unholy city of Ur, and in the influence of the new nomadic life upon the little deistic family group," while he himself is drawn to Father Forbes's sense of authority and history and "Mother" Soulsby's comforting buffalo robes and soothing responses.

Several times Theron is described as a young woman on the verge of some powerful seduction or as a young boy in search of parental guidance and protection. Salivating in the forest at Celia's knee, he describes himself as "a boy again, a good, pure-minded, fond little child, and you were the mother that I idolized." Sex is no longer a sentiment but a mysterious primal force, here somewhat inverted in boyish Theron's need to lean on strong women. Shades of Dimmesdale and Hester. Such confused sexual overtones may reveal the true sexless nature of American innocence, a sexual wasteland where easy seduction becomes easily destructive and where Theron's pursuit of Celia's pre-Raphaelite whims and Sister Soulsby's "Advance Man" social mechanics, where "the pursuit of these terrible mothers leads to an abased and enervating status of a very little boy."[15]

The lures for Theron, in what Larzer Ziff has called "a symbolic tale of America's progress to disunity in the latter half of the nineteenth century,"[16] are fourfold: Celia Madden, Dr. Ledsmar, Father Forbes, and Sister Soulsby. Celia fuses the aesthetic and sexual seduction, her room a triumph (if it can be called that) of decadent "Yellow-Book" art, her music the heavenly labials that will undo him, her Greek whims emblazoned too luridly in Frederic's overwrought prose. Ledsmar derides such decadence, proclaims his faith in rational science, and observes coldly the opiate dreams of his Chinese servant. Father Forbes combines the highly sophisticated new skepticism or "New Thought" of the 1890s with a pagan's strong belief in the necessities of ceremonial and sacredly mysterious religion. His sense of history underlines the entire novel in its presentation of the unending pagan dark that will not be scared off. Sister Soulsby preaches organization, the "good fraud" of the necessary machinery of modern life, the idea that we are all on a see-saw where good and evil

are neither separate nor valid terms by which to live. Against such odds
Theron hasn't a prayer. He follows Celia to New York, is furiously upbraided by her, collapses at Sister Soulsby's, and returns home. Our last
view of him mirrors our first. Self-confident, enamored of the cadences
of his own voice, daydreaming of political triumphs in far-off Seattle,
Theron, like Huck Finn before him, lights out for the territory, with
Alice in his cheerful, self-deluding wake. We first saw him with "features
moulded into that regularity of strength which used to characterize the
American Senatorial type," and we leave him proclaiming, " 'Who
knows? I may turn up in Washington a full-blown senator before I'm
forty. Stranger things have happened than that, out West!' "

The communal and social vision, buttressed by Frederic's often pic-
torial and cinematic prose, accounts for the realistic texture of *The Damnation of Theron Ware*. Naturalistic details abound in the historical descriptions of village life in Octavius, of the Methodist Schism, the Catholic
picnic, the debt-raising love-feast, and perhaps best of all the camp meeting. Sex, as *the* underlying instinct, underlies all, its primal thrust apparent in Celia's chambers, Theron's curiosity, Forbes's priestly powers,
the supposed affair between Alice and Levi Gorringe, the quasi-phallic
towers of the Catholic church, and the Madden house. With Celia beside
him in the dark, Theron stares up at "the majestic bulk of the big silent
house rising among the trees before them," which gives him "a thrilling
sense of the glory of individual freedom," and declares, " 'I feel a new
man already.' " And yet because we are locked, for the most part, inside
Theron's point of view, his own brief comments upon the naturalistic
and/or deterministic way of things seem merely casual attempts at self-
justification, attempts to relieve himself of the personal sense of responsibility that Frederic will not allow him to relinquish. He hungers for
Celia and all she represents and thinks that "he was only obeying the
universal law of nature—the law which prompts the pallid spindling sprout
of the potato in the cellar to strive feebly toward the light." He justifies
Alice's remonstrances and his fading affection for her by calling them
"the accidents of life, the inevitable harsh happenings in the great tragedy
of Nature. They could not be helped, and there was nothing more to
be said." Clearly in Frederic's mind natural determinism neither explains
nor excuses Theron Ware's behavior. It does not go to the roots of the
dilemma.

In order to suggest broader and deeper causes of Theron's problem,

7

52 IN HAWTHORNE'S SHADOW

Frederic must overcome mere sociological and historical causes and descriptions. He must grapple more deeply with the state of mind, the patterns of universal human experience, that Theron seems to represent. To accomplish this task, as Johnson suggests, "special conditions are required in order to achieve a sly and artful movement—which James advocated—from the Howellsian transcription of the average to the romancer's larger representation."[17] These special conditions of the romancer Frederic responded to and sought from Hawthorne's work. Stanton Garner is correct when he avows that "readers have classified him as a regionalist, as a realist, and as a naturalist, whereas his true descent from Hawthorne and Melville has largely gone unnoticed. Many sense the depth and power of *Theron Ware*, but find the source of his creative energy elusive."[18] Frederic's own short story "The Song of Swamp Robin," Garner points out, published in the *Independent* in the issues of March 12 and 19, 1891, describes the heroine of the tale as "a second Pearl, daughter of Hester Prynne," and she marries to become "Mrs. Hathorne."[19] A review of *The Damnation of Theron Ware* in the *Spectator* of 1896 suggests that there is "more than a mere touch of the vanished hand that wrote *The Scarlet Letter* in *Illumination*,"[20] the English title of Frederic's book. "Indeed," comments George Johnson once again, "in its duplicity *The Damnation of Theron Ware* might be read as an extended gloss on Hawthorne's 'Young Goodman Brown,' brought up to date and given topicality in the 'turbulent' milieu of the 1890's."[21] And Frederic himself acknowledged, "I'm not a Hawthorne, but as the small Charleston darky said to the old one, who insisted on God's superiority over the black Congressman from the Sixth District—'Yes, but don't forget—Bob Smalls he young man yet.' "[22]

It is imperative at this point to look closely at the novel in order to reveal its homage to Hawthorne, in particular to *The Scarlet Letter*. Here are the opening paragraphs of *The Scarlet Letter* and *The Damnation of Theron Ware* (italics mine). From *The Scarlet Letter*:

> A *throng* of bearded men, in sad-colored garments and gray, steeple-*crowned* hats, intermixed with women, some wearing hoods, and others bareheaded, was assembled in front of a wooden edifice, the *door* of which was heavily timbered with oak, and studded with iron spikes.

From *The Damnation*:

> No such *throng* had ever been seen in the building during all its eight years of existence. People were wedged together most uncomfortably upon the seats; they stood packed in the aisles and overflowed the galleries; at the back, in the shadows underneath these galleries, they formed broad, dense masses, about the *doors*, through which it would be hopeless to attempt a passage.

From *The Scarlet Letter*:

> . . . *all with their eyes intently fastened on the iron-clamped oaken door.* Amongst any other population, or at a later period in the history of New England, the grim rigidity that petrified the *bearded* physiognomies of these good people would have augured some awful business in hand. It could have betokened nothing short of the anticipated execution of some noted culprit, on whom the sentence of legal tribunal had but confirmed the *verdict* of public sentiment.

From *The Damnation*:

> . . . others *bearded* or *crowned* with shining baldness,—but all alike under the spell of a dominant emotion which held features in abstracted suspense and *focussed every eye upon a common objective point*. . . . An observer, looking over these compact lines of faces and noting the uniform concentration of eagerness they exhibited, might have guessed that they were watching for either the jury's *verdict* in some peculiarly absorbing criminal trial, or the announcement of the lucky numbers in a great lottery.

Another example is, of course, the famous forest scenes in both narratives, the trysts between Hester and Dimmesdale, Celia and Theron Ware. As Austin Briggs suggests, "Detail by detail, Frederic follows the climactic confrontation between Dimmesdale and Hester in the forest."[23] After the famous kiss bestowed upon Theron by the whimsical Celia, he wanders through the forest and conjures up a scene in his own mind that any reader of Hawthorne cannot fail to recognize:

When he walked alone in unfamiliar parts of the forest, he car-
ried about with him the half-conscious idea of somewhere coming
upon a strange, hidden pool which mortal eye had not seen before,—a
deep, sequestered mere of spring-fed waters, walled in by rich, tangled growths of verdure, and bearing upon its virgin bosom only
the shadows of the primeval wilderness, and the light of the eternal skies. His fancy dwelt upon some such nook as the enchanted
home of the fairy that possessed his soul. The place, though he never
found it, became real to him.

This hidden psychic spring, this primal center of the self upon which
he has half-consciously stumbled, suggests that symbol of the spring that
Hawthorne consciously used again and again, and reveals Frederic's careful
observations of Hawthorne's emblems.

The world of *The Damnation of Theron Ware* is no longer one con-
ceived in moral and ethical terms, at least in their socially rigid and traditional manifestations. Deeper urges fester beneath the surface here, "mysterious, impersonal, Titanic forces,"[24] as an early reviewer of the novel
put it. Consequently Frederic's use of or borrowings from Hawthorne
are often inverted, undermined in the way he employs them. Of the forest
scene Briggs concludes, "Frederic invokes his beloved Hawthorne perverse-
ly, however; at every turn he denies and inverts what is basic in
Hawthorne's fiction, the assumption that all human acts have large and
lasting consequences, that the acknowledgment of sin is the pre-requisite
for redemption."[25] There are no marble fauns transformed here, only illuminations which in themselves complete Theron's damnation.

The novel is rich in what Johnson has called "the enhanced lights and
deepened shadows, the legendary mists and magnified import of Hawthorne's vision of romance,"[26] and the use of light and dark does suggest the complexities of *The Scarlet Letter*. Celia, Father Forbes, Catholic
ceremonies, the church itself—all these supposed illuminations are bathed
in radiant light:

The door opened, and Theron saw the priest standing in the door-
way with an uplifted hand. He wore now a surplice, with a purple
band over his shoulders, and on his pale face there shone a tranquil
and tender light.

He entered a room in which for the moment he could see nothing but a central glare of dazzling light beating down from a great shaded lamp upon a circular patch of white table linen. Inside this ring of illumination points of fire sparkled from silver and porcelain, and two bars of burning crimson tracked across the cloth in reflection from tall glasses filled with wine. The rest of the room was vague darkness, but the gloom seemed saturated with novel aromatic odors, the appetizing scent of which bore clear relation to what Theron's blinking eyes rested upon.

Directly facing him was the arched and mullioned top of a great window. A dim light from within shone through the more translucent portions of the glass below, throwing out faint little bars of partly-colored radiance upon the blackness of the deep passage-way. He could vaguely trace by these the outlines of some sort of picture on the window. There were human figures in it, and—yes— up here in the centre, nearest him, was a woman's head. There was a halo about it, engirdling rich, flowing waves of reddish hair, the lights in which glowed like flame.

The room in which he found himself was so dark at first that it yielded little to the eye, and that little seemed altogether beyond his comprehension. His gaze helplessly followed Celia and her candle about as she busied herself in the work of illumination. When she had finished, and pinched out the tape, there were seven lights in the apartment—lights beaming softly through half-opaque alternating rectangles of blue and yellow glass.

The light always remains outside of and beyond Theron. He walks into it as if entering a spotlight of some kind. Usually he remains standing in darkness looking at these strange lights. The point, I feel, is revealed by Frederic's technique. The illuminations, however brilliant, are false, for Theron remains in the shadows of his own unenlightened ignorance. They are so theatrically suggested as to shed no inner light whatsoever. Theron's surrounding aura of "non-light" reveals how unilluminated he really is, a sort of voyeur peering into places in which he does not belong. Light and dark as moral values have been intriguingly reversed, for the

light suggests an evil with which Theron's own ignorant darkness cannot cope: "It was for all the world as if he had wandered into some vast
tragical, enchanted cave, and was being drawn against his will—like
fascinated bird and python—toward fate at the savage hands of these
swollen and enraged genii." The technique is surely Hawthorne's, even
in its moral complexities and its calculated inversion of expected values,
and it is suggestive of the elusive use of light and dark in *The Scarlet
Letter*. Perhaps it is Frederic who has simplified the technique in its repeated
and similar patterns throughout the novel, and in doing so has undercut
the very moral complexities which Hawthorne pursued and which Frederic
found relatively unpersuasive.

Stanton Garner continues: "In technique the novel is Hawthornesque,
except for Frederic's deceptively realistic prose. Most of the proper names
are heavily allusive and the passage of the seasons symbolizes a reversal
of the regeneration of *Walden*. It moves from emblem to emblem, em-
bodying meaning in those still-life pictures which have been characteristic
of classic American fiction from its beginning."[27] This emblematic, still-
life approach Frederic employs, although far more cinematically than
Hawthorne, in the novel. One thinks, as Garner points out, of those
carefully set scenes—Celia and Theron in the forest, Celia's room as an
indication or emblem of her inherent paganism, the squalor of the par-
sonage as an emblem of the parsimonious, fundamentalist squalor of Octavius, the woodland path as an emblem of the loss of faith of these moral
wanderers. There is, I feel, a deeper level in this careful arrangement of
scenes, as though one were passing through various and developing states
of consciousness.

In his famous essay "The Haunted Mind," Hawthorne describes that
state of consciousness between sleeping and waking, what Richard Wilbur
has called the hypnagogic state, in which his mind, becoming a seemingly passive spectator, watched warily as his imagination became a mirror to reflect such phantoms "without the power of selecting or controlling them."[28] For Hawthorne this amounted to a genuine moral
dilemma, because such uninitiated conjurings startled and seemed to overwhelm his moral sensibilities. Such a mind he knew to be haunted, and
in this state he readily identified himself, the artist, with the wizards and
warlocks of old. Frederic recognized this dreamlike quality in Hawthorne,
this subterranean drift that underscored the more conscious, emblematic
construction of his fiction, and tried to imitate it. He describes Theron

as "letting his mind wander at will through the pleasant ante-chambers of Sleep, where are more unreal fantasies than Dreamland itself affords." At one time Theron longs to be hypnotized by Sister Soulsby's eyes and connects such conscienceless languor with his own spiritual development:

> He needed another sort of companionship,—some restful, soothing human contact, which should exact nothing from him in return, but just take charge of him, with soft, wise words and pleasant plays of fancy, and jokes and—and—something of the general effect created by Sister Soulsby's eyes. The thought expanded itself, and he saw that he had never realized before,—nay, never dreamt before—what a mighty part the comradeship of talented, sweet-natured and beautiful women must play in the development of genius, the achievement of loftly aims, out in the great world of great men.

It is a position for which Hawthorne would have had only revulsion and contempt. Again, Frederic describes the forces unleashed by the spell of a preacher's voice at the camp meeting, the very same spell Theron longs to achieve and decides is the culmination of spiritual growth: "They would hear a strange, quavering note in the preacher's voice, catch the sense of a piercing, soul-commanding gleam in his eye, not at all to be resisted. These occult forces would take control of them, drag them forward as in a dream to the benches under the pulpit, and abase them there like worms in the dust." And finally that "strange, hidden pool," some remote and "deep, sequestered mere" of the soul, Theron conjures up himself as a "half-conscious idea," a kind of walking hypnagogic state into which he passes willingly. It is this dreamlike "sub-text" of *The Damnation of Theron Ware* that provides the novel with its primary hold on the reader, related perhaps to singular sexual instincts, but founded most probably on that same psychic and romantic power that the best of Hawthorne's strange allegories generate.

One other aspect of *The Damnation of Theron Ware* suggests the strong and irrefutable influences of Hawthorne. The characters themselves fit the Hawthornian mold. Theron, of course, suggests the golden-tongued Dimmesdale, though, whereas Dimmesdale transforms himself into an allegorical object lesson of sin, Theron sheds ideas and sensations like clothes and ends as he began, secure in his cheerful, self-deluding "innocence."

He recognizes nothing but marches to that self-deluding American Dream: "Go West, young man!" Ledsmar is Chillingworth, Dr. Aylmer, and Dr. Rappaccini reborn, the heartless scientist, the cold observer. Celia might as well be a sister to Hester, Zenobia, and Miriam, though her exaggerated paganism makes her the least believable character in the book. Father Forbes is a new voice on the scene, a Catholic figure with a perceptive historical sensibility. Hawthorne's priest in *The Marble Faun* could only hope slyly to seduce poor dove-haunted Hilda! The most interesting and misunderstood character may be Sister Soulsby. Does she represent some good amalgamation of necessary social control and common sense, or is she more evil in her effects on Theron Ware? Since all the characters remain somewhat ambiguous, even confused, we cannot pin easy labels on them, or as distinct labels as we could often pin on Hawthorne's characters. Yet it seems to me that Sister Soulsby is akin to Hawthorne's Westervelt in *The Blithedale Romance*, a representative of the modern manipulative world, not to be trusted, however practical and useful her tools of trade.

There is much evidence against Sister Soulsby throughout the novel. For one thing, Ledsmar likes her: "I don't know when I've seen two such really genuine people. I should like to have known more of them." And the two of them share the serpent imagery in the book; he worships them; she applauds the "wisdom of the serpent." She may in fact be the Devil of the piece in the guise of Maternal Assistance. She transforms Theron's view of himself, tells him that Alice worships him, that his congregation is not good enough for him, that Methodism is of course a primitive sham. It is after her completion of the love feast that Theron surrenders to her methods and that the vigorous pursuit of his damnation begins. Her eyes suggest "the image of two eagles in a concerted pounce upon a lamb." She, like Westervelt, has been a professional hypnotist. How easily she can cultivate the eager sensibilities of the ignorant Theron! Theron notices that "her answers were all so pat," an ironic allusion perhaps to "Stand Pat Hanna," the manipulative Mark back of McKinley in the election of 1896.[29] Perhaps Theron's damnation is assured when Soulsby takes control and convinces him that all his beliefs, however precariously held, are mere stage scenery and window-dressing, that he must become a conscious fraud, an actor superior to his audience. She blurs whatever diluted moral sense he has left. Her methodology asserts that his way has been corrupt, that it must now be replaced. Does she, in fact, instill in him the belief in universal corruption, so much so that the only way to beat it is to join it? Such arguments on a romantically oriented and ignorant psyche like Theron's work toward his inevitable downfall.

Sister Soulsby proclaims her own divinity—"Now I say that Soulsby and I do good, and that we're good fellows"—and so of course her fraud, by definition, is bound to be a good fraud. Perhaps this is Theron's ironic moment of illumination, initiated as he is into the industrialized faith of the Gilded Age, the faith in the divinity and power of the machine. Perhaps this is why Frederic entitled his novel in England *Illumination*, for it would allow the English to scoff at such illuminations by pious frauds. In America it became the *Damnation*, allowing American readers to take their own fall from grace more seriously. If, as Larzer Ziff maintains, *The Damnation of Theron Ware* records "the loss of innocent purpose in America,"[30] then Sister Soulsby has engineered that loss. In New York when Theron in disgrace flees to her, Brother Soulsby enters, "bearing a small lamp in his hand, the reddish light of which, flaring upward, revealed an unlooked-for display of amusement on his thin, beardless face." Theron has remembered the good Sister because of his seeing "a big picture of a woman in tights, and the word 'Amazons' overhead," and we all can imagine how helpful an Amazon would be in retrieving the lost souls of male ministers! The ambiguous character of Sister Soulsby and Frederic's own ambiguous response to modernism may indicate one more instance in which Hawthorne's gallery of stock characters appealed to him.

All that I have mentioned so far clearly indicates that Frederic was consciously striving to attain and inhabit the literary territory that his "literary parent," Hawthorne, had so clearly staked out before him. Yet one would have to agree again with Johnson that "when all this has been remarked, however, we are left with a work which is primarily 'rhetorical' in Yeats' sense of the term, a finicky niggling preciseness in structure and allusion masking an imaginative deficiency. A tour de force, the book remains at the last more complicated than complex, a flawed monument to an endeavor audacious, artful, and American."[31] Of all the critics, Johnson has most carefully investigated the major problem with the novel, the point of view. Both romantic and realistic (or naturalistic) attributes are entangled in that point of view. Here we get back to the two Theron Wares. One is the product of a particular cultural and historical environment, the ignorant, immature minister lured on by alien ceremonies, as

Garner describes him, "a classic instance of egocentric innocence confronted with the allure of exotic philosophies it fails to comprehend—
indeed, is prevented from comprehending by an inherent voluptuousness
concealed beneath a surface of affable charm."[32] If this be the heart of
the novel, then all the romantic or Hawthornesque touches can only be
self-justifications on Theron's part for his actions, as his comments on
determinism must be, and we cannot take them seriously. The romantic
elements, however inverted or transformed, can only be seen as the attempts of this comically ignorant creature to view his life in some broader
and finally fraudulent perspective. Is he a romantic trapped in a naturalistic
universe? It cannot be that simple, for Frederic's landscape, however
relegated to Theron's own view of things, itself partakes of romantic
allusions—the lights and shadows, the reversal of the seasons in relation
to Theron's supposed growth toward self-knowledge, the names of the
characters and their particular attitudes. These notions do not depend on
Theron's point of view to exist in the novel. If we can believe in the
wider representational aspects of Frederic's book, then what are we to
do with the naturalistic aspects of it—the role of sexual longings, primitive
instincts, and uncharted yearnings? Can both the romantic and the
naturalistic elements be fused in the hypnagogic reality of Theron's experiences? And if that is true, why did Frederic not make that reality
more apparent, more visible to the reader?

The fault may lie in Frederic's original working title for the novel,
Snarl. He seems to have wanted to suggest both aspects, to invest his
book with a cultural and social inevitability and at the same time with
a more universal and representative allegorical framework that would
develop beyond that more exclusive inevitability. In any case he did not
succeed. The elements of Hawthorne, and they are several, just do not
fuse with the historical realism of the novel. Even Hawthorne knew he
had to create a mythic or legendary past, to get away from the present
time and place, to allow his romantic and allegorical ideas to flourish.
Johnson suggests that if "the author relies on a 'normal' central consciousness to invest a 'normal' societal situation with a romantic signification, his reader cannot accept both the hero's point of view and the pur-
ported significance of his career."[33] The reader just cannot take Theron
seriously. Society's roles and Hawthorne's significations battle each other
instead of clarifying and absorbing each other. The fusion never takes
place. Frederic was not an artist capable of such control or finesse.

But the fact remains that Frederic was trying to forge a newer "romanticism" in *The Damnation of Theron Ware*, trying to penetrate the simplistic and iron forces of a naturalistic universe to reach the primal forces of the human psyche, that dark realm which has always been the primal core of the best American literature. Perhaps *The Damnation of Theron Ware* reveals that there never really was a viable naturalist aesthetic at all, that the factual realism and accumulation of scientifically accurate force fields in the American novel were just not enough to get at the heart of the American experience. Is this why they were abandoned so readily, why even the fiction of Theodore Dreiser, despite its Spenserian underpinnings, repeats and extends certain representational patterns of American experience that may be called romantic? Frederic clearly saw the roots he was after but he could not sufficiently blend or absorb them into the realistic caste of his fiction. They remained roots, snarled and confused, breaking loose from that fictional mold and hanging suspended in open space. It was left to a genius like Faulkner to accomplish finally the convergence of social and mythic patterns in the American psyche, to complete that attempt that had failed Hawthorne so utterly in *The Marble Faun*. Frederic may have sensed this need, this direction American literature would take, but he was not the artist to accomplish it. Perhaps the best way in which to view *The Damnation of Theron Ware* is not as an example of literary naturalism but as the midpoint between Hawthorne's allegories and Faulkner's myths.

Frederic did, however, sense the center of the haunted mind, that dark and pagan core from which all growth appears as mere illusion and in which experience can only be repetitious, cyclical, and eventually destructive. As Father Forbes, perhaps the closest character in the book to Frederic's own ideas, suggests: " 'You see, there is nothing new. Everything is built on the ruins of something else. Just as the material earth is made up of countless billions of dead men's bones, so the mental world is all alive with the ghosts of dead men's thoughts and beliefs; the wraiths of dead races' faiths and imaginings.' " Perhaps Frederic penetrated to the dark central core of American literature in which "the world was all black again,—plunged in the Egyptian night which lay upon the face of the deep while the earth was yet without form and void. He was alone on it,—alone among awful, planetary solitudes which crushed him." From this perspective Father Forbes's description of the human race sounds strangely like a description of the continual images and emotions in our own literature: "The human race are still very like savages in a dangerous wood in the dark, telling one another ghost stories around a camp-fire." What Hawthorne shied away from, what Faulkner finally dealt with, Frederic had some awareness of, but he could not articulate that muted vision. It remained "like some huge, shadowy, and symbolical monument" with its roots in Hawthorne's aesthetic, its visible branches in the naturalistic atmosphere of his age, and its core somewhere between "giving forth from its recesses of night the sounds of screams and curses" and glowing like some "spectral picture of some black-robed, tonsured men, with leering satanic masks, making a bonfire of the Bible in the public schools."

FOUR

Faulkner, McCullers, O'Connor, Styron: The Shadow on the South

C.P. SNOW may have best summed up the thrust of literary modernism, however condescendingly, when he described it as the writer's attempt "to represent brute experience through the moments of sensation."[1] Certainly Stravinsky's music, Picasso's early work, Joyce's stream of consciousness concentrated on man not as a civilized being, a carefully cultured intellect espousing sex as sentiment, but as a primitive creature, raw with emotions, experiencing sex as primal force. Freud shattered the civilized soul, layered it into superego, ego, and id. "Repression" became the common word of the Twenties.

In effect the romantic idea of the self generated the modernist primitive man. That modernist self occupied the center of an otherwise emptied universe: it existed in present time only, both victim and creator of cyclical patterns deep within its mysterious, labyrinthine mind and body, a naturalistic creature reproducing the similar psychological patterns of its fellow beings, creature of membranes and myths. At bottom, forces and desires shaped the self and placed it within repetitive cycles of primitive needs and notions: Jung's archetypes squirmed and festered within every groin and gratification. All time and space shivered, became relative from such a perspective: Einstein was right. The primitive self at the center, shorn of outmoded values, the creaky shibboleths of the Victorian era (permanently destroyed by the Great War, subverted before the trenches by such American writers as Crane and Dreiser), lived only in moments, in "the inscrutable elusiveness of flux,"[2] moments flowing into moments, the mind a myriad of Bergsonian glimpses.

Clearly the realistic tradition of nineteenth-century fiction—the idea of sequence, chronology, historical accretion—could not withstand this new vision of this more primitive self. New literary forms paralleling those in music, painting, and physics had to be devised to accommodate the flux, the heart and heat of darkness within.

Writers such as Joyce, Proust, and Conrad revolutionized the stream of consciousness in their fiction. Images, events, fragments of feeling bubbled and shimmered in the ongoing rush of a character's mind and emotions. Individual characters created their own truths, their own visions of experience, with the swiftness and awkwardness of early films, overlaid with past memories, present anxieties, future fears. Fragment abetted fragment as writers juxtaposed one moment to the next along an intuitive emotional "free fall" of narrative. "The twentieth century had addressed itself to arts of juxtaposition as opposed to earlier arts of *transition*,"[3] suggests Roger Shattuck. It seemed as though the "and therefores" and "so thats" had been left out: images, events, bits, and pieces replaced the chronological narrative line, the character's feelings and thoughts, while the novelist's own psychological connections and correspondences approximated his sense of the world as flux, adaptable finally to no creed, headlong in its intensity. Even the modernist-artist's image of himself took on the exclusivity of a vision of some scrupulous Manichean devout, supreme in his isolation and apparent wisdom.

Every stream needs its bed: gravity eventually pulls all free-falling objects to earth. Joyce and Eliot used myths to direct the flow, outside structures such as old legends and tales, outmoded religions, forms stolen from the altar and reerected in secular pursuits. For them, present chaos demanded past order to frame it. Violation, collapse, and fragmentation rebounded off Catholic masses, heroic Greek myths, ancient love poetry. "In using the myth, in manipulating a continuous parallel between [the present] and [the past], Mr. Joyce is pursuing a method which others must pursue after him," Eliot wrote in 1923. "It is simply a way of controlling, of ordering, of giving a shape and significance to the intense panorama of futility and anarchy which is contemporary history. . . . Instead of narrative method we may now use the mythical method. It is, I seriously believe, a step towards making the modern world possible for art, towards . . . order and form." In manipulating past and present, Eliot and Joyce resorted to several tones—awe, outrage, satire—but irony appeared greater than all of them and became the touchstone of modernism, the strategy of the self-protective distant eye in a world momentarily threatening to unravel once and for all.

Hemingway insisted on reproducing "the real thing, the sequence of motion and fact which made the emotion." Emotion remained that real thing, the psychological self at the center of a collapsed world, and to capture the movement of it, the motion of the flux, along with the visible events within which that motion took place, became Hemingway's creed. He applied poetic imagism to fiction: all events were rendered dramatically visible, as sharp as a photograph, the hard-edged focus of a camera's eye. Interior revelation, explanation, transition submitted to the tyranny of the image. Pound wished to see things directly, a wish as extraordinarily revolutionary as it was outrageously naive: images shorn of prior expectations, outworn values, fraudulent ideologies. Capture the fact, the image, stare obsessively at it, focus on that instant, that precise moment of observation, and the rest, the significance, will fall into place, an aura around it, a seething within it. Think in images to avoid the excrescences of personality that clogged so much nineteenth-century poetry and fiction. Literature like science can be a craft, an artifact, precise and sharply focused. All the rest blurs the truth. History lies. Explanations stanch the flow and curdle the inscrutable onrush of reality, of mind and emotion bereft of withering beliefs and shattered faiths. Rites of spring embody true "moments of sensation." The rest remains suspect.

Literary modernism seems tailor-made for the vision and techniques of Hawthorne's romance, thus opening new vistas to that older literary form. The individual self's battle against his/her own consciousness and the primitive world which both surrounds and is embodied within that consciousness rekindles Hawthorne's Manichean vision with a vengeance. Hearts of darkness and haunted minds appear inseparable, just as mythic methods encompass the character's or author's consciousness as the doomed shadow of the past encompassed Hawthorne's. A world of moments produces a literary landscape of scaffold epiphanies, those same episodic tableaux that surface again and again in Hawthorne and Melville, and the poetic spell of language seduces the reader once again into darker "neutral territories" of fevered minds and distraught souls. Isolation and disconnection, those staples of the failed rescues of Hawthorne's romance, thrive in the often imprisoning banks of the stream of consciousness, and the threat of solipsism lurks within every imaginary rush and turn.

Besides Hemingway, and in some respects Fitzgerald, the greatest practitioner of literary modernism in the United States was William Faulkner. In his work a crumbling traditional society and revolutionary literary techniques clash with a ferocity unmatched by any other American writer at the time. His work and the continuing development of southern fiction reveal both the triumph of literary modernism and the long shadow of Hawthorne's romance.

At the center of Faulkner's vision lies "the human heart in conflict with itself," that central Manichean enigma that baffled Hawthorne. Faulkner, however, as we shall see, embraced the theories of modernism. In his recreation of multiple perspectives, with their various narrators fed on rumor, gossip, legends and their own often rigid explanations of events, along with Faulkner's own overarching belief in that inscrutable flux inherent in the very nature of things, he managed to break out of Hawthorne's finally stultifying allegorical forms. An omniscient narrator could no longer present several allegorical meanings in allegorical fashion, carefully moving from Adultery to Able to Angel: the world shivered and became ultimately fluid. Though the Manichean heart remained, modernism dispersed it, and the rigidity of Hawthorne's romances became the relentless fluidity of Faulkner's.

The human heart in conflict with itself: the center of Faulkner's romances. The unfathomable mystery of human motive and personality lies beyond human comprehension, though characters scramble to grasp some ultimate significance. The elusive centers of his masterpieces: the banished Caddy, a creature of love and promiscuity, violation and innocence; the dead Addie, raging about the disconnections between word and deed; the crucified Joe Christmas, an invention of such Manichean conflict that he seems an allegorical blank, more design than person, black and white cancelling each other out, the perfect victim whose life can only be fully experienced in his mutilation and death; the dead but heroically legendary Thomas Sutpen, innocence and will, design and destruction at odds with one another; the raped Temple and the mechanical Popeye, victim and villain.

Faulkner's great romances stem from elusive selves at the center of things, as narrators circle around them in search of their own meanings, their own designs. These self-conflicts infect the narratives. Faulkner projects his Manichean vision into the intense gloom and light of his characters' tales and speculations. His oxymoronic style, rife with paradox, doubling back, viewing and reviewing the past, spawns the Manichean conflicts, intensifies them, and weaves a rhetorical spell that entraps the reader, draws him into the search for significance, lures him into a welter of gothic possibilities, dreamlike episodes, the "scaffold epiphanies" of tall tales and unfulfilled curses. And in the remote and far reaches of a decaying South, the romantic atmosphere is complete. As Arthur Kinney suggests, "This sense of the novel as a series of discrete scenes which through repetition, parallelism, and juxtaposition intimate a broader meaning for the whole is fundamental to Faulkner's narrative poetics,"[4] and one could easily extend that definition to include the form of Hawthorne's, as well.

Faulkner employs both individual streams of consciousness and the Hemingwayesque cinematic presentation of "hard" images to approximate the flux of his vision. Benjy, Quentin, and Jason pursue Caddy as obsessively as Rosa, Mr. Compson, Quentin, and Shreve pursue Sutpen. The shattered Bundren family conjures up the dead Addie, as Faulkner himself juxtaposes Horace and Popeye at the spring, Joe Christmas and Gail Hightower in Jefferson. Each perspective thrives on the ultimate inability to resolve the central character's mystery or motives: all remain oxymoronic allegorists in some fashion or another, struggling through "not onlys" and "but alsos" toward some motionless abstraction that does not exist. All contradict, indict, speculate and add to the continuum of the human mind and spirit, an ease with ultimate flux that terrified Hawthorne and may have forced him to cling to his later static and studied style in the still-born passages of *The Marble Faun* and *The Blithedale Romance*. The allegorical method, linking image and idea at the very moment each occurs, "translating" the image into immediate speculative idea, reveals a basically monistic mind in search of an ultimate truth to nail to the scaffold. Faulkner's modernist methods shatter that dying literary form, as all social, mythic, and individual patterns converge into one ongoing stream of narrative. Truth remains multiple, relative, a process inherent in the human mind, at times terrifying (one thinks of the intensity of Quentin's obsessions, of Horace Benbow's, of Joe Christmas's) but finally inescapable.

One senses the conflict in Faulkner raging unabated in his great romances. Past battles present; a vanished moral code confronts its continued violation; Sartoris battles Snopes; Colonel Falkner haunts the young William Faulkner; black opposes white; the "new South" stands as a withered bitter outrage in contrast to the nostalgic sanctuary of an "Old South" that never existed. Value batters fact: how can one decide which is which or transform the latter into the former? Life, the motion and flux of it, seems threatened by motion and flux. Significance attracts, but the static quality of the sanctuary it seems to promise suggests only death and withdrawal. Outrage, the fierce fuel of Manichean conflict, the sensation of a lost believer stumbling into a Manichean age, triumphs. And all of these thrive in a kind of simultaneous suspension, conflict become an eternal unrelenting rite.

In a short sketch entitled "An Innocent at Rinkside," Faulkner's observation of a hockey game epitomizes his ultimate vision of the world:

> The vacant ice looked tired . . . it looked not expectant but resigned . . . .
>
> Then it was filled with motion, speed. To the innocent, who had never seen it before, it seemed discorded and inconsequent, bizarre and paradoxical like the frantic darting of the weightless bugs which run on the surface of stagnant pools. Then it would break, coalesce through a kind of kaleidoscopic whirl like a child's toy, into a pattern, a design almost beautiful, as if an inspired choreographer had drilled a willing and patient and hard-working troupe of dancers—a pattern, design which was trying to tell him something, say something to him urgent and important and true in that second before, already bulging with the motion and the speed, it began to disintegrate and dissolve.

Out of perpetual motion, "bizarre and paradoxical," the conflict at the heart of things, come momentary pattern and design, as if a choreographer, a god, had arranged it; but just as quickly and as certainly, as if in a split second on the edge of ultimate collapse, design disintegrates and dissolves. Flux is all, however momentarily the intimations of patterns emerge. And art attempts to trap it, like "the roof which stopped and trapped all that intent and tense watching, and concentrated it downward upon the glare of ice frantic and frenetic with motion; until the by-product of the speed and the motion—their violence—had no chance to exhaust itself upward into space and so leave on the ice only the swift glittering changing pattern.''

Add to this Faulkner's sense of his native Mississippi. Like Hawthorne's Salem, Calvinism lurks in all decaying corners: the sense of evil, the unrelenting self-scrutiny, the self-righteous rigor of the Scotch-Irish. Guilt and damnation interpenetrate the South's defeat in war; doom shadows the violent land: the witch-hanging judge in Hawthorne's family, the peripatetic colonel in Faulkner's, grandfathers immersed in their country's, their region's, past. Biblical patterns of justice and retribution intermingled with tall tales and frontier legends and that sense that the present constitutes a falling off from the past, a diminishment, a tragic, inexorable loss of some deep, unredeemable kind. And both men admire and fear the Hollingsworths and Chillingworths, the Sutpens and Percy Grimms of this world.

The southern fascination with rhetoric and urgently nostalgic images of its past fueled Faulkner's vision. As past continued into present, as the self became mesmerized with introspection and obsessed with further introspection—Quentin, Gail Hightower, Darl Bundren, Rosa Coldfield, Horace Benbow—paralysis resulted. How many of Faulkner's characters sit in dark rooms, their present become only the self-hypnotic reiterations of past deeds, past sins, yearning for an ultimate answer, sinking more deeply into paralysis. Past and present tumble into one another, separate categories collapse, a solipsistic incestuous stasis results, as introspection feeds on introspection, paradox on paradox, word on word. Incest becomes the ultimate paralysis, the ultimate sin, as does miscegenation: the collapse of opposites into one mesmerizing trance. And there stands Faulkner's ultimate indictment or presentation of himself and his South: the belief that intensity of feeling parallels and is equal to depth of knowledge, that the stronger the emotion, the rage, the more one knows and understands. Emotion and reason become one, collapse into one another in a final Manichean nightmare that leads to suicide, spiritual and physical paralysis, the long dark cry of Quentin's at the end of *Absalom, Absalom!*: *"I don't hate it . . . I don't! I don't! I don't hate it! I don't hate it!"* Language expresses vehemently the opposite of the complex of emotions and feelings: word and deed confirm their final opposition as they simultaneously reveal a feeling so intense that no amount of language can strike at its core. The heart in conflict with itself at once erupts and dissolves. Emotion consumes reason. The fierce outrage flings itself into a distant and vanished present.

One early critic of Faulkner was correct when he referred to Faulkner's works as "romance of the appalling."[5] They are myths of violation and loss, dark romances written in the shadow of *The White Rose of Memphis*, the moonlit romances of a false South "gone with the wind." Conflict is all; only death can quench but never resolve it. Manichean mystery reigns supreme amidst the constant flux, and all are swept before it.

Addie Bundren's outrage in *As I Lay Dying* turns upon itself and others. To her, other people remain secret, separate, selfish. Only in whipping them can communion come, "only through the blows of the switch could my blood and their blood flow as one stream." Only through sexual violation can self-definition or at least a guise of wholeness be achieved: the self as violated victim renews itself, "time, Anse, love, what you will, outside the circle." The self must submit to the "terrible blood," to impulse, dissolving into a kind of "not-self" in order to achieve self-recognition. To live is to be aware of the terrible boiling blood, the aloneness that contains it. All else is false. Primitive passion alone, directed to undercut every social and cultural convention, restores Addie to her original hating, vengeful self. Addie's father told her that life is only getting ready to stay dead a long time. From such a perspective, everything but mindless instinct appears false; everything has no value. Surrendering to the terrible blood approaches whatever life there can be. And after that, after Jewel's birth, balance the books, clean the house, give Anse his remaining children.

Under such direct attack, all values, ideas, significances buckle and shatter. Words become mere masks, the false facades of the terrible blood. Words are "no good"; they "don't ever fit"; they are merely "shapes to fill a lack," "lifeless vessels" into which the real violation and violence of life are poured carelessly. Word and deed meet only in constant battle: "I would think how words go straight up in a thin line, quick and harmless, and how terribly doing goes along the earth, clinging to it, so that after a while the two lines are too far apart for the same person to straddle from one to the other." Manicheism: the dark fluid blood demanding its sacrifice; the rest, like the words "sin" and "salvation," mere garments to be tossed aside, discarded. There is none of Flannery O'Connor's "wise blood" in Addie Bundren, no mysterious Christian mystery between mind and matter, word and deed. Only Manichean separation which leads Addie to her "swift and secret" liaison with the Reverend Whitfield, subverting any conventionally Christian notion of sin, lying with God's instrument whose duty it is to sanctify sin in order to eradicate it, knowing that the sin of her actions is "the more utter and terrible" because of her conscious notion to upend all values.

Is this Faulkner's answer to *The Scarlet Letter*? Hester seems to have had no compulsion to seek out a minister in order to seduce him and undermine the significance of his spiritual role. Addie, apparently convinced that "my daily life is an acknowledgment and expiation of his sin. . . . I know my own sin. I know that I deserve my punishment. I do not begrudge it," shocks the conventionally Calvinistic Cora Tull, who is stunned by the extent of Addie's pride and vanity in such knowledge. Addie is intent on eradicating any sanctified notion of sin, since words are mere fleshless screens for the terrible blood, the interior fluid darkness of the self. Hester expresses artistry in her elaborately designed letter; Addie can only whip her students and lash out at those around her, revenging herself upon Anse and her family by making him vow to cart her corpse into Jefferson: the ultimate revenge, deed fastened to the word. Certainly Hester questions the social order after her torment and is convinced that what she has done "had a consecration of its own"; but Hawthorne expresses no sympathy for the muddled state of her questioning—it can lead to no truth, only to further darkness— and leaves the entire idea of consecration open to speculation. Addie consecrates nothing except her own sexual fury, allowing for the time when "the wild blood boiled away." Then she cleans house, rights the records, a Manichean self-possession that can only then "get ready to stay dead a long time."

Whitfield suggests Dimmesdale in his substitution of the will, the word, for the deed. Addie is dead before he arrives at the Bundren house. He need not confess to anyone. His secret is safe with her. His spiritual pride, the idea of triumphing over Satan, of being assured of God's forgiveness, suggests Dimmesdale's own, and his utter hypocrisy mirrors that Puritan minister's. On his final scaffold Dimmesdale transforms himself into parable, the world's ultimate sinner, a life-sized allegory for his bewildered flock: the individual sin submits to the greater glory of the dying minister as ultimate Christlike figure, taking all sin upon himself. Whitfield too speaks of "my Gethsemane," enlarging his careless sexual straying into Christlike proportions and pronouncing pompously upon the Bundren place, "God's grace upon this house."

As in all of Faulkner's great romances, the central character's dilemma shadows the entire narrative, which, like light across a spectrum, splits up into various angles of vision, differing facets of that crucial central self. For Darl, word and deed become permanently disconnected; Jewel and his horse exist only in action, "as deed"; in Vardaman's childish, mythical view of the world, word and deed remain permanently fused: mother and fish, both dead, become one. Dewey Dell seeks relief from her one deed; Cash, forever seeking a balance, grows more compassionate, less abstract throughout the journey and embodies a more sympathetic human approach. And Anse, full of inaction, as lazy and shiftless as Cora thinks all the Bundrens must be, opposes the horizontal road beckoning travel to the vertical shape of man suggesting stasis. Addie's word is Anse's "man"; her deed, his idea of the snake, "because if He'd a aimed for man to be always a moving and going somewheres else, wouldn't He a put him longways on his belly, like a snake? It stands to reason he would." Snakes and deeds—the inherent evil in all actions?—a Manichean suggestion that permeates this mock-heroic narrative and colors the Bundren saga with its sense of ultimate doom.

What could be more Hawthornesque than the beginning of Faulkner's greatest gothic romance, *Absalom, Absalom!*? The "neutral territory" or withdrawn setting of Miss Coldfield's "dim hot airless room," the sense of doom and the past's lingering in her "eternal black which she had worn for forty-three years," the alternation of light and heat with the cooler dark, and of course the rhythm and rhetoric of a growing trance, a hypnotic spell conjured up to lure the reader from the light of common day, from the ordinary world: "From a little after two o'clock until almost sundown of the long still hot weary dead September afternoon . . . ." A compulsive confession in the dark room "with that air of impotent and static rage," in "the dim coffin-smelling gloom," tales "about old ghost-times." Hawthorne led us to the Pyncheon House. Faulkner lures us into its very heart, into a dreamlike suspension.

And at the center of this romance, beyond and within the masks, the demonic conjurings, the shadows of doom, the classically tragic posturings and theatrical renderings "in a land primed for fatality and already cursed with it," lurks Sutpen himself, the enigmatic master of design, whose "innocence" can fathom only a measurable morality, a logical, legalistic "mistake" that has destroyed his entire enterprise. But even he joins the other storytellers around him in trying to figure out exactly what happened; "his very calmness was indication that he had long since given up any hope of ever understanding it." "His code of logic and morality . . . in which he struggled to hold clear and free above a maelstrom of unpredictable and unreasoning human beings," fails him. The Manichean clash between logic and humanity, reason and emotion, fatally undermines his design. His own self-reliance, the mountain man's innocence of "a country all divided and fixed and neat with a people living on it all divided and fixed and neat because of what color their skins happened to be and what they happened to own," this democratic Adam's shock at Tidewater hierarchies, coupled with no sense of retribution, "no sins of the father come home to roost," damn him in such a place as the Old South, as American innocence itself was doomed to repeat the human mistakes and sins inherent in its own frail but unrecognized humanity. Each seeks his own design in Sutpen's fall, although, as Grandfather Compson recognized, even language will fail, leaving "the little surface corners and edges of men's secret and solitary lives . . . sinking back into the darkness where the spirit cried for the first time." Even beyond Sutpen lies that inscrutable flux, the dark and ultimately impenetrable spirit in all men, the heart of Hawthorne's American romances.

Sutpen's design spawns further Manichean confrontations: brother kills brother: white kills black: incest and miscegenation, twin negations at the gothic center of Faulkner's South, that black hole within the Southern nightmare. And as Judith suggests, "You are born at the same time with a lot of other people, all mixed up with them, like trying to, having to, move your arms and legs with strings only the same strings are hitched to all the other arms and legs . . . only each one wants to weave his own pattern into the rug." The self battling "society," the others: layers of further unresolvable conflict at the heart of things, "ripples moving on, spreading, the pool attached by a narrow umbilical water-cord to the next pool which the first pool feeds, has fed, did feed . . . the old ineradicable rhythm." And deeper at the center of things the perfectly circular conversation between Henry Sutpen and Quentin Compson: the perfectly closed circle as ultimate trap, ultimate interpenetration, confrontation,

self-hypnosis. Is it any wonder that Quentin remains "an empty hall echo-
ing with sonorous defeated names," a walking ghost, shadow-creature
of a Manichean mind?

Significances clash. Are we witnessing a heroic contest stemming "from
some of the old virtues"? Can we "salvage at least from the humbled
indicted dust something anyway of the old lost enchantment of the heart"?
Or is there "no such thing as memory: the brain recalls just what the
muscles grope for: no more, no less: and its resultant sum is usually in-
correct and false and worthy only of the name of dream"? Are there
"larger, more heroic" figures in the past? Or do victims thrive no matter the time and place, and only our nostalgia creates enlarged puppets
of our illusions? In any case the ferocity with which each character hungers
to tell his/her version of the Sutpen legend—Rosa, Mr. Compson, Grandfather Compson, Quentin and Shreve, yes, and even Sutpen himself:
Chinese boxes, realm leading on to further realm—attests to the metaphorical and allegorical imagination of the human mind. The sheer boun-
tifulness and exuberance of *Absalom, Absalom!* testify to the human spirit
and its desire to fabricate, weave, invent, explain, and propose, the only
"truth" perhaps that we can know. And the dark intensity of the romance
reflects Faulkner's southern consciousness at its most mercilessly Manichean,
driven, torn, ravaged by the heart in conflict with itself. It is the ultimate
testimony to Faulkner's art.

The character of Joe Christmas and the savage Manicheism of *Light
in August* provide a final example of Faulkner's art and vision. Bigotry
and the Puritan impersonal ideal underlie this "epileptic" assault upon
the small-town South. This is the Protestant legacy: "Pleasure, ecstasy,
they cannot seem to bear: their escape from it is in violence. . . . And
so why should not their religion drive them to crucifixion of themselves
and one another?" Their "bleak and bloodless logic" demands vengeance,
demands the rigid conflicting categories of their radically polarized faith.
They cannot pity one another, for to pity one another "would be to admit self-doubt and to hope for and need pity themselves." Examples
abound: the fierce fundamentalism of McEachern, the racism of Doc Hines,
the nymphomaniacal corruption of Joanna Burden, "the abject fury of
the New England glacier exposed suddenly to the fire of the New England
Biblical Hell"; the distorted Christian vision of Gail Hightower, "offer-
ing instead of the crucified shape of pity and love, a swaggering and un-
chastened bravo killed with a shotgun in a peaceful henhouse"; and the

smug self-righteousness of the townspeople, "with pistols already in their pockets . . . to canvass about for someone to crucify." Such Puritanism culminates in Percy Grimm, the young Nazi "priest" with the face of an angel, pure in his vengeance.

Caught in this virulent crossfire, Joe Christmas emerges as ultimate negation, ultimate victim. He exists to be crucified as black to white, male to female, self to society. He exists "contemplative and remote with ecstasy and self-crucifixion," a self who achieves self-realization at the moment of self-destruction, the two inseparable, the scapegoat made martyr to Manichean murder.

Gavin Stevens, imprisoned as well within his society's social categories, views Christmas as a man torn between his white and black blood. This is true as far as it goes, metaphorically logical in Faulkner's southern terms, the white suggesting hope, illusion, social acceptance, recovery; the black, violence, corruption, sex, death. Here are Faulkner's polar antitheses writ large, unending conflict that can know no Emersonian leap of faith into the "bipolarity of unity." Christmas's death parodies Christ's. His death becomes a fixed memory for the town. And in the present, "they are not to lose it." They will never forget it. In the future "it will be there, musing, quiet, steadfast." But what does it mean? What does it signify? It remains "of itself alone serene, of itself alone triumphant." Ironies abound. It carries nothing beyond itself. It remains significantly solitary. The impersonal negation of Christmas's life as victim may carry a certain triumphant serenity about it, but it is the ecstasy of self-crucifixion, a black hole of self-knowledge. Christmas's "I am" reflects inexorably his "I am not." He remains a tortured Manichean soul, so ravaged by his society's contraries—black and white, male and female, individual soul and Puritan law—that he becomes a bleak and dark abstraction, an attitude more than a character, that dark negation of pity, love, and human sympathy at the center of Faulkner's South that is obsessed with memories of war, dubious heroics, and the terrifying knowledge of defeat within a country that had never known it. The people must crucify someone. They demand outrage as their final sanctuary. Joe Christmas fills their need, and Faulkner's. They demand blood, the blacker the better (and there is no proof of Joe's blackness, only careless epithets hurled at an orphan), and they get it. In his sexual mutilation lies their finest hour.

A deeper, sexual-psychological conflict darkly underscores the black-white, Puritan-pleasure, society-self confrontations of *Light in August*. In

Christmas's mind men "could always count upon one another, depend upon one another; . . . it was the woman alone who was unpredictable." The world of men remains cold and hard, built securely along impersonal lines of bully and victim, master and slave. The world of women, however, "the lightless hot wet primogenitive Female," shares the overheated fecundity of the black race in white eyes. To tumble into this abyss, to open chasms of emotion and pity, is to sacrifice the simplicities of Calvinist cruelty and prejudice, and for Christmas, the product of such battle lines, this can only mean ultimate self-destruction. The woman "would try to get herself between him and the punishment which, deserved or not, just or unjust, was impersonal . . . a natural and inescapable fact." And since Christmas's personality is based solidly on his complete rejection of the personal, women threaten him with their "affinity and instinct for secrecy, for casting a faint taint of evil about the most trivial and innocent actions." Sex becomes vengeance, riddled with the Calvinist's horror of pollution and decay, the terrible fluids of sex. This grim undercurrent of foul blood and polluted sex almost unbalances the book, exacerbated as it is by Joanna Burden's sexual vampirism. Oedipal shadows loom large here: man to exist must escape woman, but in doing so he destroys himself, and yet if he surrenders, he surrenders to the black abyss, to death, to the hot wet smothering pall of the female.

Faulkner's poles of outrage and sanctuary are visible here. His characters consistently strike poses and attitudes of outrage, astonishment, awe. They cannot believe what is happening. Events, actions, motion outrun their amazed comprehension of them, leaving them numbed as if caught in someone else's nightmare. They become trapped like figures on a Grecian urn in "formally erotic attitudes and gestures," creatures of a consciousness at war with itself, torn between Puritan obstinacy, the need for stasis and control, and a more life-giving, romantic flow, the need to accept or struggle with the motion of life (epitomized by Lena Grove, the walking womb, a lobotomized earth-mother), the emotional tumult of which, though incomprehensible, is their only antidote to death.

Faulkner's oxymoronic style, riddled with paradox and conflict, describes motion before comprehension can master it, seems to flounder in impulse and instinct which precede the mind's ability to try to understand them. Readers get lost, feel the sway, the pull, the tug of events which involve them viscerally, demanding a comprehension which usually comes much later in the narrative, if at all. Significance remains contradictory in the fierce pummeling the events inflict upon the reader. It is "like a fellow running from or toward a gun aint got time to worry whether the word for what he is doing is courage or cowardice." Running breeds tension, the breathlessness of *Light in August*. Action precedes idea, as in Addie's mind deeds undercut any attempt to describe them in words. It opposes the Puritanical need to signify. What remains is conflict, rhetorically experienced in Faulkner's ongoing rush of language, his torrent of words overwhelming his characters, each of them struggling for "his grip upon that blending of pride and hope and vanity and fear, that strength to cling to either defeat or victory." It is the persistent clinging that Faulkner admires, half of him demanding that it signify, the other half seeing in that almost allegorical obsession, certain death.

Hence, Faulkner's interest in so many different narrators, the descendents of literary modernism, each grappling with the facts of motion, each trying to come to terms with them, to try to comprehend them. This quest remains Faulkner's own, as it was Hawthorne's, and his characters follow him completely in this: the black man's telling of Christmas's breaking into a revivalist meeting, the furniture dealer's picking up Lena and Byron Bunch, Joanna's revealing her family history, Hightower's recalling his doomed past, Byron's relating events to Hightower, Mrs. Hines's tales of Milly and Doc, Gavin Stevens's fascination with Christmas's "passive suicide." Talk permeates, creates the book, a patchwork quilt of conversations, recollections, speculations, rumors, gossip, characters talking their way toward some momentary stay against confusion, just as their conclusions and surmises buckle and dissolve in the face of the relentless spiraling of events themselves.

The apotheosis of talk, the southern consciousness turned madly inward upon itself, culminates in Hightower's obsession with his grandfather, final proof that "memory believes before knowing remembers," again the circular center at the heart of things, Henry and Quentin locked in conversation. Emotion precedes knowledge, *is* knowledge in a blind leap of faith and feeling in which categories crumble and the Manichean mystery assumes mind-ravaging proportions; and memory swallows it all, before knowing can ever hope to catch up with it. "I have been a single instant of darkness," Hightower declares and echoes Quentin, Christmas, Rosa, Addie, as "the sandclutched wheel of thinking turns on with the slow implacability of a medieval torture instrument." Faulknerian doom traps all; memory rapes the consciousness, stuns and traps

the imagination like some ravenous "gnosis" spawned in the South's
defeat. Characters shudder, bound to their shared bitter dead-end nightmares of nostalgia and loss, all-consuming and unforgiving.

All of Faulkner's fiction from *Sartoris* or *Flags in the Dust* to *The Mansion* reveals his essential Manichean vision. It permeates the entire
Yoknapatawpha saga. His is not the simply historical southern saga that
Malcolm Cowley supposed—and for the most part half-created in the Viking edition of *The Portable Faulkner* in 1946—but is part and parcel of
Hawthorne's romantic vision. As Hyatt H. Waggoner has pointed out,
"With Hawthorne, he warns us against expecting redemption by a celestial
railroad. His tragic vision, again like Hawthorne's and like Melville's,
does not deny democracy but sustains it. Nor does it suggest that we
try to escape the world: rather, that we do what we can to transform
it, and be prepared to endure it. His tragic vision does not deny or restrict
freedom, it demands and magnifies it, but recognizes the forces that limit
it."[6] And as Faulkner himself admitted in his praise of Melville's *Moby-
Dick*, "I think that the book which I put down with the unqualified
thought 'I wish I had written that' is *Moby Dick*. The Greek-like simplicity
of it: . . . a sort of Golgotha of the heart become immutable as bronze
in the sonority of its plunging ruin; all against the grave and tragic rhythm
of the earth in its timeless phase. . . ."[7]

Man himself is finally Faulkner's most Manichean creation. He is a
constant source of agony and awe. Like the "Old South" embodied, he
is permanence amid change. He is a pole of force around which all motion must coalesce. He experiences life as an outrage when the motion
of the world beyond and outside him fails to recognize not his authority
nor his being but the mere fact of his existence. Thus by retelling events,
by investigating his past, by examining past actions, those flexible bits
and pieces of fluid motion, he is, in effect, trying to stop them, to isolate
and suspend them, to give them meaning and at the same time to establish
his right to give them meaning.

Man's self-consciousness is a reality that rivals the reality of the universe.
He would be the omnipotent god of his own universe if he were not
overawed by the presence of that "other" universe which threatens him
without apparent motive. Essentially this is Faulkner's dilemma: two uni-
verses struggling to be God, the one seemingly unconscious of its power
and authority, and therefore as demonic as it is divine, the other conscious only of its weakness and inadequacy. So Faulkner set his men and

women in motion, driven as they were by the same personal demon that drove him, that all-consuming role played by the South in his life and in his fiction, the region he could only love and hate inexplicably. He sent them to snatch meaning out of time, to render one "something" immobile, immutable, and eternally meaningful. The search, fatal if successful, continues unabated; man's reward is his endurance; man's hope, his possible transcendence; man's confidence, his folly; man's business, life's outrage. Such Manichean conflict persists throughout the whole of Faulkner's fiction.

Faulkner's Manichean vision parallels Hawthorne's. His use of modernist techniques—inseparable, of course, from the vision itself, a product of his oxymoronic style—liberated it from the crumbling allegorical fortifications of Hawthorne's last romances and brought it into the mainstream of twentieth-century American fiction. Southern writers followed that path in their own manner—McCullers, O'Connor, Styron, to name just a few—and continued the tradition of the American romance well into the new century. In them we can continue to see the power of that vision and the forms of the romance they used to express it.

"I suppose my central theme is the theme of spiritual isolation," Carson McCullers once said. "I have always felt alone."[8] Her rural South of mill towns and fly-specked cafes, the Columbus, Georgia, of her youth, suggests Hawthorne's Salem in its sense of decay, her vision of alienation and loss more keenly felt, perhaps, in a society which still prized community and tradition. In such a vacuum her characters seem driven inward to a world of private reverie and dream, in her darker fictions into a world of nightmare.

Narcissism plagues McCullers's characters, whether children or adults. An unrelenting solipsism darkens as her people age, the spontaneity of childhood lost in the blind pursuits of adulthood. Sex fuels a gothic world, a place ruled by psychological determinisms, separate selves locked into their fierce habits and obsessions. Her creatures seem possessed by alien forces, the unconscious motivations of lonely, alienated souls, characters fumbling within the primitive mainstream of modernist art. Hence the sense of dread that stalks McCullers's landscape, "that Sense of the Awful" that Tennessee Williams described, "which is the desperate black root of nearly all significant modern art."[9] Individuals are trapped in a gothic Manichean world that knows no exit. At her best McCullers captures that world, unmarred by the adolescent sentimentalities of *The Heart Is a Lonely Hunter* and *The Member of the Wedding,* where child-heroes thrive in an asexual realm still open to the possibilities of a life lived along a sensitive, vague edge.

McCullers referred to art as a "flowering dream," the reflection of her vision of the world around her. Her best books reflect that dream-world, the territory of romance akin in kind to Hawthorne's and Faulkner's. That dreamworld also reflects the modernist forms of Eliot's "The Waste Land" with its emphasis on cyclical patterns and its individuals trapped in mythic repetitions in a world that has lost any recognition of the possible liberating visions of ancient mythic rebirths and renewals. The psychological determinism of McCullers's fictional world approaches ritual in its ceremonial scenes and intensities, just as the characters in a romance spill over into the world of allegory, creatures of a metaphoric design that rules their lives and their actions. These often parallel Hawthorne's romantic designs in form if not in style.

McCullers's style for the most part remains objective and concrete in an imagistic manner. The bizarre events and characters in *Reflections in a Golden Eye,* for instance, are reported in an almost clinical manner, as though the writer were viewing her world through a jeweler's eyepiece, with that sharply focused clarity of the imagist poet. Consequently her world ultimately reflects Poe's more than it does Hawthorne's. Any moral sense is replaced by the cold eye dispassionately watching the playing out of events, the setting up of confrontations, the psychic inevitabilities of warring opposites and inner frustrations. The battle between will and instinct rages. The trap of the world is complete in a claustrophobic Manichean manner. And McCullers becomes "a peacock of a sort of ghastly green. With one immense golden eye. And in it these reflections of something tiny and . . . grotesque."

Reflections in a Golden Eye, McCullers's second book, reveals that descent into a nightmare world that Frye describes as the dark romance, in which "life [is] so intolerable that it must end either in tragedy or in a permanent escape."[10] Identities crumble; personal actions become restricted, locked into a world of mirrors and self-reflections; sudden metamorphoses—the Captain's passion for Williams—occur; animals, such as Leonora's horse Firebird, become companions and express a kind of freedom human beings cannot; and the whole is represented by a "symbolic visual emblem,"[11] like the scarlet letter or in this case the golden eye of the painted peacock. Imprisonment sets the tone of the entire book, and the inevitable demonic recognition leads to "the realization that only death is certain."[12] Faulkner's South falls in upon itself, a black hole absorbing all the light within it.

Of the book, McCullers said that once "relieved of the moral and physical strain of *The Heart Is a Lonely Hunter* I wrote *Reflections in a Golden Eye* in the spirit of a somewhat ghostly plane. . . . It's really a fairy story—everything is done very lightly."[13] Nightmare would be more to the point. The withdrawn setting, the territory of romance, appears immediately: "An army post in peace time is a dull place. Things happen, but then they happen over and over again. . . . all is designed according to a certain rigid pattern." Monotony engenders violent and bizarre action; the rigid caste system with its traditions of rank and service, the Old South in microcosm, breeds hostility and envy, the kind of social protest all romances create against the more conservative, realistic world of the novels Hawthorne described. The emphasis on patterns throughout the book primes the reader to discover allegorical designs, just as McCullers's description of her tale like ingredients in a recipe (". . . a murder was committed. The participants of this tragedy were: two officers, a soldier, two women, a Filipino, and a horse") draws attention to the modernist objectivity and external, dramatic "reporting" of her style.

The atmosphere of the book includes intense gloom and explosive light. Captain Penderton's wild ride on Firebird occurs in a dark wood, the same sanctuary from the post where Private Williams suns himself naked. "Green shadowy moonlight" haunts the tale, as well as that "misty lavender glow" after sunset with "a hint of darkness . . . already in the air."

Reflections abound and reverberate. Firebird's name suggests the phoenix, the opposite of Anacleto's golden-eyed peacock. A drugged Penderton feels the presence of "a great dark bird . . . with fierce, golden eyes . . . enfold[ing] him in his dark wings." Penderton glimpses himself as a small grotesque doll, "mean of countenance and grotesque in form," and he resembles a broken doll when he tumbles off Firebird in the forest. Such images reinforce the gothic claustrophobia of the army post, of McCullers's alienated characters, of the world as prison and pit.

But it is the sheer Manichean vision of *Reflections in a Golden Eye* that drives this fictional nightmare. Polarities abound, redouble, repeat, mirror one another. Captain Penderton and Private Williams: a warped aesthetic will and subconscious instinct. Penderton broods on homo-sexual desires, demands orderliness and rigidity in all his actions, thinks of death and withdrawal. Williams displays the "strange rapt face of a Gauguin primitive" and thrives on naked sojourns in the woods, "for there was one thing that this soldier could not do without—the sun." Penderton's wild ride on Firebird, convincing him that death is near, explodes into "a great mad joy," a mystic delight in physical motion on the edge of extinction. His fall and his subsequent vision of the naked Williams, who can soothe and control the wayward horse in a way Pender-ton cannot, produces that sudden metamorphosis from smoldering ascetic to passionate lover, and he stalks Williams on the post after their return to it.

If Williams is the Caliban of the fable, Anacleto, Alison Langdon's houseboy, is the Ariel, a "rare bird" who ritualizes everything in his delicate Filipino manner and hates the people he must associate with. If Williams suggests unformed natural impulse tainted with violence and voyeurism, Anacleto represents the other pole of consciousness, the too-refined, artificially artistic will. Each is impotent; each is confined in his own world; each suggests the poles of consciousness between which the Pendertons and the Langdons struggle for self-gratification and fulfill-ment. And each of these couples reflects the Manichean battle between flesh and spirit, a precarious balance and an ongoing war that is "resolved" only by Leonora Penderton's affair with Morris Langdon. The over-wrought, nervous Alison twitches and spies, lost in a world of childish dreams of retreat, and eventually expires of a heart attack, after her final statement about the state of affairs: "My God, what a choice crew!" Confrontation redoubles yet again with the settings in the book, the clash between the rigid army post and the freer, darker, sunnier forest beyond it.

The mind itself is at war with itself: "The mind is like a richly woven tapestry in which the colors are distilled from the experience of the senses, and the design drawn from the convolutions of the intellect. The mind of Private Williams was imbued with various colors of strange tones, but it was without delineation, void of form." Design battles colors; the intellect battles the senses. And in the end, will murders instinct, Penderton kills Williams: "The Captain had slumped against the wall. In his queer, coarse wrapper he resembled a broken and dissipated monk. Even in death the body of the soldier still had the look of warm, animal comfort." Monk and animal: a final Manichean split. The rigid pattern is complete.

In *The Ballad of the Sad Cafe*, perhaps McCullers's masterpiece, the nightmare realm continues, a place where tradition exists only unconsciously as a series of habits and empty rituals. It is a world trapped in a meaningless and therefore grotesque present, resulting in a labyrinth of dark corridors and Manichean gestures. Strange signs and superstitions permeate this world, as they do in old ballads and folk tales: numbers, events, beliefs, a witch's brew. Narcissism triumphs. Lovers love those who love others in a complete circle of disconnection. The imprisonment of *Reflections* conquers all.

"The Twelve Mortal Men" is McCullers's choral conclusion to her ballad. Here the chain gang is working, and yet from them arises a melody that can be heard, and has been heard constantly throughout the book, in the town. "The voices are dark in the golden glare," and it seems as though "the sound does not come from the twelve men on the gang, but from the earth itself, or the wide sky." It is a transcendent harmony of love and despair, mixed "with ecstasy and fright," the essentials of the human condition. It is a lament sung for the inevitable realities of that condition, a song sung by common men bound together by their common mortality, a Hawthornesque brotherhood both black and white. They sing not in spite of their chains but because of them. Unlike the participants in the nightmare which has just been completed, they know they must act together in order to survive the mutual degradation that fate has seen fit to thrust upon them. They can see their chains and acknowledge their common bonds. The music sinks down, but it can rise again. In the wake of such a cruel and relentless fate, and not in spite of but because of that fate, McCullers captures a faint glimmer of human endurance and brotherhood, even though she can see "just twelve mortal men who are together."

McCullers's vision of the dark labyrinth of the human heart and the brotherhood of all men bound to their separate but equal fates links her to Hawthorne's "truth" of the human heart, but significant differences exist. In McCullers's world, an abnormal fear of adult sexuality permeates everything. This may be linked to her relationship with Reeves McCullers, the man she married, divorced, and later remarried, who eventually committed suicide. It also may reflect the dark side of her sentimental attachment to childhood and children, acknowledging the fact that the South is "a very emotional experience for me, fraught with all the memories of my childhood."[14] Nostalgia breeds paralysis and claustrophobia and leads to such sentimentalized faith, a kind of bastardized Wordsworthian belief (another primitive undercurrent in modernist art, perhaps), in the "poetry in children. It always strikes me that they are so capable of losing and finding themselves and also losing and finding those things they feel close to. . . . Mrs. Roosevelt says, 'Children are the only people that tell the truth.' I agree with her."[15] Here is no charming, enigmatic, demonic Pearl. Southern sentimentality has fallen in upon itself as it does in other ways in Faulkner's work, but here unrelieved by distance and rhetorical exorcism.

McCullers's world remains as Manichean as her vision, an ultimate trap within or beyond which there is no other, save the murky psychological motives of her characters. A quest for moral significance collapses in such a Poe-esque void. Romance can never be delivered from nightmare, since the descent only ends in death. In the final paragraph of *Reflections in a Golden Eye*, still a strange and powerful fiction, Leonora "stared about her as though witnessing some scene in a play, some tragedy that was gruesome but not necessary to believe." Hawthorne sought belief, however fragmented and scattered in his final romances, or at least sought a vision of the world that suggested a morally significant pattern. McCullers like Poe stages gruesome scenes and pursues them to their inevitable conclusions, a mesmerizing, chilling art but one that harbors no tragedy, since there exists no necessity of belief, no moral significance finally. It took a Flannery O'Connor to shape the gothic and grotesque contours of modernist southern fiction to a moral pursuit, a more morally conscious level between the Manichean forces of utter disbelief and fanatical faith. McCullers recreates a modernist dread, itself perhaps the sentimental side of her childhood simplicities and reveries, and stalks it to its Manichean conclusion. But nightmare leads on only to further nightmare, a dark design of momentary stays against confusion that dissolves into the spiritual paralysis of her gothic art.

"Hawthorne said he didn't write novels, he wrote romances; I am one of his descendants,"[16] Flannery O'Connor declared in a letter to a friend. She reiterated, "I think I would admit to writing what Hawthorne called 'romances', but I don't think that has anything to do with the romantic mentality. Hawthorne interests me considerably. I feel more of a kinship with him than with any other American. . . . I write 'tales' in the sense Hawthorne wrote tales—though I hope with less reliance on allegory."[17] Was O'Connor merely indulging in self-defense, or was she making a legitimate literary point?

At first glance no two writers could seem so unlike one another: Hawthorne, the New England "Calvinist"; O'Connor, the orthodox Catholic. Hawthorne blasts his self-reliant anti-heroes, men such as Hollingsworth, Ethan Brand, the Reverend Hooper, obsessed with their own prideful visions and one-dimensional prophecies; O'Connor celebrates her backwoods prophets, the "Jesus freaks" from a blighted rural South, expressing as they do a faith, however distorted, in the Christian idea of mind and matter, spirit and flesh made mysteriously whole. Hawthorne's characters seek salvation in human sympathy, in love for one another; O'Connor's pay heed only to God's mysterious grace in the universe and aspire to some pinnacle of isolation. Her heroes would be Hawthorne's villains. O'Connor's grotesques seek a separate peace with their God and exist in a world so objectively drawn, so grotesquely shaped in the best modernist tradition of external gesture and concrete surface, that it hardly ever resembles Hawthorne's more speculative, probing landscape of doubt and dark design.

Yet O'Connor, commenting about novels that deal only "with the movement of social forces, with the typical, with the fidelity to the way things look and happen in normal life,"[18] sounds like Hawthorne's descriptions in his prefaces. Her thirst for extremes, exaggeration, and distortion, and her description of "the prophet-freaks of Southern literature" as "not images of the man in the street" but "images of the man forced out to meet the extremes of his own nature"[19] suggest Hawthorne's "truths of the human heart" as well as Faulkner's "human heart in conflict with itself." Her belief that the "tradition of the dark and divisive romance-novel has combined with the comic-grotesque tradition"[20] may be her way of expressing not only her descent from Hawthorne's romances but her own modern commitment to modern southern literature as well, and to both of them as reflections of one another. Certainly Hawthorne and Faulkner would celebrate her description of "the business of fiction to embody mystery through manners, and mystery is a great embarrassment to the modern mind."[21]

If Hawthorne warned against the tragic potential of transcendental self-reliance, only to find himself adrift in Manichean doubts and discrepancies, O'Connor expresses no such doubts: "The Manicheans separated spirit and matter. To them all material things were evil. They sought pure spirit and tried to approach the infinite directly without any mediation of matter. This is also pretty much the modern spirit, and for the sensibility infected with it, fiction is hard if not impossible to write because fiction is so very much an incarnational art."[22] All well and good. O'Connor's Christian orthodoxy is made perfectly clear in her letters and essays: man, "incomplete in himself," remains "prone to evil, but as redeemable when his own efforts are assisted by grace"; grace works through and transcends nature; Christ provides ultimate meaning; the "rest is the devil's destruction."[23] Yet she realizes that Christian writers "may be unconsciously infected with the Manichean spirit of the times and suffer the much-discussed disjunction between sensibility and belief,"[24] Eliot's modernist curse. As Frederick Asals suggests, "The inherent dualism of O'Connor's imagination is so radical that the deep revulsion against all forms of matter, the opposition of it to the spiritual, and the absolute separation of the worldly from the other-worldly results in a work [*Wise Blood*] that can only be called 'Manichean.' "[25] And when O'Connor goes on to explain that "my subject in fiction is the action of grace in territory held largely by the devil,"[26] one wonders just how much her orthodoxy has succumbed to the Manichean vision ostensibly surrounding and within her.

Both Hawthorne and O'Connor knew the dungeon of the heart, the demonic, godlike power of the creative artist, the scent of old Adam's sins, the scorn of rationalist, self-sufficient men ("The Aylmers whom Hawthorne saw as a menace have multiplied"[27]) and viewed the world in stark polarities. But O'Connor may describe herself and Hawthorne best when she views him as "that fastidious, skeptical New Englander who feared the ice in his blood."[28] That temperament led to paralysis, withdrawal, conscious displacement and dislocation, and when "tenderness is detached from the source of tenderness, its logical outcome is terror."[29] O'Connor's comments on Hawthorne's daughter Rose, who converted to Catholicism, reveal her own personal descent from that fastidious romancer: "She discovered much that he sought, and fulfilled in a practical way the hidden desires of his life. The ice and blood which he feared, and which this very fear preserved him from, was turned by her into a warmth which initiated action. If he observed, fearfully but truthfully; if he acted, reluctantly but firmly, she charged ahead, secure in the path his truthfulness had outlined for her."[30] O'Connor's prophets thus charge ahead. Hawthorne's tragedies become her dark comedies. Catholicism or fundamental Christian faith thaws the ice in the blood, shatters the belabored self-scrutiny of Hawthorne's darker characters and Faulkner's paralyzed Quentins and Hightowers, and Francis Marion Tarwater, part Swamp Fox, Manichean mixture of tar and water, "moved steadily on, his face set toward the dark city, where the children of God lay sleeping."

One may sympathize with the truck driver in *The Violent Bear It Away* who mutters, "You ride through these states and you see they all belong to it. I won't see nobody sane again until I get back to Detroit" (Joyce Carol Oates might vehemently disagree!), but that book presents O'Connor's art in the best and warmest light, excluding some of the brilliant short stories.

The Violent Bear It Away fully reveals O'Connor's affinities with Hawthorne's romances. As Asals describes it, "*The Violent Bear It Away*, with its dense concentration, exquisite sense of form and structure, and movement between the examination of inner struggle and dramatic scenes of confrontation, is reminiscent of the methods of Hawthorne's *The Scarlet Letter*. In fact, O'Connor may well have borrowed her central configuration of three complexly intertwined adults (if young Tarwater may for the moment be so considered) circling around a mysteriously supernatural child from her predecessor's masterpiece."[31] And the three baptism scenes in the book may parallel the three scaffold scenes in *The Scarlet Letter*, according to Leon Driskell and Joan Brittain.[32]

The dark woods, that place of mystery with its mysterious rim and edge, its atmosphere of lightning and dense shadow, its black caves and swollen red sun, suggest Hawthorne's romantic settings, however "unneutral" in this case. Natural and supernatural merge, shimmer; such primal elements as fire, water, and air seem charged with significance, redolent with mystery. Episodes generate other dreamlike episodes, the frantic, almost dizzying progress of men obsessed. The sins of the fathers, in this case the urge for Christian prophecy, permeate O'Connor's landscape. Her characters are "doomed" and compelled to surrender at last to their obsessions, burdened with the curse of children to believe.

"The man forced out to meet the extremes of his own nature," in this case the child Francis Marion, parallels Hawthorne's allegorical truths of the human heart in Manichean conflict with one another—until Tarwater charges ahead. Rayber the rationalist battles the old dead prophet to rescue Tarwater from that prophet's obsessions. And yet he too is divided between the bubbling fanaticism in his own blood and his fierce repression of it. O'Connor, turning the screws, doubles and redoubles the battle between rational will and virulent prophecy. Old Tarwater and Rayber's father, the dead insurance agent, battle for Rayber's soul. Rayber too was kidnapped and taken away to Powderhead when he was a young boy. Tarwater and Rayber battle to save Rayber's son, Bishop, Tarwater on the verge of baptizing him, Rayber trying to prevent that ceremony from taking place. Rayber is Old Tarwater's nephew; Francis Marion is his; both Rayber and Old Tarwater lost their sisters in a disastrous car wreck. These parallels increase the subjective intensity of the tale, along with O'Connor's further correspondences between Old Tarwater and Bishop, Bishop and his father Rayber, young Tarwarter and Rayber, Tarwater and his father the divinity student, who committed suicide after the wreck. These excruciating similarities increase the visceral experience of the Manichean clash between reason and emotion, between the dead rationalism of the modern world and the mad, haunted prophecies of the Old Christian fanatic in the dark woods.

Young Tarwater is himself set upon by false prophets. T. Fawcett Weeks, the salesman, speaks only of a worldly materialism that insists on working hard and that mouths a conventional idea of love that "was the only policy that worked 95% of the time." Lucette Carmody, the evangelist-child in the tabernacle, preaches her "Born Again" faith and belief in resurrection. The man from Detroit chalks it all up to southern insanity, the fundamentalist "crazies" of the Bible Belt. The homosexual rapes Tarwater, a perfumed emblem of the materialist sexuality of a soulless modern world. And Buford Munson, the black who from the beginning has seen to Old Tarwater's Christian burial, plants a cross on the old man's grave and reveals to Tarwater that no matter the fire, the flight, the fury, the murder of Bishop, the mad lectures of Rayber, Christian ceremony has been accomplished all along. It is Tarwater's ultimate sign in the dark woods that his struggle is over, his duty just begun.

Several critics of O'Connor's fiction, although a minority of them, suggest that her world is so grotesque, her characters so programmed to act as demonic grace compels them to, that any genuine Christian vision shatters and collapses.[33] She created such literal surfaces, such projections within them of rage and violence, such a flat, constricted, Manichean world, that no possible action could ever seem a Christian mission, a religious act. O'Connor's modernist art, filled with mechanical, animalistic gestures, demonic acts, the Manichean trap of lust and alienation and dread, an objective, almost cartoonlike style, suggests a world of such spiritual vacuity that nothing genuinely spiritual can occur. In such a world, where Tarwater's baptizing Bishop occurs simultaneously with his drowning of him, demonic forces must rule the landscape, and Christian gesture proves as hollow and as violent as any other.

O'Connor insisted that she had to flatten her fictional world, to distort it cruelly in order to make room for the Christian mystery that was to arise from and within it: "It should reinforce our sense of the supernatural by grounding it in concrete, observable reality."[34] And in such a world, in such a palpably physical and visible prison, "violence is strangely capable of returning my characters to reality and preparing them to accept their moment of grace. Their heads are so hard that almost nothing else will do the work."[35] Or is this merely the ice in the blood conjuring up grim, claustrophobic landscapes where only blind rage can ever hope to break through and out of it? And if the violent action of gesture replaces genuine human emotion, as Josephine Hendin perceptively suggests, are we not left not with Christian vision but with violence for violence's sake, the ice in the blood shattering a Manichean world of mere concrete detail and physical action, justified in the sheer emotional rage at that world that reflects the ice itself?

O'Connor's solution may involve several strategies at once. If the world of dark woods and evil city is as awful as it is made to seem, perhaps it forces the characters to take a stand. Such vacuous negation may breed violent acts of revelation. Violence may be necessary in such an empty place, an ultimate act of human will and choice to free itself from the dead constriction of rational self-sufficiency. Free will and predestination may be flip sides of the same coin, O'Connor forcing us to feel the sheer necessity of an act of faith. And in such a landscape, perhaps the descent of God's grace can only appear as one other demonic possession, one more dark will wrestling with an abandoned world. As Joyce Carol Oates suggests, "[O'Connor] sees man as dualistic: torn between the conventional polarities of God and the devil, but further confused because the choice must be made in human terms, and the divine might share superficial similarities with the diabolical."[36]

What O'Connor creates in fact is a world that is not as Manichean as modernist eyes may envision it to be. "The natural world contains the supernatural,"[37] she insisted, and in order to prove this she used several methods. She conjures up a religious impulse in her characters, in young Tarwater, in powerfully naturalistic images: religious zeal takes on the thrust of hunger, the lust of sex. It operates as a primal force in her characters' personalities. Seeds sprout; blood trembles; eyes stare and throb; a palpable, silent waiting hovers around every action, every gesture. Spiritual belief becomes a physical force, a bloodied instinct in pursuit of resolution or satisfaction. The natural images in *The Violent Bear It Away* bristle with biblical overtones; the sun, the woods, water, fire are charged with primal mysteries, culminating in the apocalyptic twelfth chapter of the book. Spiritual assurances come wrapped in images of Manichean conflict and physical doom. The moon appears and disappears; Tarwater's eyes are "singed . . . black in their deep sockets"; his shadow is "jagged"; light and dark battle for some final obeisance; Tarwater's path to his fate is suggested, not definitely envisioned; and moving toward the dark city suggests a staggered march toward self-destruction and death.

Self and nature reflect one another in the strange forces that operate within and through them. Ascent into Christian truth appears as a descent into madness, exactly as it would appear in such a world. It is the relentless and mysterious power of such forces, demonic/divine, that O'Connor manages to convey in her images, the doubling and redoubling of her gothic tale, the strange ongoing borders of her sacred wood. And that may account for what Carlson describes as her Byzantine art: "Byzantine art does not reject the natural world but views it only in relation to the supernatural world, thereby rejecting vague realistic curves for the vigorous yet sharply defined line and angle. Its premise is that art never imitates the natural world but instead discovers form within matter."[38] Mystery animates that matter, drives it toward revelation in that presentation of "line and angle."

What O'Connor firmly establishes in her hard-edged landscape is the possibility of ambiguity, and in such a modern Manichean maze, in so secular and physically visible a place, ambiguity becomes an act of reconciliation, a revelation of the possibility of spiritual powers and forces. Faith in sheer materialism wavers when ambiguity can be seriously entertained. A possible doubt as to the pervasive nature of a purely materialistic universe, however unresolved, suggests that certain spiritual dimensions may coexist or emerge from the psychological trap of mere action and reaction. The choice between Tarwater's free will and a predetermined course set mysteriously for him becomes ours, finally, for he both submits and chooses, though in his eyes, if not in ours, the choice is his to make. Ambiguity abounds in *The Violent Bear It Away*: the baptism and drowning, Bishop's murder and Tarwater's act of self-definition, self-transcendence; an act of violence reflecting an act of faith; psychological compulsion mirroring spiritual awareness, the force of a religious impetus toward belief; physical rape establishing spiritual deliverance; crucifixion promising resurrection. And, in grand southern fashion, intensity of feeling—the dark, incestuous, tortured implosions of this book—mirrors the depth of Tarwater's eventual belief and knowledge. In a Manichean world the Christian mystery, if seen only in terms of ambiguity and its emotional force, survives. Paradox reconciles. Ambiguity liberates.

Hawthorne, enclosed in dark dualistic designs, could not apply allegorical methods successfully to an ambiguous, paradoxical vision: he could only reproduce his own uncertainty, his essential dread in the Manichean notion of eternal combat, spirit and matter perpetually at odds with one another, both mired in subjective moods imprisoned in the ice in the blood. For O'Connor, to establish ambiguity was enough. The suggestion of the possibility of the power of Christian faith in so cruel and faithless a world represented a positive act, a liberating vision. Both romancers quarreled with paradox, wrestled with dark designs and ever darker necessities, but Tarwater charges ahead, no matter the odds against him. However Manichean that final paragraph, Tarwater is converted and convinced of the rightness of his actions.

O'Connor's grotesque parables lack human sympathy finally, as McCullers's tales do. It is as if their handling of literary modernism resulted in a Manichean disconnection within themselves, in too cool a distance from their characters. O'Connor rescues Old Tarwater from the curse of her modernist style because of his warmth, his madness, his energetic, country-charged speeches. And her opening line mixes the grotesque and the humorous with just the right balance between the drunken boy, the determined black, the decorum of Christian ceremony, and enough "dirt on top to keep the dogs from digging it up." O'Connor like Hawthorne never did thoroughly escape from the ice in the blood, but in her best moments, in *The Violent Bear It Away*, she exorcised and transformed it, a fully fictionalized "wise blood" after all.

Many of William Styron's strengths as a writer come from those that we associate with southern fiction. Baroque rhetoric powers his narratives; Faulkner's ghost lingers in his language. He evokes the kind of doomed, guilt-ridden landscapes we associate with the southern vision of the world. The problem of evil haunts him at all levels—social, psychological, meta-physical—and spawns the moral quest, the search for values of his heroes amid the stark realities of pain and suffering. Manichean conflicts ravage his prose, his outlook, his characters, as if an ultimate nihilism or irrevocable Greek fate savaged the vestiges of his own Christian faith or background. Such a wartorn spirit leads to certain death, to spiritual paralysis. He stalks the "riddles of personality" like the best romancers and sets up voices of "normalcy," moderate spokesmen, as clear-eyed witnesses to extraor-dinary events and persons: Culver to Mannix, Peter Leverett to Cass Kin-solving, Stingo to Sophie Zawistowska and Nathan Landau. A kind of existential, finally unexorcised sense of guilt relentlessly hounds him.

Styron writes in the tradition of the southern gothic romance, mov-ing from revelation to revelation, surprise to surprise, pacing his fiction as a series of building climaxes, each more shattering than the preceding one. He mounts scaffold epiphanies on ascending rungs of plot, as he did from the very first with *Lie Down in Darkness*: "It finally occurred to me to use separate moments in time, four or five long dramatic scenes revolving around the daughter, Peyton, at different stages in her life. The business of the progression of time seems to me one of the most difficult problems a novelist has to cope with."[39] The secret remains "a sense of architecture—a symmetry, perhaps unobtrusive but always there, without which a novel sprawls, becoming a self-indulged octopus. It was a mat-ter of form."[40]

Styron's gothic architecture comes complete with its aura of damna-tion and doom, a dusky cathedral filled with omens and auguries, night-mares and demonic shadows. And at the end of labyrinthine corridors appear the inevitable horrors: Peyton's suicide, Cass's murder of Mason Flagg, Nat's murder of Margaret Whitehead, Sophie's surrendering her daughter Eva to the gas ovens of Birkenau. Sambuco, "aloof upon its precipice, remote and beautifully difficult of access," the enclosed white temple of Nat Turner's dreams, "those days" of the 1940s in *Sophie's Choice*—here are the removed, withdrawn settings of dark romances. Nathan Landau wonders, however, if such a structure for fiction could be "a worn-out tradition," and John Gardner, reviewing *Sophie's Choice*, discussed the ambiguous relationship between the evil of Auschwitz and "the helpless groaning and self-flagellation of the Southern Gothic novel."[41] The question is raised by both Styron and Gardner whether or not this kind of romance has outlived its usefulness, however passionately and grippingly recreated.

The ambiguous nature of Styron's vision may serve to undermine his gothic structures. For one thing, he often relies too heavily upon psychological explanation, a kind of rational reductionism that reduces metaphysical speculation to Freudian solution. In *Lie Down in Darkness* Styron deals with what his character, Albert Berger, calls, "this South with its cancerous religiosity, its exhausting need to put manners before morals, to negate all ethos . . . a husk of culture" in the new suburban middle-class South, a world obsessed by its own narcissistic corruptions. These may be the result of the Old South gone dead, but a stronger case can be made for oedipal tensions and familial dislocations along a purely psychological grid: nostalgia and self-indulgence, however alcoholic, however wounding, seem almost disconnected from any southern past or for that matter any past at all.

The trouble with the elegantly rendered and moving *The Confessions of Nat Turner* is that the religious fanatic *cum* prophet tells his own tale. All explanations and suggestions—psychological, tragic, Christian, heroic—tend to look like mere self-justifications. Nat as both interpreter and actor may see himself moving from Old Testament vengeance to New Testament charity and contrition, but within his own psychological maneuverings and suggestions, even this broadly mythic and religious design dissolves. The tidy psychology of the case study threatens to undermine the realities of any political action, any historical commitment. Manichean contrasts—black and white, good and evil, master and slave—produce a kind of paralysis, a deeply felt and exquisitely written blank like the smooth white sides of that dreamed windowless enclosure.

Styron once suggested that "all my work is predicated on revolt in one way or another. And of course there's something about Nat Turner that's the ultimate fulfillment of all this. It's a strange revelation."[42] But as he described himself, he remains a "provisional rebel."[43] His sufferers are witnessed at a distance, Mannix's "revolt" by Culver, Cass's angst by Leverett, Sophie's choices by Stingo. It is as if he has his cake—the rebellion, the guilt—and eats it, too—the "resurrection" and the increased awareness of his witnesses. If many of Styron's rebels participate in a kind of self-mutilation or self-flagellation, his witnesses experience this as well, but at a distance. And as we shall see in both *Set This House on Fire* and *Sophie's Choice* (for me his most passionate and fierce romances), violence and revenge are just barely, if at all, transmuted into Christian symbols. At times the Christian imagery seems itself "provisional," a literary laying on of uncertain hands. We get finally not tragedies but melodramas, exorcisms rendered "safe" by the remarkably unscathed witnesses.

The whole question of Styron's notion of evil remains ambiguous. In *Lie Down in Darkness* Styron writes: "Too powerful a consciousness of evil was often the result of infantile emotions. The cowardly Puritan . . . , unwilling to partake of free religious inquiry, uses the devil as a scapegoat to rid himself of the need for positive action." Evil becomes a dodge, an excuse for inaction, as if once again the Manichean polarities produced only stalemate, fashioned in a fierce baroque prose style. And Styron adds: "Perhaps the miseries of our century will be recalled only as the work of a race of strange and troublous children, by the wise old men in the aeons which come after us."[44] Infantile emotions, troublous children, a hint of adolescent angst sounded in a void? Evil as howling self? Is there something to Mailer's indictment of *Set This House on Fire* as the "magnum opus of a fat spoiled rich boy who could write like an angel about landscape and like an adolescent about people?"[45] Does gothic doom become, then, rhetorical, a literary attitude, a Faulknerian mannerism laced with a fatal Fitzgeraldian glamor, overwrought in a gothic style?

Of *Set This House on Fire* Jonathan Baumbach suggests that the book "attempts the improbable: the alchemical transformation of impotent rage into tragic experience. Styron's rage is the hell-fire heat of the idealist faced by an unredeemably corrupt world for which he as fallen man feels obsessively and hopelessly guilty."[46] This suggests also Gardner's assessment of Styron's writing as "a piece of anguished Protestant soul-searching, an attempt to seize all the evil in the world—in his own heart first—crush it, and create a planet fit for God and man."[47] The Manichean battles in this book reveal the passionate intensity of this alchemical urge.

The sacred and the profane, the prudish and the prurient, God and nothingness, being and nihilism, doom and nostalgia, Anglo-Saxon and Italian notions of honesty battle it out in *Set This House on Fire*. Peter Leverett, the moderate realistic lawyer, confronts Cass Kinsolving, the guilt-ridden visionary artist. Each has been attracted and played sycophant to that "gorgeous silver fish . . . a creature so strange, so *new*" that is Mason Flagg. Flagg represents a Manichean vision in his "dual role of daytime squire and nighttime nihilist," a distinctively American Jekyll and Hyde, "able in time of hideous surfeit, and Togetherness's lurid mist, to revolt from conventional values, to plunge into a chic vortex of sensation, dope, and fabricated sin, though all the while retaining a strong grip on his two million dollars." Is this Styron's "provisional rebel?" He celebrates the new frontier of sexual adventure as would a gnostic libertine corrupt in his faith and reveals "that slick, arrogant, sensual, impenitently youthful, American and vainglorious face," the spoiled, self-indulgent American child, filled with unfulfilled desire, itself desirous of further increase. He suggests Styron's America in the Fifties, "a general wasting away of quality, a kind of sleazy common prostration of the human spirit," in times "like these when men go whoring off after false gods" in a realm of "moral and spiritual anarchy." Is it any wonder that Peter Leverett's father cries out for "something ferocious and tragic, like what happened to Jericho or the cities of the plain, a promise to bring back tragedy to the land of the Pepsi-Cola . . . ?"

The Manichean vision acquires metaphysical proportions in Cass's mind. He "dreamed wild Manichean dreams, dreams that told him that God . . . was weaker even than the evil He created and allowed to reside in the soul of man." He is haunted by dreams of "women with burdens, and dogs being beaten, and these somehow all seemed inextricably and mysteriously connected, and monstrously, intolerably so," the dog beaten to death but refusing to die, "which suffered all the more because even He in his mighty belated compassion could not deliver His creatures from their living pain."

Peter Leverett suffers a recurring nightmare of a shadow beyond the window in the dark, a friend bent on betrayal and murder but for no apparent reason. It is Cass who suggests "that whosoever it is that rises in a dream with a look in his face of eternal damnation is just ones own self, wearing a mask, and thats the fact of the matter." Evil becomes the self trapped in itself, a spirit at war with itself, a narcissistic and ineradicable sense of guilt that will not be overcome, despite Cass's ex-

planations of exile, orphanhood, ignorance, the war, his wife's Catholicism, his own "puddle of self" at the base of his artistic nature, his Anglo-
Saxon background, his terror, his Americanness, his actions toward blacks.
"To triumph over self is to triumph over Death," Cass declares. "It
is to triumph over that beast which one's self interposes between one's
soul and one's God." Between that soul and God lurks the Manichean
beast of the self, the solipsistic, psychological center around which Styron's
metaphysical and sociocultural explanations of Manicheism pale. At one
point Cass discusses "this business about evil—what it is, where it is,
whether it's a reality, or just a figment of the mind," a cancer in the
body or something "to stomp on like you would a flea carrying a bubonic
plague." He decides that "both of these theories are as evil as the evil
they are intended to destroy and cure." Evil thus remains either "the
puddle of self," which Styron belabors in the book, or the mystery of
endless pain that knows no justification, a cruel beating down of the human
spirit that in the end, like that puddle, suggests a perpetual entrapment,
an imprisonment of both mind and matter, a Manichean mystery that
can know release only in the worship of a demonic God or the furtive
celebration of sex and sensation.

Both Leverett and Kinsolving press on to make their personal nightmares
make sense. "Passionately he tried to make the dream give up its meaning," Styron writes of Cass. He might just as well be writing about his
use of the gothic romance to surrender up the significance of his Manichean
vision, incapable or unwilling because of his own southern background
or Christian tradition, to recreate *only* a Manichean vision in the tradition of Poe: "Each detail was as clear in his mind as something which
happened only yesterday, yet when he tried to put them all together he
ended up with blank ambiguous chaos." The details confront the overall
design: we have reached a standstill, an impasse. "These various horrors
and sweats you have when you're asleep add up to something," Cass
maintains, "even if these horrors are masked and these sweats are symbols. What you've got to do is get behind the mask and the symbol. . . ."
Kinsolving suggests Melville's Ahab who, in penetrating the mask, reduces
ambiguity to palpable design and submits willfully to the Manichean fire-
worshippers at his side. He becomes his own devil. Cass cannot.

Set This House on Fire cries out for tragedy to alleviate its pain. Styron
instead settles for melodrama, the *deus ex machina*, the Fascist-humanist
Luigi, who will not allow Cass to wallow in any more of his guilt. Luigi

to Cass plays the wise father to the angst-ridden American adolescent: Cass is "relieved" of his guilt.

Kinsolving and Leverett meet years later to go fishing on a river they knew as boys to talk of their pasts. If at first both seem like opposites, they in fact blend into one southern sensibility: bewitched and entranced by Flagg, they succumb to a rampant, unanchored nostalgia that swallows everything before it, an omnivorous sentimentality, "the sad nostalgic glamor," the southern mind's ravenous appetite for "a hundred gentle memories, purely southern, which swarmed instantly through his mind, though one huge memory encompassed all." Nostalgia begets narcissism or vice-versa: intensity of feeling replaces knowledge as the keystone to awareness. But this nostalgia is not seen as tragic, as a Manichean flight from adulthood: it survives "pure" in its sweeping intensities, its rhetorical sweeps—it is the ominous flip side of Cass's dread, of Styron's gothic plot and structure. Catastrophe, doom, guilt, phantoms, and diabolical enchantment draw Leverett to Flagg, Cass to Flagg, Leverett to Cass, but rampant childhood nostalgia surmounts and floods them all, feeding upon itself.

As Flannery O'Connor suggested, "When tenderness is detached from the source of tenderness, its logical outcome is terror."[48] That nostalgic tenderness cancels out the gothic terror: Manichean confrontation has produced spiritual stalemate. As Joyce Carol Oates suggests in reference to Norman Mailer, "He has constructed an entire body of work around a Manichean existentialism [with] a firm belief in the absolute existence of Evil [and] a belief in a limited God, a God who is a 'warring element' in a divided universe . . . [H]is energetic Manicheanism forbids a higher art. Initiation . . . brings the protagonist not to newer visions . . . but to a dead end, a full stop."[49] Melodrama deflates tragedy and, for all its passion and power, leaves a world split between suffering and sentimentality, a dark design of untransmuted spiritual impotence, mesmerized by a Manichean reality but unable or unwilling to succumb to its fatal power and terrifyingly realized inevitability. Perhaps "ultimate" rebellion would insist on such a vision. "Provisional" rebellion can only disguise it in Christian images and psychological explanations. The void which surrounds Cass's tirades, that outer world which dissolves in the wake of his internal cries, may reflect only his own narcissism, suggesting that Styron is intent upon withdrawing into a safer hollow from the very Manichean vision he has so fiercely created.

The Manichean vision of *Sophie's Choice* is announced in Styron's opening quotation from André Malraux's *Lazare*: "I seek that essential region of the soul where absolute evil confronts brotherhood." Nathan is both Sophie's savior and her destroyer; love battles death; Calvinist southerners are mesmerized by New York Jews; North and South fight over virtue or the lack of it; black and white, slave and master become both victims and accomplices of one another; out of the adversity Poland has suffered comes not compassion and charity but sustained anti-Semitic cruelty; sex in Stingo's 1940s breeds both liberation and guilt; Sophie "could not bear the contrast between the abstract yet immeasurable beauty of music and the almost touchable dimensions of her own aching despair"; every choice is fraught with disaster. Survival itself produces the ineradicable "toxin of guilt." Poland reflects a defeated South with "her indwelling ravaged and melancholy heart," the sense of inestimable loss, a legacy of "cruelty and compassion." Opposites attract, becomes entangled, lead to suicide as ultimate paralysis. George Steiner's "two orders of simultaneous experience are so different, so irreconcilable to any common norm of human values, their coexistence is so hideous a paradox" that they like "gnostic speculation[s] imply, different species of time in the same world." And evil itself becomes the banality of duty and obedience, the belief in the "absolute *expendability* of human life," the reality of Auschwitz that cannot be finally understood.

The most "common norm of human values" Styron undermines is Christianity, at the same time that he uses Christian imagery, apparently without irony, to describe the scope and mythic archetypes of his material: "I mean it when I say that no chaste and famished grail-tormented Christian knight could have gazed with more slack-jawed admiration at the object of his quest than I did at my first glimpse of Sophie's bouncing behind." A good line, but the Christian quest motif sticks to the entire form of Styron's use of the gothic romance: it leads, however disastrously, to understanding and significance in ultimately religious terms. Stingo's own "Protestant moderation" invests sex with guilt and his "residual Calvinism" sparks his imagination with visions of doom and desecration, but on the train with the "dark priestess" toward the end of the book, the black woman, he goes into "a bizarre religious convulsion, brief in duration but intense" and reads the Bible aloud with her; not the Sermon on the Mount—"the grand old Hebrew woe seemed more cathartic, so went back to Job." The archetypal victim, but a victim of residual faith, a kind the agnostic Stingo does not share. He disguises himself as the Reverend Entwistle to get a room with Sophie and admits that "the Scriptures were always largely a literary convenience, supplying me with allusions and tag lines for the characters in my novel," but what are we to make of Stingo's impression of Dr. Jemand von Niemand, the man who forces on Sophie her most chilling choice? He must have done so, Stingo speculates, because he thirsted for faith, and to restore God he first must commit a great sin: "All of his depravity had been enacted in a vacuum of sinless and businesslike godlessness, while his soul thirsted for beatitude." The great sin will shadow forth a greater faith "to restore his belief in God."

At the conclusion of the book Stingo reads lines from Emily Dickinson at the graves of Sophie and Nathan: "Ample make this bed. / Make this bed with awe; / In it wait till judgment break / Excellent and fair." And after a night of Poe-esque dreams on the beach, being buried alive and awakening to find himself buried in sand like "a living cadaver being prepared for burial in the sands of Egypt," he welcomes the morning, blesses "my resurrection," and explains: "This was not judgement day—only morning. Morning: excellent and fair." The ironies are apparent, but so is the stab at symbolic resurrection, waking from the gothic nightmare, returned to the land of the living. It is as if Stingo/Styron wants it both ways again, provisionally damned, provisionally saved, without O'Connor's sterner choices or Faulkner's deeper consciousness. Auschwitz disregarded "Christian constraint"; Stingo will not, despite the revelations of Sophie. He clings to his genteel moderation despite the "Sophiemania" that engulfs him and "laid siege to my imagination."

Gothic romance usually demands the waking from the nightmare, a return to normalcy after exorcism. But Stingo, like Peter Leverett and Cass Kinsolving before him, will not surrender to being exorcised; he clings to what the narrative, the romance, proves to be falacious and outmoded doctrines. Perhaps the gothic romance cannot embrace absolute evil; the term itself curdles the narrator's will to embrace it. Others will die; Stingo, Leverett, and Kinsolving will survive because of the very harried faith they have been "taught" during the romance to outgrow. Stingo's attraction to "a certain morbidity" is not the same thing as the "tragic sense." It is too guarded, too self-protected, too distanced from the real Manichean vision of things by splendid baroque rhetoric and vocabularies of doom and dark auguries. He loves the doom as he loves a nostalgic South; it is "the feeling in my bones," shiveringly enjoyable, a frisson of the spirit. And within that emotional solipsism, absolute evil proves sheerest poppycock.

And yet *Sophie's Choice* works, with its escalating confessions, its incestuously ominous rhetoric, its sheer dramatic scope and power, as we learn of the real nature of Sophie's father, her many lovers from the murderer Josef to the lesbian Wanda, the incredible choice of surrendering her daughter to the ovens. Stingo's climax literally occurs in bed—at last—with the pale, radiant Sophie; hers occurs in her suicide pact with Nathan: sex and death, twin dark towers of Manichean castles: semen and cyanide brutally intermingled. "Everyone's a victim. The Jews are also the victims of victims, that's the main difference." There is the frightening core of *Sophie's Choice*, evaded or at least displaced by Stingo's awakening from premature burial to the possibility of morning and of resurrection. Sophie weaves tale after tale before her "patient confessor," each until the end a "fabrication, a wretched lie, another fantasy served up to provide a frail barrier, a hopeless and crumbly line of defense between those she cared for, like myself and her smothering guilt." But the Christian fabrications, the literary allusions, are themselves frail barriers and should crumble completely before the overwhelming presence of guilt, even as "small" in comparison to Sophie's as is Stingo's in relation to his mother's death, his native region, and the money he inherited from the slave sold down river, Artiste (appropriately named). Gothic romance, aligned to Christian images of demonic nightmare, the dark night of the soul, and resurrection, itself crumbles as it did in *The Marble Faun*, undone by the pit of Rome, or in *The Blithedale Romance*, overwhelmed by the harsh reality of power, of masters and slaves beneath the veils. In Stingo's narrative it does seem a "worn-out tradition."

Perhaps Styron writes at the end of southern romance, or perhaps he has stretched the form to include a vision of the world that it cannot contain, that murky spurious mixture of Christian archetype and Manichean vision. Styron's world mirrors McCullers's in the intensity of its narcissism and the trap of irrevocable guilt. Rational psychological explanations cannot encompass such a fierce conjuring up of guilt; they can only reduce and confine it. Styron's guilt will not be confined in any rational, religious scheme or design: it overwhelms every attempt to comprehend it, existing as some great Manichean "black hole" that can result only in ultimate withdrawal (the ascetic of suicide) or in sexual revelry (the libertinism of Mason Flagg, of Stingo's starving lust). Rhetoric, however intense and poetic, cannot transmute it into anything finally significant other than its own dark, irrevocable existence, men and women entombed for life. As Rilke suggests in Styron's opening quote, "death, the whole of death,—even before life's begun . . . this is beyond description."

In Styron's world we are in Poe country, in that vast southern literary mind of intense, unmitigated emotion feeding upon itself to the exclusion of everything else. Faulkner transcended it by his genius, the depth of his complexity of vision; O'Connor surmounted it through an ultimate religious faith, garbed in grotesque disguises, in the grim visages of serious clowns. McCullers and Styron seem trapped within it, McCullers more certain of the Manichean shadows of her vision, setting it up as dark fable, as inevitable as death itself. Styron pussyfoots around it, hanging onto Christian images, archetypes, symbols despite the splendid proofs that they do not apply. Perhaps this is where the southern tradition in American fiction ends, grappling with absolute evil outside its borders, serving up horrors as it would serve up childhood fantasies. Styron excels at it. His fiction drives itself toward a revelation he cannot or will not accept. And all the magnificent rhetoric in the world will not gloss over the provisional nature of his vision, not mere ambiguity but at last evasion. The line between paradox and paralysis is a thin one. Styron's marvelous conjurings up of the former lead finally to the latter, and perhaps this is the absolute evil in contemporary society that haunts him the most.

FIVE

John Cheever:
Suburban Romancer

HAWTHORNE and Cheever share the literary tradition of the American romance, as fashioned by Hawthorne. They share the basic elements of the romance form: the stylized characters, the atmospherics, the elements of prophecy and transformation, allegorical patterns, perilous journeys, "a penchant for the marvelous," the use of legends, myths, and fables as stylized patterns to "get at" the mysterious roots of human motive and desire. Cheever shares with Hawthorne the particular form of the American psychological romance as well, in which the self, not society or social forces, stands at the center of the fictional realm, marked as it is by the distinctly Manichean conflict between good and evil, light and darkness, both of these as equal and ominous combatants, both at times hopelessly intermingled and confused. Both Hawthorne and Cheever create fictions mixing dreams and actuality, creating that psychological land-scape of mind and matter which the isolated self occupies. Their episodic structures reflect the emblematic quality of incidents and images; these become miniature epiphanies of an entire theme or vision. Both authors visibly explore their own material, creating their own distance from it in order expressly to invite the reader to join them in their quest. The veneer of social comedy in Cheever's work differs markedly from Haw-thorne's more tragic vision, but as American romancers they remain re-markably similar.

At the time of his death, June 18, 1982, John Cheever had at last gained the modest wealth and popular acclaim that had eluded him. The prizes had always been there—four O. Henrys, the National Book Award, the Howells medal, topped by the Pulitzer for his collected stories in 1978. But the critical response had always lumped him with other novelists of suburban manners, such as John O'Hara and J.P. Marquand, confusing

what he called his "target"—"Suburbia was a reflection of the aspirations of my time"[1]—with his true vision of the world, the distinctly
moral vision of good and evil and human choice that dogged Hawthorne
and generated his romances. His critics acted as though there was "some
confusion between architectural decorum and moral probity . . . as if there
were some connection between real-estate values and serenity."[2] So did
his characters. Cheever did not.

When, on September 9, 1979, at the MacDowell Colony in Peter-
borough, New Hampshire, he became the twentieth recipient of the Edward MacDowell Medal, annually given for an "outstanding contribu-
tion to the arts," Elizabeth Hardwick observed that in rereading many
of Cheever's stories, "I began to see some kind of symbolic approach
closer to Hawthorne than to, say, Fitzgerald whom he once might have
reminded me of."[3] At Cheever's funeral John Updike memorialized
"the magic certainty of his prose" and saw him as "a teller of tales purely." In his review of Cheever's last book, *Oh What a Paradise It Seems*,
Updike wrote: "Cheever's instinctive belief in the purity and glory of
Creation brings with it an inevitable sensitivity to corruption; like
Hawthorne, he is a poet of the poisoned."[4] And the *New Yorker*, bid-
ding farewell in its too fanciful prose, finally grasped the vision: "Like
Hawthorne's, his characters are moral embodiments, rimmed in a flickering
firelight of fantasy."[5]

In remarks written to me on the first page of *The Leaves, the Lion-Fish
and the Bear* (1980), Cheever scrawled enigmatically: ". . . and with my
cordial regards to the memory of that pioneer environmentalist Nathaniel
Hawthorne." One had only to look at the beginning of *The Wapshot
Chronicle*: "Looking back at the village we might put ourselves into the
shoes of a native son (with a wife and family in Cleveland) coming home
for some purpose—a legacy or a set of Hawthorne. . . ."

Oh What A Paradise It Seems with its romancer's frame—"This is a
story to be read in bed in an old house on a rainy night"—presents a
final fable of Cheever's vision, replete with the decorous sensitive hero,
the articulate Lemuel Sears. It celebrates "the miraculousness of the
visible world"[6]—rain, love, light, streams, landscapes. It presents correspondences between mood and luminescent matter, the Manichean mingling of emotions, rootlessness, innocence, homelessness and a fervid
nostalgia for home, a "gypsy culture" spawning "spiritual vagrants,"
"nomads" in search of a lost past which had never existed. It also in-

cludes Cheever's ironic jabs at fast-food franchises, psychiatry, the rites and rituals of suburban cocktails, and "people—and he counted himself among them—who had lost the sense of a harvest." Cheever's lean lyric line, conjuring up correspondences between light and man's moral choices, a seeming paradise of physical beauty and spiritual freedom, confronts a tale of pollution and murder.

Sears recognizes the "contrary polarities in [his] constitution," as he slips fluidly from heterosexual to homosexual love. He is convinced "that the polarities in his constitution were acutely incompatible and that the only myth that suited his disposition was Dr. Jekyll and Mr. Hyde." Cheever's lifelong wrestling with his own homosexuality adds a special poignance to the Manichean Jekyll-and-Hyde struggle of his characters and structure of his fiction. This Manichean spirit surfaces in all of Cheever's other romances in much greater scope, as we shall see, between the Wapshot brothers, Nailles and Hammer, and the Farraguts. We find it muted here in this slighter book—even Farragut has been murdered after all, at last—but it colors the whole and attests to this final hard-earned testimony of faith.

Spiritual confinement haunts Cheever's world: the dark Manichean world of Falconer Correctional Facility/Daybreak House, the world as final trap, dreary prison, sexual narcissism; the habits, routines, and traditions of St. Botolph's; the suburban rites of Bullet Park, rites set adrift in sacred groves completely disconnected from the past; the characters' own desires, sexual and metaphysical; the weary, rootless presence of an American railway station at dusk. Cheever's language creates both his characters' urge to transform that prison-world, however comfortable, however dreaded, and their lazier desire to accept their confinement as an indication of their worldly success and fashionably good manners. For Eliot Nailles, himself the epitome of suburban manners, language invokes his own suburban style. He too easily confuses the decorum and physical grace of Bullet Park with some ultimate holy city of faith. The superficiality and artifice of suburban living breed a drug-induced "wonderfulness" he will not shake. For Cheever, however momentary, however illusory, language can invoke grace itself. The lyric line transcends irony and produces epiphany, however hedged and guarded. The prison remains dark, chaos threatens every line, but momentarily characters can experience the sensation of resurrection and rebirth in the lyric lines of Cheever's prose. Sears on the ice:

He skated and skated. The pleasure of fleetness seemed . . . divine. Swinging down a long stretch of black ice gave Sears a sense of homecoming. . . . It seemed to Sears that all the skaters moved over the ice with the happy conviction that they were on their way home. Home might be an empty room and an empty bed to many of them, including Sears, but swinging over the black ice convinced Sears that he was on his way home. Someone more skeptical might point out that this illuminated how ephemeral is our illusion of homecoming. There was a winter sunset and in this formidable show of light and color he unlaced his skates and returned to his apartment in the city.

The litany of home, appreciated and experienced in the swiftness of skating, might be recognized, if one were skeptical, as illusory and fraudulent. Emotion confronts the reason. And yet the lyric line, the lyric thought, risen from the "pleasure of fleetness seemed . . . divine." Cheever swings over black ice, recognizing the blackness, the dashed hopes, the essential return to a lonely apartment in the city. But the light and color in nature have proved "formidable" at the moment, and that divine sense of connection and consummation between mind and matter descends like grace in the long, elegaic, lyric peroration of his vision. Images touch deep memories, instinctual havens of archetypal experiences, a psychic wholeness, however unrealizable, recognized momentarily as having been realized somewhere, sometime in the very nature of the soul. Such sensations create the sense of moral choices. The trap shudders ever so slightly: a state of grace in a tale of corruption and pollution. And Cheever's fable, framed by the voice of the old romancer, recognizes the delight and the risk: "By framing a painting the artist, of course, declared it to be a distillate of his deepest feelings about love and death. By junking the frame he destroyed the risk of a declaration."[7]

"The constants that I look for," Cheever wrote in the preface to his collected stories, "are a love of light and a determination to trace some moral chain of being." The contrary polarity exists, however: "Calvin played no part at all in my religious education, but his presence seemed to abide in the barns of my childhood and to have left me with some undue bitterness." Bitterness and light: Cheever's Manichean poles. His characters, trapped in social roles, confined to suburban villas, are made for comedy more than for tragedy. The lyric line captures their rambling monologues, their incongruities, the non sequiturs of their existence. Cheever loves shifting tenses and voices, "changing keys"[8] in his tales, as the characters search for significance, bombarded by strange episodes, fragmented events.

Literary modernism influenced him in his belief in juxtaposition and jump cuts, as did the romancer's art. For him, "linear plot is unreal, debased, useless, false."[9] He enjoyed the sudden illuminations, the revelations that could occur as one episode spilled over and bumped into another episode. Continuity was kin to Robert Frost's momentary stay against confusion; the essence of contemporary life was its jagged metamorphoses, its sudden leaps and diversions, within which the comic and tragic remained closely interwoven. His fiction, whether short or long, reflects this basic vision. The long books reflect no gerrymandered jumble of short stories awkwardly thrust together but his experience of the fractured modern world, the gypsy culture in full cry. "A trout stream in a forest . . . seemed for Sears to be the bridge that spans the mysterious abyss between our spiritual and our carnal selves," but it is a ghostly bridge, ancient and unreliable, that can vanish and topple into the rushing flood of a world in endless flight from itself. Sacred groves within seeking natural correspondences without vanish in the next sudden shift of voice and events.

Cheever's characters often view themselves as shaped by the social demands of their environment, whereas Cheever, in his fragmentary plotting and episodic structure, undermines this superficial "suburban gloss," reduces suburbia to a state of mind, and thereby presents it as one more psychological projection of man in an infinite state of flux. If his characters feel that they are products or victims of an infinite network of social obligations, of status-seeking, money-making, and object-consuming, Cheever reveals them as trapped in certain psychological states, embodiments of traditional moral patterns of good and evil. In such a realm, reality easily slips between the visible physical world and the dreamworld, between suburban splendors and nightmarish visions, and Cheever's episodic structure, like Hawthorne's, emphasizes exactly that. As suggested, critics have often argued about the episodic nature of Cheever's longer fictions, viewing them as clumsy attempts to stitch together random short stories and odd bits and pieces culled from the imagination of a writer, essentially, of short stories. In fact such episodic notation mirrors the emblematic form of the romance that Hawthorne employed.

Hawthorne's persistent use of allegorical symbolism is often replaced in Cheever's fiction by a similar use of the manners and mores of suburbia: both conventions help tie together the various episodes and fragments. Each episode in a Cheever book can be seen as an emblem of the entire theme and vision of the book. Each incident repeats, comments upon, or embroiders the basic vision or situation of Cheever's fictional world. Each emblem is one more link in the chain of his sensibility. The experience of loneliness, isolation, nostalgia, moral conflicts with good and evil, surface in each of his separate events. His plots are not so much incremental as spasmodic, dreamlike (thus matching the dreamlike texture of his tales), and quirky. These fragments reflect the actual modern experience of characters' lives and help to break up and subvert the cocoon of manners and illusions of suburban permanence these people seek refuge in. Cheever's romances stalk modern man's moral identity, and the wild and wonderful nature of his eccentric episodes, the mingling of the marvelous and the actual, reveal the psychological complexities of a fragmented world. Truth may lie, as in *The Wapshot Scandal*, "at the center of the labyrinthine and palatial structures" of his quixotic plots, and that truth may be the acknowledgment that all events in modern life seem to take "such eccentric curves that it was difficult to comprehend." In each episode the self *in extremis*, however comically rendered, resembles Hawthorne's allegorical scaffold scenes in *The Scarlet Letter*: monologue may replace emblem, but the intent and effect remain the same.

Cheever's habitual use of two querulous brothers in his fiction to express opposite visions of reality crosses several biographical, psychological, thematic, and structural boundaries. His own brother, Frederick, who was seven years older and who died an alcoholic, became in Cheever's eyes "the strongest love of my life."[10] Cheever's father, Frederick, was forty-nine when John was born, owned a Lynn shoe factory, lost his business in the 1929 crash, attempted suicide, and deserted the family when John was fifteen. His mother, Mary Liley, an Englishwoman, opened a gift shop in order to make ends meet and seems to have been the kind of independent woman who undermined her husband's pride. After his famous expulsion at seventeen from Thayer Academy, Cheever went to live with his brother Frederick in Boston, and they both took a walking tour of Germany in the summer of 1929. Cheever admitted to fantasizing about killing his brother at times, and that between them grew up "an unseemly closeness";[11] theirs was in effect "a Siamese situation."[12]

In the short story "The Brothers" (1937), Tom and Kenneth Manchester seek each other out after the divorce of their parents. They cling to an intense affection between them, almost desperately, "as if sharing it with others would be some betrayal of their pleasure." The collapse of their family "brought the brothers still closer together . . . cherishing their habitual round, their aimless comings and goings, the little certainty they had rescued from the wreck of their home." They both have an extremely intense appreciation of family and place, of "the familiar hills" that now seem desolate but hardy in the autumn of "the New England of their fathers." In the course of the story both boys—Tom is seventeen, Kenneth is twenty—pay habitual weekend visits to the farmhouse of Amy Henderson, a widow, who has a daughter, Jane. Jane is attracted to Kenneth, but Kenneth is so used to relating only to his brother that he remains oblivious and indifferent to her feelings. Tom recognizes what is going on and tries to allow them time together, but Kenneth recognizes nothing.

Finally Tom realizes that their own present refuge in each other cannot continue: "It was the first time it had occurred to Tom that their devotion to each other might be stronger than their love of any girl or even than their love of the world." He realizes that theirs is "a love that held no jealousy and no fear and no increase," that their mutual devotion might deform them and turn their sanctuary into some place of sterile affection. Consequently Tom decides to move to New York. Kenneth returns to the farm alone. Jane has already decided to move to Chicago and live with Amy's sister. On "one of the first great nights of autumn [when] the wind tasted of winter and of the season's end and moved in the trees with the noise of a conflagration," Kenneth "felt the pain that Tom had brought down on both of them without any indignation; they had tried to give their lives some meaning and order, and for love of the same world that had driven them together, they had had to separate." He is left "like a stranger at the new, strange, vivid world." Maturity, the recognition of separate selves, the interposition of sexual completion and need, all have emerged to sever the boyhood refuge and brotherly closeness. Separation, however painful, becomes necessary in order for each to establish his own personality and life. In the story it is difficult to tell one brother from the other, as if their relationship circumscribes any separate reality or personality they may have had. They are left with the realization of going their separate ways and the deep sense of loss and loneliness which accompanies the necessary split. It is a loss that most Cheever characters carry with them and that can never be healed.

In "The Lowboy" (1959) and especially in "Goodbye, My Brother" (1951), the psychological split between brothers becomes apparent. In simplistic and rather stark terms one brother comes to represent a love of natural beauty, an appreciation of humanitarian values and so-cial/religious ceremonies, an enlightened spirit, and a sense of decorum and grace. He becomes, in short, the Cheever "hero." The other seems obsessed with the decay and ugliness of the world, embodied as they seem to be in a brutalized materialism and a rootless, selfish self-concern, and with the forces of destruction which can be directed to sweep away the illusions of decorum and grace. In "The Lowboy" the "bad" brother, Richard Norton, radiates the "aura of smallness" and selfishness of the "spoiled child." He has risen from a sad and chaotic family past "into a dazzling and resplendent respectability," the facade of which he wishes to maintain at all times. He insists on having the lowboy which the nar-rator, the "good" brother, at first wishes to have, since it is a family heirloom. Richard demands it; the narrator surrenders it. Richard takes it home and sets it up exactly as it had been in the family, complete with silver bowl, "on its carpet of mysterious symbols."

Richard's "wayward attachment" to the lowboy, however, transforms him. In the narrator's mind, because it is linked to a chaotic and sor-rowful family past, "the fascination of the lowboy was the fascination of pain." Richard becomes quarrelsome and argumentative. The narrator, noting the transformation that has taken place—"Oh, why is it that life is for some an exquisite privilege and others must pay for their seats at the play with a ransom of cholers, infections, and nightmares?"—returns home to smash all the family heirlooms that remain, and exclaims: "We can cherish nothing less than our random understanding of death and the earth-shaking love that draws us to one another. . . . Cleanliness and valor will be our watchwords. Nothing less will get us past the armed sentry and over the mountainous border."

At first the psychological conflict is clear: Richard views life in its darker terms, having "committed himself to the horrors of the past"; the nar-rator delights in the "green-gold" light of a spring day: "It was astound-ing in its beauty, and seemed . . . a link in a long chain of leafy trees beginning in childhood." And yet it is the narrator after all who tells the story, who seems entranced by his brother's darker visions. It is the narrator who conjures up the entire nightmare vision in the story of family ghosts returned on a dark and rainy night to observe the lowboy in Richard's house. It is the narrator who evokes the drunks and the suicides and the cripples in his family tree and confines Richard's position "to observation." Even on that burgeoning spring day the narrator admits that "it was the shadow that was most mysterious and exciting, the light one could not define." His tale of his brother's transgressions is in effect his own personal exorcism; the "dark" brother becomes a psychological projection of his own darker obsessions and his need to triumph over them by proclaiming "cleanliness and valor." His is a vigorous—and, as we shall see, stylistic—attempt to get beyond the sentry and mountains into a realm of light and transcendental vision, and his brother's failure to do so almost assures and is necessary for his own success.

The same is true for the marvelously constructed "Goodbye, My Brother," the story Cheever chose to place first in his 1978 collection. Lawrence Pommeroy views a bigoted and narrow universe, steeped in its own decay and gloom. His world feasts on the same kind of "spiritual cannibalism" that motivated his Puritan ancestors. He reminds the narrator, his brother, of a "Puritan cleric" with his "habits of guilt, self-denial, taciturnity, and penitence." "His baleful and incisive mind" embodies that Calvinistic New England legacy of "undue bitterness" which resides in Cheever's fiction. The narrator is determined "to trace some moral chain of being." He admires "the harsh surface beauty of life," those "obdurate truths before which fear and horror are powerless," and records his sensuous moments: the roses smelling like strawberry jam, the grapes smelling of wine, the sky filled with "continents of shadow and fire." The Pommeroys gather at their summer house at Laud's Head and more or less systematically run Lawrence out of the family.

And yet once again the narrator admits that he and Lawrence are "very close in spirit." The phrase looks in both directions at once, for it suggests both that they are not really close at all and that they are extremely close. For all his railing against the vestiges of Puritanism in Lawrence, the narrator reads as much "significance and finality into [his] every gesture" as he does in Lawrence's, even though he considers his own vision blessed and Lawrence's "sordid." The narrator sees the world in terms of signs, portents, revelations, and religious ceremonies: swimming becomes a ritual baptism, an "illusion of purification" in which the family can "shed our animus in the cold water." His use of the word "illusion" suggests that he may suspect the foundations of his own good faith in the beauty of life, and when he goes to meet the summer ferry on the island and discovers that for all its whistles and clangings and smell of brine, it is "a voyage of no import," he realizes all too swiftly that "I had hit on exactly the kind of observation that Lawrence would have made." Throughout the story he ascribes certain dark feelings and thoughts to Lawrence by using such phrases as "it must have occurred to him" or "as if he saw" or "I knew that the buoys . . . would sound to him like half-human, half-drowned cries." At last fed up with Lawrence's gloom, his inability to enjoy himself, his acidic remarks about the family and a party at the club (the men dress up in their old football uniforms, the women in their bridal gowns, for the "come-as-you-wish-you-were" party), the narrator strikes him with a root on the beach. It is a repetition of a similar incident twenty-five years before, when the narrator hit his brother with a rock. This visionary Cain strikes out at the Puritanical Abel.

Lawrence, stunned, leaves the Pommeroy clan once and for all. He will not return to Laud's Head for summer vacations. His goodbye is one more in a long series of goodbyes, or so the narrator describes it. For a man intent on denying the reality of Lawrence's gloomy vision, the narrator spends a lot of time recreating the depth, the imagery, and the scope of that vision. But his own lyric appreciation of the world around him triumphs, once the darker brother has been exorcised. The story ends with that lyric vision completely in control, with its poetic rhythms and mythic overtones similar to modernist imagist verse (as arranged below), but it is a vision which in this case has been earned by the narrator's wrestling with his own Puritan heritage:

> My wife and my sister were swimming
> —Diana and Helen—
> and I saw their uncovered heads,
> black and gold in the dark water.
> I saw them come out
> and I saw that they were naked,
> unshy, beautiful, and full of grace,
> and I watched the naked women
> walk out of the sea.

In Cheever's four novels (or, more accurately, romances) his creation
of the two antagonistic brothers becomes not only the major psychological
focus but also the major thematic and structural one: "A mythology that
would penetrate with some light the density of the relationship between
brothers seems to stop with Cain and Abel and perhaps this is as it should
be." "Mysterious polarities" dictate the major pattern of Cheever's fiction; the darker brother proves to be "one of those figures who stand
outside the brightly lighted centers of our consciousness and defeat our
love of candor and our confidence in the sweetness of life." Such psychological states, represented by the opposing brothers—a romantic pat-
terning of obsessive, symbolic, and almost allegorical types, in place of
fully realized, well-rounded novelistic characters—reflect Cheever's larger
themes, "the clash between night and day, between the head and the
groin." As he makes explicit in *The Wapshot Scandal*, "We are born between two states of consciousness; we spend our lives between the darkness
and the light, and to climb in the mountains of another country, phrase
our thoughts in another language or admire the color of another sky draws
us deeper into the mystery of our condition . . . here is a whole new
creation of self-knowledge, new images for love and death and the in-
substantiality and the importance of our affairs."

In *The Wapshot Chronicle* and *The Wapshot Scandal* Coverly and Moses
Wapshot enact the episodic drama of spirit and flesh. Coverly clearly
possesses "an alert and sentimental mind"; he is Icarus, "something mysterious and unrestful" to his father Leander; he suffers the extreme
rootlessness of the modern age and nostalgically longs for the more traditional (however illusory) confines of St. Botolphs. Yet to him is granted
"a searing vision of some golden age . . . a vision of life as hearty and
fleeting as laughter and something like the terms by which he lived."
Moses on the other hand, the more sensual of the brothers, basks in his
"judicious and tranquil self-admiration." His "taste for the grain and
hair of life" underscores "the kind of good looks and presence that sweeps
a young man triumphantly through secondary school and disappoint-
ingly enough not much farther." "He was the sort of paterfamilias who
inspires sympathy for the libertine," given the frigidity of his own code
of decency and his hypocritical philandering when it comes to "sexual
commerce." Coverly's awe in the face of life, his appreciation of the
beauties of the natural landscape and his own father's sacramental and
"unobserved ceremoniousness of his life," and his Christmas dinner for

the blind contrast with Moses's petty adulteries with the widow Wilston at the Viaduct House on Christmas Eve and his cynical belief that "the brilliance of light, the birth of Christ, all seemed to him like some fatuous shell game invented to dupe a fool like his brother while he saw straight through into the nothingness of things."

In *Falconer* Ezekiel Farragut, the Coverly brother, accidentally murders his brother Eben: "They looked enough like one another to be taken for twins." Eben is an alcoholic, abusive and cruel; he summons waiters by clapping his hands, and "his marriage could be dismissed, if one were that superficial, as an extraordinary sentimental and erotic collision." Ezekiel, heroin addict and murderer, yet celebrates "the simple phenomenon of light—brightness angling across the air—" which strikes him as "a transcendent piece of good news"; he continually marvels at the "invincible potency of nature" within a ceremonial sense of traditional religion and form. Ezekiel strikes Eben with a fire iron when Eben exclaims that their father really wanted to make their mother have an abortion and avert Ezekiel's birth. Ezekiel's dark night of the soul comes to an end when he hides himself in the burial sack of the dead prisoner Chicken and manages to be reborn into freedom.

Cheever's most apocalyptic and allegorical brothers are not brothers at all, yet they represent most clearly the conflict between social order and decency and individual chaos and dark dreams. In *Bullet Park* Eliot Nailles represents the perfect suburbanite, assured of his own sense of duty and decency, having "less dimension than a comic strip" in his solidly monogamous relationship with Nellie, viewing his love for his wife and son Tony as "a clear amber fluid that would surround them, cover them, preserve them and leave them insulated but visible like the contents of an aspic." He "thought of pain and suffering as a principality, lying somewhere beyond the legitimate borders of western Europe." His fragile suburban insulation is first threatened by Tony's spiritual paralysis—"There is a tendency in your income group to substitute possessions for moral and spiritual norms. A strict sense of good and evil, even if it is mistaken, is better than none"—and by Paul Hammer's kidnapping and attempted crucifixion of his son. Hammer, Nailles's nemesis, is an illegitimate child; his very existence is already "a threat to organized change." Nailles believes in "the mysterious power of nomenclature . . . nothing short of death could separate John and Mary. How much worse was Hammer and Nailles." He is a creature of his own mysterious dreams and believes that "the nature of man was terrifying and singular and man's environment was chaos." Moral prerogatives and duties appear to him as no more sturdy than a fragile kite string in the wind. He threatens "whole artificial structures of acceptable reality," such as Nailles's suburban existence, sees no genuine emotion or value whatsoever in Nailles's existence, listens to his mother's railing against the selfishness and vacuousness of American civilization—"Never, in the history of civilization, has one seen a great nation singlemindedly bent on drugging itself"—and decides that he will crucify Tony Nailles to "wake that world." In *Bullet Park* Cheever starkly draws his battle lines.

Cheever conjures up St. Botolphs at the beginning of *The Wapshot Chronicle* and *The Wapshot Scandal* in a similar fashion to Hawthorne's method in *The House of the Seven Gables*. In his opening paragraph Hawthorne at once establishes his setting, his mood, and his relationship with the reader. The romantic spell is at once conjured up, unlike the more dramatic and objective beginnings of so many contemporary novelists (such as Pynchon, Coover, and Kosinski) which plunge the reader immediately *in medias res*, into swift actions as yet undefined, or into sardonic ironies deliberately employed to disconnect the reader from any immediate emotional commitment. Hawthorne's setting is an old New England town, steeped in age and shadows from the past. The meditative mood implicitly reveals the strong and mysterious influences of the past upon the present, thus creating an atmospheric medium of mellow lights and shadows, unlike the broad daylight world of more realistic novels. Hawthorne's old Pyncheon house, "rusty," "huge," and "weather-beaten" suggests the romantic precincts of old castles and moldering ruins. At the same time Hawthorne consciously includes the reader in his created spell, speaking of "*our* New England towns" and revealing immediately the effect of the old house on him during "occasional visits to the town aforesaid." Hawthorne at once elicits the reader's sympathies and includes him in his own quest toward "tracking down" the mysteries hidden in the old house. The reference to "antiquities" promotes a certain nostalgia for the shadowy past as well, a fascination with long-ago times and dreamlike, legend-haunted landscapes.

For Cheever, St. Botolphs is "an old place, an old river town." It exudes "an aroma of the past" and suggests "an impression of unusual permanence" on its green. The snow falling on Christmas Eve in the opening paragraph of *The Wapshot Scandal* exhilarates and refreshes old

Mr. Jowett, the stationmaster, "and drew him—full-souled, it seemed—out of his carapace of worry and indigestion." The snow's "whiteness seems to be a part of our dreams." Setting and mood complement Hawthorne's own, and Cheever immediately includes the reader in "*our dreams.*"

The difference between Hawthorne's and Cheever's opening paragraphs, however, is more immediately apparent. With every reference to the "then" of the past and the impression of permanence which only *seems* permanent, Cheever immediately drops his reader into the "now" of the modern world. His mood of romance appears far more fragile than Hawthorne's: burdened with nostalgia for a lost Eden that may or may not have existed, his characters—and readers—are swiftly made aware of the discrepancy between human yearning and the realities of modern guilt, rootlessness, and disconnection. Thus if St. Botolphs was once a great inland port, now it displays only a table silver factory. Windows that first strike one as being "as delicate and reproachful as the windows of a church" are in reality looking out from the offices of a dentist and an insurance agent. St. Botolphs now looks prosperous only when an Independence Day parade is forming. Similarly old Mr. Jowett is singing "Oh Who Put the Overalls in Mrs. Murphy's Chowder" on Christmas Eve, "although he knew that it was all wrong for the season, the day and dignity of a station agent, the steward of the town's true and ancient boundary, its Gates of Hercules." That last Herculean image appears both ironic and romantic, at once part of Mr. Jowett's own self-inflation and of Cheever's comic exaggeration, and as part of a genuine conjuring up of an old New England village on the snowy, legendary eve of Christmas.

In his four romances Cheever's own creation of suspended, enchanted moments at the beginning of each book grows less and less romantic. St. Botolphs in *The Wapshot Chronicle* is presented in a full-bodied, historical manner: the village exists in the "real world" just as he describes it. In *The Wapshot Scandal*, however, Cheever announces his own separation from the Wapshots and their world: "It was always in their power to make me feel alone, to make it painfully clear that I was an outsider." By the end of the novel he announces his decision never to return to St. Botolphs again, and the village itself dissolves into "nothing at all." By the time of *Bullet Park* the mood of the opening paragraph has become far more plaintive and somber, and the romantic reverie is now clearly

116 IN HAWTHORNE'S SHADOW

a solitary thing: "Paint *me* a small railroad station then. . . ." The setting is still "at the heart of the matter," the reader is still included in the reverie—"*You* wake in a pullman. . . . *We* travel by plane"—and "your country" still suggests that strange, romantic aura, "unique, mysterious, vast," but the world looks lonely and empty, a place of weary travelers coming and going. "The spirit of our country seems to have remained a country of railroads," and although that spirit is not entirely rootless and transient, "a somber afterglow" permeates the opening of the book.

Finally, in the opening paragraph of *Falconer*, Cheever seems to have done away with the aura of romance altogether. His concentration upon the escutcheon over the main entrance to the prison, with its fatalistic and lethal images of arrows, swords, blindness, and pikes, leads him to dwell on this "last emblem" the prisoners will see before they go to their separate cells. That emblem suggests to him "man's endeavor to interpret the mystery of imprisonment in terms of symbols." Cheever's distance from his emblem, his critical apprehension of it drained of much of the romantic and legendary aura of his first three romances, reminds us of Hawthorne's opening paragraph in *The Marble Faun*. Hawthorne too stands far back from his own creation, outside the realm of mystery and romance, when he observes "the pretty figure of a child, clasping a dove to her bosom, but assaulted by a snake" and views it in stark allegorical terms as "a symbol . . . of the Human Soul, with its choice of Innocence or Evil close at hand." Both writers seek refuge in an immediate emblematic statement, though Cheever's still suggests an ultimate "mystery"—the true province of romance, perhaps—in place of Hawthorne's unrelenting allegorical interpretation.

Both writers create a dream texture in their tales, suggesting that "reality" exists in some "neutral territory" between the visible physical world and the interior imaginary one. Cheever suggests that "the mind itself is such a huge and labyrinthine chamber that the Pantheon and the Acropolis turn out to be smaller than we had expected." Man is indeed "a microcosm, containing within himself all the parts of the universe. . . . The distillations and transmutations release their innate power." More explicitly he describes St. Botolphs as "a place whose streets were as excursive and crooked as the human mind."

All Cheever's romances and many of his best short stories are crammed with dreams, nightmares, reveries, memories, omens, spells, and epiphanies. Consciousness invests everything with a nagging, ghostly uncertainty: visions undermine the explicit codes of suburban manners. Transformations suddenly occur. The social environment becomes not a straitjacket of independent rules and regulations but a state of mind, forever shifting and shimmering, in no way as permanent and exclusive as the inmates of Shady Hill and Proxmire Manor would have it. The world becomes "something mysterious and unrestful," a bewildering dreamscape of loneliness and rootlessness. Reality becomes "no more inviolable than the doors and windows that sheltered her." Even morality may become a fragile manner "influenced by landscapes and kinds of food." Rites and ceremonies tremble and shudder in a world where "total disaster seemed to be some part of the universal imagination." A primordial chaos threatens everything. Tony Nailles can only be "rescued" by a mysterious Swami who regards himself as a "spiritual cheerleader" and chants his litanies, which appear as artificial yet as mesmerizing as a game of grandmother's trunk or an adolescent's howl damning the suburban world. The world embodies "the landscape for some nightmare or battlefield" in which old men sell "phallic symbols and death's heads." Only in *Falconer* does Ezekiel Farragut, if only gratuitously and momentarily, break free of a dark, imprisoned world and rejoice at the genuine revelation of light. And Lemuel Sears does grasp "that most powerful sense of how singular, in the vastness of creation, is the richness of our opportunity."

Hawthorne intrudes upon all his romances: he invites the reader to explore his fictional material with him. The same is true in much of Cheever's work. When Daniel Hoffman described Hawthorne's style as "both detached and committed, both amused and serious, both dubious and affirmative,"[13] he could just as easily have been describing Cheever's. And when he suggests that Hawthorne's style, whether affirming or denying, points "to something other than the literal context of its assertions," the same can be said of Cheever's. In relying on allegorical signs, Hawthorne suggests both multiple significances and the possibility that there may ultimately be no significance at all. In comparing the "fabled then" of our nostalgic American heritage and the "prosaic now" of our contemporary American experience, Cheever uses all kinds of allegorical, mythic, legendary, Christian images and yet suggests that all may be ultimately chaotic and empty. "Nothing at all" remains in *The Wapshot Scandal*. Eliot Nailles goes off to work wonderfully drugged at the end of *Bullet Park*, suggesting that no matter how decent and decorous suburbia may be, it cannot handle or deal with real suffering. Only in *Falconer* and *Oh What a Paradise It Seems* do Cheever's "heroes" rejoice, their love of light carefully supported by traditional Christian imagery and ritual. In *The Wapshot Chronicle* Leander Wapshot's earthy, cere- monious love of natural beauty and rites of human passage, circumscrib- ed carefully by the often eccentric traditions and habits of an old New England village, helps to see Coverly through, and even though Farragut views his Wapshot-like family unsparingly without the soft focus of sen- timent and legend (they "were the sort of people who claimed to be sus- tained by tradition, but who were in fact sustained by the much more robust pursuit of a workable improvisation, uninhibited by consistency"), he yet admires their "pure, crude and lasting sense of perseverance."

Cheever consistently plays off romantic images against more mundane ones. His texts are filled with heraldric, archaic, biblical, abstract moral images connected with fables and myths and old traditions, against which are juxtaposed the common, ordinary images of everyday existence. The style therefore reflects in its "distilled dissolution," in its constant down- ward movement "from fable to floor,"[14] the over-all vision of decay and collapse, the experience of disenchantment, which underlies all of his fic- tion. As Hawthorne suggests in *The House of the Seven Gables*: "If we look through all the heroic fortunes of mankind, we shall find this same entanglement of something mean and trivial with whatever is noblest in joy or sorrow. Life is made up of marble and mud. . . . What is called poetic insight is the gift of discerning in this sphere of strangely mingled elements, the beauty and the majesty which are compelled to assume a garb so sordid."

If the style of the American psychological romance often reaches the intensity of poetry (one thinks most often of Faulkner), if it strives to achieve a heightened consciousness with exaggerated effects and reveals a fascination for an atmosphere of mystery, of light and dark, and mixes the marvelous and legendary with the mundane and ordinary, then Cheever's style matches that of the romance. It is his tone, however, that is very different from that of other romancers.

Cheever believes that decorum is "a mode of speech." His lucid, careful language reflects a certain propriety of behavior and observance of "good manners" which in no way reflects the overheated, zealous prose of a Faulkner or an Oates. His is similar to the neoclassic sense of propriety and "rightness," the same cool, even-tempered prose style that suggests in its tone Hawthorne's. Cheever's tone at all times is dignified, formal (one constantly must recognize how, in many ways, *Falconer* is both a stylistic and a thematic breakthrough in his fiction), and sharp-eyed: he seems determined to maintain a stoical sense of duty in the face of any disaster or nightmare. He seems to carry out a particular and often personal obligation and promise to himself, intent on searching for those images of light and lyric regeneration as keenly as the narrator in "Goodbye, My Brother" and Ezekiel in *Falconer*, at the same time carefully recognizing the darker and more prevalent forces of his age. The reader is constantly aware of his handling and shaping of his material to find revelation in it, as he is of Hawthorne's.

Cheever's coolly controlled prose achieves a romantic, ironic, and comic tone all at the same time. He celebrates moments of lost communion and conjures up images of our genuine nostalgic yearnings, while at the same time undercutting the reality of such a past Eden in the juxtaposed "disbalance" of his images, all the while maintaining a comic distance toward present chaos in his mock-heroic manner. Episodes such as the apocalyptic Easter egg hunt in *The Wapshot Scandal*, the discovery of Coverly's possible homosexuality in *The Wapshot Chronicle*, the tribal rites and passions of suburbia in *Bullet Park*, and the rigors of prison life in *Falconer* share this careful blend of human desire, frustration, and that gentle comic distance and observation that make us laugh at our human foibles. Cheever's laughter is a gentle one, a sympathetic one, for his characters, trapped in their own images of suburban convention and social regulation, often are trying to recapture and portray whatever shred of dignity and decorum they can muster. Cheever approves of their attempts, however foolish, sympathizes with their failures, however self-generated, and mocks them for their hankering after objects and status and the last refuge of the scoundrel, respectability. His style alerts us to his own decorum in the light of contemporary confusions, to his characters' gropings toward some vision of the same light, and to the darker awareness that the strength of our yearning may produce nothing finally but fragmented fury and a wistfully misplaced ideal of a lost sanctuary.

In many ways Cheever's style contradicts the fragmented and episodic structure of his romances and short stories. His decorous tone, which can be mistaken for the glossy finish of suburban conventions in those tales seemingly mesmerized by the comfortable crises of *New Yorker* fictions, is often the result of a lyric and graceful repetition of images and

objects; his plots, which reveal modern psychological existence as essentially chaotic and disconnected, are the result essentially of a romancer's
technique and vision that are intent upon breaking through the public
display of social conventions and peering more deeply into the nature of
man in both his moral and his psychological dimensions. When tone and
plot seem too much at war with one another, then Cheever does seem
to be engaged in the "soft sell of disaster,"[15] of not taking the very visions he conjures up seriously enough. His best tales are perhaps those
in which the lyric style and a lyric vision complement one another or
in which dreams, meditations, and digressions open up the surface of the
tale and allow for Cheever as author and as involved participant in the
story to "think out loud" about the ramifications of his art, his search
for a moral chain of being, and his pursuit of a lasting, recognizable vision. "The World of Apples" and "Angel of the Bridge" suggest the
first kind of tale, as do the epiphanies within the romances; "The Country Husband" and "The Death of Justina," one of his short masterpieces,
suggest the latter.

The story of "The Death of Justina" is a comic one in which suburban conventions conflict with higher, more necessary duties. The narrator's wife's old cousin, Justina, expires in her chair after lunch. The
narrator lives in Zone B of Proxmire Manor; no one can be moved or
buried there. Zone B doesn't recognize death. Proxmire Manor has ex-
luded it from its glossy suburban precincts. The narrator finally makes
a deal with the mayor, and Justina is finally buried in a place like a dump
to which the dead "are transported furtively as knaves and scoundrels
and where they lie in an atmosphere of perfect neglect."

The vision of "The Death of Justina" embraces a wider territory.
Cheever observes the American landscape of a "half-finished civilization,"
seeing only "utter desolation." Proxmire Manor exists as a sanctuary in
a wasteland, where the homes of friends are "all lighted and smelling
of fragrant wood smoke like the temples in a sacred grove, dedicated to
monogamy, feckless childhood, and domestic bliss but so like a dream."
Americans seem atrophied in consumerism, relying upon Elixircol tonic
to rid them of all maladies, victims of apocalyptic commercialism in the
narrator's dream of a strange supermarket. In this modern American scene
disappointment exists everywhere; a "terrifying bitterness" stares out of
the "anthracite eyes" of a melting snowman on the hill. The narrator
momentarily surrenders to the nostalgic image of his grandmother and

sleigh bells, when in fact she worked as a hostess on an ocean liner before her death. The realization of death hovers in the air, in Justina's sudden demise, in the narrator's forced surrender of smoking and drinking. Elixircol will not rout it, nor will Justina's undertakers, who mask the reality of death with "a violet-flavored kiss. . . . How can a people who do not mean to understand death hope to understand love, and who will sound the alarm?" And finally even the efficacy of art itself is doubted: certainly "fiction is art and art is the triumph over chaos (no less), and we can accomplish this only by the most vigilant exercise of choice, but in a world that changes more swiftly than we can perceive there is always the danger that our powers of selection will be mistaken and that the vision we serve will come to nothing." Cheever admires decency and despises death, but in the world of "Justina" can this be enough?

In the course of the story Cheever relies upon meditations, dreams, memories, visions, digressions, and biblical quotations to express the various dimensions of his concerns, his questions about modern suburban morality, consumerism, our recognition of the fact of death, our psychological disconnection and uncertainty. The tale opens with Cheever's own meditations on the nature of his art. These are followed by the narrator's meditations on the state of his health, on the conventions of his social environment— "death is not the threat that scandal is"—and on his own unsettling ideas and dreams, that the soul lingers in the body after death and that he sees a face in his English muffin, "a pure force of gentleness and censure." The concerns of Cheever and the narrator are obviously similar, but the narrator is more specifically a product of his social milieu, and Cheever is standing outside and above that milieu, raising the wider question of moral chaos and change and their effect upon us and upon art in general.

The narrator's return to Proxmire Manor is acknowledged as "a digression and has no real connection to Justina's death but what followed could only have happened in my country and in my time and since I was an American traveling across an American landscape the trip may be part of the sum." No "real connection" perhaps in terms of the bare bones of the plot or the fuller body of social conventions, but connected of course to the very essence of Cheever's vision of art, death, and the American psyche. Cheever parodies the slick television commercials for Elixircol and replaces the final one, which the narrator must write, with the complete Twenty-third Psalm. In that tight, succinct litany of faith must come man's true acknowledgment of need and the dispelling of his own grief.

For the vision of the apocalyptic supermarket, a scene of nightmarish guilt drowning in darkness, Cheever creates a dream, at first beyond the scope of and disconnected from the fact of Justina's death, yet again another dimension of his vision. This strange scene, which Cheever describes as "the strangeness of a dream where we see familiar objects in an unfamiliar light," suggests one more emblematic encounter with Cheever's vision of loneliness, moral blight, and eventual death.

All these various forms—dreams, meditations, authorial intrusions, digressions—are the romancer's stock in trade, his mingling of the marvelous and the mundane, his fictional "tricks" to open up the placidly seeming world of Proxmire Manor and reveal the psychological interior of modern man's distressed and discordant soul. Justina's death becomes the object of these fantasies and hallucinatory asides. It suggests the fanciful delight Hawthorne takes circling the corpse of Judge Pyncheon. Stunned by the fact of death, Cheever weaves his tale out of the fabric of romance and swells his vision of contemporary disenchantment.

Before he was buried beside his parents in Norwell, Massachusetts, Cheever in the last seven years of his life achieved what Updike referred to in his tribute as a "willed act of rebirth." His lyric line "willed" that vision of possible redemption, always conjuring it up in darker contexts, which Hawthorne could not have shared, despite his own fragile glimpse of enchanted communions. That may have been what Updike called the "something intensely graceful about him that made life a pleasure." Lemuel Sears shared that vision at the last: "The illusion of eternal purity the stream possessed, its music and the greenery of its banks, reminded Sears of pictures he had seen of paradise. The sacred grove was no legitimate part of his thinking, but the whiteness of falling water, the variety of its sounds, the serenity of the pools he saw corresponded to a memory as deep as any he possessed." In the depth of that memory of sacred groves lurk the visions of the American romancer's, of Cheever's, art.

SIX

John Updike:
The Beauty of Duality

CRITICS have casually linked John Updike's fiction to Hawthorne's over the years. His recreation of details with the sharp eye of a Vermeer parallels Hawthorne's delight in the Dutch realist painters. Calvinism hovers over his characters like storm clouds gathered in the soul, whether in Rabbit's sense of sin or in Piet Hanema's ideas of divine judgment. Two of his books, *Couples* and *A Month of Sundays*, suggest Hawthorne's *The Blithedale Romance* and *The Scarlet Letter*, the latter in effect a response to Dimmesdale's adulterous dilemma, however suspect in John Gardner's terms as "a piece of neo-orthodox Presbyterian heresy (Christ has redeemed us in advance, so let's fornicate)."[1] Critics have also hinted at the similarity of the two writers in terms of their sensibilities, their self-conscious use of symbolism, their penchant for allegory, and their juxtaposition of lyric celebration with ironic deflation. As David Lodge perceptively suggests, "Both writers like to temper romance with realism, lyricism with irony; both tend to rely on ambivalent symbolism at crucial moments in their narratives; both are highly literary, highly self-conscious stylists."[2] As John Vickery sees it, "Like Hawthorne, Updike uses terminology and conceptions of the universe, not to get at or demonstrate theological abstractions, but to express man's condition in an understandable way. Whether or not they believe in or support institutionalized religion is irrelevant to their themes."[3]

On May 23, 1979, at the American Academy of Arts and Letters, Updike delivered an address on "Hawthorne's Religious Language." In this address, reprinted in 1981, Updike described Hawthorne's sensibility in sharply defined Manichean terms: "From Christianity Hawthorne accepted the dualism, and made it more radical still. Orthodox doctrine bridges matter and spirit with a scandalous incarnation, Jesus Christ. In

Hawthorne, matter verges upon being evil; virtue, upon being insubstantial. . . . *The Blithedale Romance* . . . in its smallest details conveys Hawthorne's instinctive tenet that matter and spirit are inevitably at war. . . . The axis of Earth-flesh-blood versus Heaven-mind-spirit with a little rotation becomes that of the World versus the self."[4] Clearly such an address was meant to reflect on Updike's fiction and vision as well.

Radical polarities pervade and permeate Updike's books. Matter and spirit clash and duel relentlessly; woman and man, earth-goddess and sky-god, sex and religion, past and present grapple and interpenetrate one another completely. Every soul experiences this raging battle. "Yes, I do feel that to be a person," Updike admits, "is to be in a situation of tension, is to be in a dialectical situation."[5] His novels document this unending conflict, almost to the point of standoff: a hushed equilibrium between warring forces may be achieved momentarily, but the underlying tension suggests that such a suspension can shatter at any moment.

In his often-quoted review of Denis de Rougemont's *More Love in the Western World*, Updike neatly explains Manicheism: "Manichaeanism, denying the Christian doctrines of the Divine Creation and the Incarnation, radically opposes the realms of spirit and matter. The material world is evil. Man is a spirit imprisoned in the darkness of the flesh. Women are Devil's lures designed to draw souls down into bodies; on the other hand, each man aspires toward a female Form of Light, who is *his own true spirit*, resident in Heaven, aloof from the Hell of matter . . . an Eternal Feminine that preexisted material creation."[6] Updike goes on to explain that we need not rely on heresy to reveal man's essential nature— "Do we need a heresy, or even a myth, to explain it? Might it not simply be that sex has become involved in the Promethean protest forced upon Man by his paradoxical position in the Universe as a self-conscious animal?"[7]—but still the radical heart of that heresy does encapsulate the spirit and the matter of that "paradoxical position" in his fiction.

Cheever's expression of the Manichean vision appears within the forms of romance he chose to use. Updike's penchant has always been for a kind of expansive psychological realism; thus the Manichean vision must be necessarily submerged in the ordinary experiences and events of the novel. Hawthorne insisted that in America in general and in the novel in particular "actualities" . . . [are] terribly insisted upon." In this terrible insistence upon the actualities of life, on the surfaces and incidents of daily existence, Updike may blunt the thrust of his vision. In fact a further

Manichean battle exists between these luminous surfaces and his own Manichean vision of the individual's response to them, a state of war within Updike's sensibility that has never been entirely resolved.

Rabbit, Run (1960) reveals the mysterious heart of Updike's vision. Rabbit skates on surfaces, yet he feels a sense of continuity and spiritual uplift that, however shaken, cannot be eradicated. "All I know is what feels right," he tells Janice. "That's the whole secret, really, getting the ball in front of your hands, where you get that nice lifty feeling." Immediate impressions come to him like spiritual glimpses; in fact, he cannot separate the two. The imprisonment of such sporadic "highs" complements them. His "gnosis" of speed, sex, and physical grace feels threatened by all outside interlopers. Interpreters stand ready to translate him into their own terms. Janice ironically sees him as a saint, and Eccles, in a less ironic manner, picks up the term. To the prostitute, Ruth Leonard, he first appears as a Christian gentleman, then as Mr. Death. To Mrs. Smith in her garden he represents life. And to Tothero, the retired coach, he is running itself: "You can't run enough. . . . A boy who has had his heart enlarged by an inspiring coach . . . can never become, in the deepest sense, a failure in the greater game of life."

Eccles, hounded by his corrosive unbelief, fills Rabbit's head with greater ideas, calling him a mystic, so much so that later on when Rabbit is with Ruth he declares, "I'm a mystic. . . . I give people faith." Eccles presses the point: "We're trying to *serve* God, not *be* God," he tells him and goes on to add suggestively, "This was all settled centuries ago, in the heresies of the early Church." Fleeing from the cemetery and Becky's burial, these Manichean ideas come to haunt him once again as if justifying his actions, his very existence: "He obscurely feels lit by a great spark, the spark whereby the blind tumble of matter recognized itself, a spark struck in the collision of two opposed realms, an encounter a terrible God willed." "There's something that wants me to find it," Rabbit tells Eccles, as if setting Eccles up to provide him with a justification, a definition of his vagrant quest. Rabbit, yearning for articulate transcendence, finds it in Eccles's suggestions and discussion: it corrupts his idea of himself, produces that "idle remote smugness" Ruth sees in him: "I'd like to get hold of the bishop or whoever and tell him that minister of his is a menace. Filling poor Rabbit full of something nobody can get at . . . he just lived in his skin and didn't give a thought to the consequences of anything."

Updike's feelings about Eccles are not ambiguous. Kruppenbach's monologue makes that clear: the role of the minister is to stand for faith, hard-won and diligent, as an example to others: "In running back and forth you run from the duty given you by God. . . . All the rest, all this decency and busyness, is nothing. It is Devil's work." Running may feel good, but it leads nowhere. Rabbit's is finally "a magic dance empty of belief." His Manichean immersion in sex and basketball—the drive to occupy the hole without the encumbrance of the net—confirms him as trapped in a particular social and historical milieu, however momentarily transcendent his feelings.

And yet at the beginning of the novel, when Rabbit comes upon the boys playing basketball, he delights in "the way [one of the boys] moves sideways without taking any steps, gliding on a blessing: you can tell." Physical grace approximates moral vision, a religious rite: in Rabbit's eyes it becomes a substitute for it. This is clear when he hits that golf ball high into the air:

> The sound had a hollowness, a singleness he hasn't heard before. His arms force his head up and his ball is hung way out, lunarly pale against the beautiful black blue of storm clouds, his grand-father's color stretched dense across the east. It recedes along a line straight as a ruler-edge. Stricken; sphere, star, speck . . . a final leap: with a kind of visible sob takes a last bite of space before vanishing in falling. "That's *it*!" he cries and, turning to Eccles with a smile of aggrandizement, repeats, "That's it."

The right feeling demands the right spatial sensibility, and vice versa: "When he looks up, objects seem infinitely solid and somehow tip, seem so full they are about to leap. His real happiness is a ladder from whose top rung he keeps trying to jump still higher, because he knows he should . . . the true space in which we live is upward space."

Originally Updike meant to subtitle the novel, "A Movie." This makes sense, since he wrote the book in the present tense. His cinematic prose reproduces Rabbit's running, his physical gestures. We view Rabbit's actions mostly from outside as visual events, a rush of dazzling surfaces. Feelings, sentiments, intimations of immortality fly fast and furiously by, depending upon the moment, the mood, and the appropriate motion. In effect, while Rabbit runs Updike writes. Running and writing reflect one another. Depth is sacrificed to visual image: the physically graceful ex-basketball player and sexual athlete parallels the stylistically graceful writer. And there are both the novel's visceral pleasures and its central problem.

Updike creates that moment of the golf shot cinematically. We see the ball in the air, a small moon contrasted against dark clouds, associated in Rabbit's mind with his grandfather. We not only see; the prose reproduces the actual motion of the swing in a series of visual images: "Stricken; sphere, star, speck." The prose captures Rabbit's elation: momentarily action and feeling coalesce perfectly. Coordination rings true. It seems a romantic, transcendent moment, a Wordsworthian spot of time, Emerson's transparent eyeball as first circle defining its own horizons. But "it" remains elusive: motion substitutes for vision for both Updike and his hero. What are we to make of "it" ultimately?

Updike is as trapped in his cinematic prose as Rabbit is in his physical grace. The poetry of each stirs the other's outlooks. But the moment doesn't last. It remains visceral, emotionally but not spiritually transcendent. And at the grave site, when a vision of unity sweeps through Rabbit, we get the motions of transcendence without the lasting faith or vision: "And meanwhile his heart completes its turn and turns again, a wider turn in a thinning medium to which the outer world bears a decreasing relevance." Here is a mysticism of motion for its own sake, a physical reckoning so poetically rendered it approaches spiritual revelation but fails to materialize into articulate thought or vision, except for, "Don't look at *me*. I didn't kill her." True, but how could they not misunderstand what he is saying? If language as both incarnation and communication fails to adhere to feelings and thoughts, what then are we left with? The graceful silence of a ball whooshing through a basket?

Updike's brilliantly cinematic style and Rabbit's physical grace can acknowledge nothing but blankness beyond: neither one can go any further than the trap of style and society that surround them. Both commit the sin "of flight . . . and conceit"; momentary poetic conceits celebrate flight. Intimations of Christianity remain hollow and perverse; running and writing shudder when pressed to perform incarnations of their own. Updike's upbraiding Rabbit suggests the limits of his style as well: "Harry has no taste for the dark, tangled, visceral aspect of Christianity, the *going through* quality of it, the passage *into* death and suffering that redeems and inverts these things. . . . He lacks the mindful will to walk the straight line of a paradox." Updike achieves paradox here by omission; it shimmers in the background but then sputters, never catches fire. His prose and Rabbit's running cannot finally go through to anything; death and redemption remain abstract notions off-stage, cardboard creatures conjured up but "unfelt," the vague dark underpinnings of mood and manner.

Rabbit grasps at something: "Funny, how what makes you move is so simple and the field you must move in is so crowded. Goodness lies inside, there is nothing outside, those things he was trying to balance have no weight. He feels his inside as very real suddenly, a pure blank space in the middle of a dense net." The image reverberates: the self entrapped, within a kind of ultimate radiance, simplicity, paradoxically pure and blank that needs the dense net to define it. It is akin to Emerson's "beautiful necessity" and the kind of Thoreauvian "universal innocence" he discovered in the woods. It is not Hawthorne's conception of the dark self at all.

The beginning of a key to Rabbit's interior—a blankness leading on to blankness and somehow synonymous with goodness: this is the empty screen when the cinematic prose has stopped—may be found in Updike's "The Dogwood Tree: A Boyhood." He writes of the soul as a camera: "It is as if the soul is a camera shutter customarily set at 'ordinary'; but now and then, through some inadvertence, it is tripped wide open and the film is flooded with an enigmatic image."[8] Rabbit: the golf ball: the flight from the cemetery. Such an image suggests a notion of the world, radically unlike Hawthorne's—on the face of it (we will examine it more closely below)—that permeates *Rabbit, Run*, that lies beyond the prose's ability to spell it out, an incandescent quivering in Updike's world:

Blankness is not emptiness; we may skate upon an intense radiance we do not see because we see nothing else. And in fact there is a color, a quiet but tireless goodness that things at rest, like a brick wall or a small stone, seem to affirm. A wordless reassurance these things are pressing to give. An hallucination? To transcribe middleness with all its grits, bumps, and anonymities, in its fullness of satisfaction and mystery: is it possible or, in view of the suffering that violently colors the periphery and that at all moments threatens to move into the center, worth doing? Possibly not; but the horsechestnut trees, the telephone poles, the porches, the green hedges

recede to a calm point that in my subjective geography is still the
center of the world.[9]

From such a perspective, Rabbit occupies middleness. We viscerally share
his grits and bumps, his satisfactions in his athletic skills leading on to,
touching the skirts of mystery and grace. And within him lies "a quiet
but tireless goodness," not blankness but an approximation of the soul
at rest at the still center of a turning world. "The heart prefers to move
against the grain of circumstances," Updike writes. "Perversity is the
soul's very life."[10] Hence Pascal: "The motions of Grace, the hardness
of the heart; external circumstances." To Hawthorne this would appear
not as Calvinism, not in the shadow of Manichean vision, but as the heresy
of romanticism, the delusion of an Emerson mesmerized by momentary
surfaces. And perhaps this is why Rabbit's dance is "magic"; it unites
middleness, periphery, and center in some silent awe. Of course he passes
the ball and "runs. Ah: runs. Runs." But what else within such a prose
style can he do?

Within his cinematic style Updike does include some characteristics
of the Hawthornian romance. Allegory stalks these pages in the characters'
names—Rabbit, Angstrom, Tot-hero, Eccles—as other critics have carefully
pointed out. Mystery hovers in the wings, impenetrable because trapped
in the running of hero and prose. The plot does ride on episodes, often
on dreams: Rabbit dreams of two disks in the sky, the moon and the
sun, an explanation of death that vanishes upon waking. His compulsive
and obsessive nature contributes to the thrust of his race from wife to
coach to prostitute to church. What triumphs, however, as it does in
most contemporary fiction, is society itself, social and cultural complications as net and web: the press of wives, houses, parents, Pennsylvania.
Social conventions hold the upper hand despite the zig-zagging. Rabbit
needs the net to define himself; he can remain pure only in terms of the
density of the net he has conjured up around him. Shades of Hawthorne's
dark dualism! Thus he remains a negative force, an actual blank, however
graceful his actions and the prose that celebrates them.

Physical grace approximates moral vision; Updike's images suggest a
romantic faith that has no place to go. But Rabbit's own solipsism and
Updike's concentration upon him leave both of them stranded. Vision
remains elusive, vague, inconclusive, not in the suggestive beauty of

paradox but in a Manichean split between thought and feeling, spiritual and physical grace. The similarity between the two suggests Manichean complacency, an acceptance of the trap of sex and action, since nothing else in this world is possible. But it also suggests a kind of fraudulent escape, a graceful dimwittedness that can create nothing but continued flight: "What kept him walking was the idea that somewhere he'd find an opening," Rabbit thinks. In this he shares his creator's hope.

In the excellent "sequels" to *Rabbit, Run*, actually fine novels in their own right—*Rabbit Redux* (1971) and *Rabbit Is Rich* (1981)—the romance elements are more and more submerged in the novelistic terrain of manners, history, politics, and economics. Rabbit's spirit continues to thrive: his interior lyricism, no matter the onset of apocalypse, age, death, and physical erosion, remains vibrant if trapped. But then he needs the security of the net—marriage, society, social conventions—in order to maintain his special grace. What Updike brilliantly succeeds in doing is presenting the particular "angst" of his age, the soul of the times in Rabbit's own class and place. In *Rabbit Redux* he is the hard-hat pursued by apocalyptic demons; in *Rabbit Is Rich*, the comfortable middle-aged man inhabiting cozily "the narrow places life affords." Running turns to jogging to working off a forty-two-inch waist.

In both novels he learns to love the net while pursuing the hole less and less: "The presence of any game reassures Rabbit. Where any game is being played a hedge exists against fury." And in *Rabbit Is Rich*, "the stifled terror that always made him restless has dulled down. He wants less. Freedom, that he always thought was outward motion, turns out to be this inner dwindling." How far he has come from that golf shot with Eccles. Now he experiences "a strange sort of peace at his time of life like a thrown ball at the top of its arc is for a second still."

In *Rabbit Redux* Updike creates Rabbit's exorcism of the Sixties. Manichean voices assail him in the thin, almost stereotypical characters of Jill and Skeeter: enthusiasm, easy sex, violence. America itself is portrayed in Manichean terms: "it acts as in a dream, as a face of God. Wherever America is, there is freedom, and wherever America is not, madness rules with chains, darkness strangles millions." History intervenes; Vietnam kills; Skeeter, the black Jesus, twists history into myth as he seduces both Rabbit and Jill by word and deed.

Rabbit realizes that his country is not perfect; history reveals as much. And he recognizes that "time is our element, not a mistaken invader."

He inhabits novelistic space. Romance is practically nonexistent. Updike does link images throughout: the moon, emptiness, the desert of Las Vegas, the abstractions of television, the black-and-white of race relations, enough so that one critic perceptively views the novel as "self-contained . . . splendid and inaccessible like a space vehicle, from a remote distance."[11] "Everybody now is like the way I used to be," Rabbit complains. "Action without thought is violence," Jill suggests, perhaps a comment on the earlier Rabbit book, in any case a touchstone to Rabbit's exorcism here.

Likewise in the superb novel *Rabbit Is Rich*, Updike captures and portrays the end of the Seventies, good-naturedly reprising both Rabbit and America in his opening line, "Running out of gas. . . ." We are immersed in history once again, the territory of the novelist. And Rabbit? "He doesn't want to think about the invisible anyway, every time in his life he's made a move toward it somebody has gotten killed." The living survive; the dead suggest sleeping gods watching. Rabbit remains more or less at ease with his feelings within the society that often fosters them, despite his run-ins with the surly Nelson, repeating his own flight into history and circumstances. "There are no depths, this is what there is," Nelson thinks of Pru, and Rabbit believes of himself and his friends "that there is nothing to know. We are each of us filled with a perfect blackness." Brilliant novel, but not romance.

To appraise the true legacy of Hawthorne that Updike has inherited, we should explore those fictions that most resemble Hawthorne's romances, *Couples*, *A Month of Sundays*, and *The Witches of Eastwick* (1984), after a look at an earlier work that reveals romantic patterns. These should be the true test, the right place to see if Updike moves in Hawthorne's shadows.

Of the Farm (1964) certainly suggests the lineaments and vision of the romance despite its evaporating into an equilibrium of thought and feeling that achieves the quiet stasis of ultimate evasion. Updike can extend a metaphorical vision, a palpable design; the farm in all its metaphorical implications permeates this book. The novel is in fact about the farm as metaphor: it borders on the realm of romance.

The opening paragraph presents that "withdrawn setting," that "somewhere else," with which romances often begin: "We turned off the Turnpike onto a macadam highway, then off the macadam onto a pink dirt road. We went up a sharp little rise and there, on the level crest where Schoelkopf's weathered mailbox stood knee-deep in honeysuckle and poison ivy, its flipped lid like a hat being tipped, my wife first saw the farm. Apprehensively she leaned forward beside me. . . . We rattled down the slope of road, eroded to its bones of sandstone, that ushered in our land." Turning off into a stranger place, off the beaten track: even the dirt road is an odd color. The Manichean vision lurks in that honeysuckle and poison ivy clustered around the mailbox. It is the first time the new wife has seen the farm. She remains apprehensive. Suggestions of confrontation and/or revelation arise, as the road, suggestive of death and decay, "eroded to its bones," ushers them in, a guide to some as-yet-secret ceremony.

Updike pursues the farm imagery everywhere: it penetrates the levels of his narrative in the manner of metaphysical vision—before psychological chit-chat undercuts and immobilizes it or at the very least erodes its authenticity. The farm is a "people sanctuary," a place of "glistening stillness, an absolute visual silence like an eighth-note rest in the flow of circumstance," a cinematic epiphany. It is Mrs. Robinson, the mother, "as if in being surrounded by her farm we had plunged into the very territory of her thoughts." And it is Peggy, woman, earth-goddess: "My wife is a field." The farm shivers with memories of Joey's childhood and prophesies death, the end of the natural cycle. Even language cannot escape its pervasive reality; it "aerates the barren density of brute matter with the penetrations of the mind, of the spirit."

The many-layered imagery of the farm takes in the Manichean vision of man and woman, sky-god and earth-goddess, "food and love, money and mud, God and the Devil. . . . Talk in our house was a continuum sensitive at all points of past and present." The vision culminates in the sermon about Man and Woman: "With one half of his being he turns toward her, his rib, as if into himself, into the visceral and nostalgic warmth wherein his tensions find resolution in dissolution. With his other half he gazes outward, toward God, along the straight line of infinity. He seeks to solve the riddle of his death. Eve does not. In a sense she does not know death."

Fine, but the novel achieves a kind of vague equilibrium, a curious static suspension, "some state of equilibrium finally free of irritation." This may parallel that "quiet but tireless goodness that things at rest . . . affirm," but its ultimate effect is to dull the vision, muddy the waters, erase complications, and achieve a kind of evaporation of everything that has gone before. The psychiatric talk undercuts the imagery; mystery becomes Oedipal tension. "All misconceptions are themselves data which have the minimal truth of existing in at least one mind," Joey acknowledges. "Truth is constantly being formed from the solidifications of illusions." But the tension, the clash, the conflict between truths Updike smooths out in the vacuous ambiguity of Joey's final line to his mother: "*Your* farm. . . . I've always thought of it as our farm." He admits, "I must answer in our old language, our only language, allusive and teasing." He has succumbed to the childhood spell, recognized all too easily the complexities of sex, women, earth, and death; he inhales all this comfortably, effortlessly, as if he feels nothing at all. The novel evades decision, anxiety, the depth of the farm imagery itself, and drifts off into Joey's glibness and insincerity. Everything cancels itself out, as if the romantic imagery and Manichean vision had been stretched so thin that they have been bleached out like bones on a desert. What pain there is dissolves in evasive action; we are left stranded.

"A romance operates on a slightly different principle from a novel," Updike suggests. "Instead of muscles, it has springs and trap doors. It's something of a valentine. It's meant to have the textures of the fabulous."[12] Updike was commenting on *Couples*, his full-blown attempt at a romance in the Hawthorne tradition. The plot suggests the springs and trap doors: Angela sleeps with Freddy Thorne in a deal to get Foxy an abortion. The Tarbox church burns down. Tarbox itself bristles with the significance of a remote setting, the emblem of "a fresh way of life," with its Blithedalian overtones, symbolic of an age and a state of mind, "suspended in this one of those dark ages that visits mankind between millennia, between the death and rebirth of gods, when there is nothing to steer by but sex and stoicism and the stars." A city by the sea, more damned and Poe-like than Hawthorne's city on the hill, suffering the Kennedys' fate: "Not wealth nor beauty nor homage shelters them. Suffering tugging at a king's robe. Our fragile gods." And the couples, spoiled children like a candy-sucking America fallen from grace, tumble in upon one another in Tarbox's ambiguous shadow.

Couples reveals the allegorical polarities of romance. Angela, in love with stars, cool, remote, heavenly; Foxy, associated with flowers, the marshes, the world ("I think of [God and the world] as the same"); Piet Hanema, married to one, drawn to the other, his name redolent of piety, anima, amen, man, sporting a nagging Calvinism he employs almost to excuse himself ("unlike most men he really didn't judge. . . . Only God judged"); Freddy Thorne, the dentist, mesmerized by death and decay, impotent priest, scavenger of death; and Ken Whitman, unlike the Whitman of lilacs, "a saint of science," cool, remote, hypnotized by photosynthesis. Angela and Piet: spirit and flesh; Foxy and Ken: flesh and spirit; Freddy as ringmaster and ironic commentator. Tarbox provides the "stage set . . . the business district, whose apex was formed where Divinity Street met Charity Street." Piet's office is on Hope Street. Even the plot achieves the formal balance of romance: Piet's four mistresses are aligned to the four major deaths in the tale: Georgene, Foxy, Bea, Carol: the hamster, Jackie's baby, John Kennedy's assassination, John Ong.

The Manichean vision permeates the world of Tarbox as indicated by the very notion of couples: "The beauty of duality. A universe of twos." Religion and sex lock horns, interpenetrate one another, do battle for what souls these couplers have: "We set our genitals mating down below like peasants, but when the mouth condescends, mind and body marry. To eat another is sacred." Nature advertises war and ambiguity; decay and rebirth intermingle; as maples starve and great forests thin during the autumn, "the marshes, needing no rain, sucking water from the mother sea, spread lush and green." And in the conflagration of the church, "through the great crowd breathed disbelief that the rain and the fire could persist together, that nature could so war with herself." "The world hates the light," Piet thinks. "No light touched them into light. The eternal loss of light." Women are traps; only men demand justice; "a condom and candy wrapper lay paired in the exposed gutter."

Scenes are pressed to reveal religious musings. The golden rooster at the top of the church spire suggests God and the new religion of sex, "with its pricking steeple and flashing cock." After the church burns and the cock falls, "the sky above was empty but for two parallel jet trails." Cut thumbs from beer cans suggest "the new stigmata"; communion hosts are juxtaposed with hors d'oeuvres; sacraments abound; faces behind a car's windshield at sunset appear "like saints under glass." And through everything images of death recur like a dirge, associated with spring, sex, guilt, parents, "the onyx immanence of death" in all things.

The allegory and imagery take precedence over plot and circumstance. Couples blend; the Saltines and Applesmiths; faces, figures blur and dissolve. They exist less as characters than as imagistic patterns, clusters of momentary feelings, sensations, men and women as moods: "Her voice dimensional with familiar shadows, the unnumbered curves of her parted, breathing, talking, thinking lips." They conform to whatever conventions others conform to, blend in, ghosts of Tarbox, rococo creatures (without the solidity of baroque) less apparent than the poetic prose that etches their visceral pleasure and pains. Piet, because he shatters the labyrinthine structure of life in Tarbox, automatically becomes a scapegoat. The best drawn, most realized character necessarily offends such grayness. Allegory threatens momentary poetic surfaces that are rigidly, almost desperately, adhered to by people willingly locked into their rites and rituals, "a cycle of parties and games." Games threaten moral design; they seek to defuse it, as "duty and work yielded as ideals to truth and fun."

The romance itself, portraying cyclical changes and the formal arrangements of a carefully contrived dance, preserves the solemnly rococo minds and manners of its inhabitants. Allegory slides into cyclical repetition: "The Hanemas live in Lexington, where, gradually, among people like themselves, they have been accepted, as another couple." Circles lead on to new circles, themselves the repetition of the old. Group sensibility smothers the self as the pattern of the dance undercuts the allegory of the initial arrangement. All slides into melancholy circumference.

At the heart of *Couples* lies the "chronic sadness of late Sunday afternoon." This corrosive melancholy underscores all things. As Foxy realizes, "After weeks of chastity I remember lovemaking as an exploration of a sadness so deep people must go in pairs, one cannot go alone." Piet experiences a depression he cannot locate, "his sense of unconnection among phenomena and of falling. The lack of sun and shadows." Loss, the fear of aging and death, time's relentless tolling, an ineradicable but vague sense of guilt: these plague everyone, a murky melancholy mood that lurks everywhere. In this place, this gray afternoon of the soul, the Manichean vision slides into moody unease, and allegory loses its hardness, its moral reasons for being. Springs and trap doors, the texture of the fabulous, lose their edge and dissolve.

The moral design, the structural allegory of *Couples*, does not work. The failure of Christianity and the failure of sex as a new, albeit ironic, creed imply judgment of a kind: if the religious imagery, the Tarbox streets, the allegorical characters are used ironically, then sex falls in upon itself, in upon the "chronic sadness" of the couples. If, on the other hand, these are used as moral touchstones, as a way of judging these characters, this town, then they are constantly undercut by the adventure of adultery itself—"the acrobatics its deceptions demand, the tension of its hidden strings, the new landscape it makes us master"—and by the descriptive beauty of the sex act. At times sex is enough; it appears transcendent; in the long run, however, it appears deficient, a Manichean dodge, the sanctuary of the "gnostic devotee." And if chronic sadness does inhabit the heart of the matter, as I think it does, consistently, relentlessly, unimpaired, then no allegory can ride sufficiently on the vague presentiments of mood and memory. Piet talks of God, "the God who nails His joists of judgment down firm and roofs the universe with order . . . a Calvinist God Who lifts us up and casts us down in utter freedom," and such Calvinist aspirations align themselves to allegorical "truths" in much American fiction, but here Piet's Calvinism, like his fear of death, seems a mere sentiment, a passing thought, a darker momentary mood. Tarbox remains stage set; it is not so much haunted as virtually uninhabited. Allegory and the confused moral and religious imagery sink into querulous feelings; structure yields to sentiment, right-angled Christian imagery to circular repetition. We get style in place of soul, an image like the "onyx immanence of death." Terror is stingless; we get elegy for lost youth, not Manichean romance.

In *Couples*, structure and texture—the moral design and the style—war with one another. Calvinist promptings, Manichean conflicts are muted by melancholy, by the joy of sex. There is something too comfortable, too comforting in this. What is "the secret stream running beneath reality"? As usual the often sensitive, perceptive Piet spills the beans: "What impresses me isn't so much human self-deception as human ingenuity in creating unhappiness. We believe in it. Unhappiness is us. From Eden on, we've voted for it. We manufacture misery, and feed ourselves on poison. That doesn't mean the world isn't wonderful." The self festers within its own Manichean doubts and conflicts. The world, somewhere out there, remains untouched, indifferent, beautiful. The world is "absolutely good, like water, or life, or existence itself," something uncontaminated by the human ego, the animal lusts. And once we all knew that and felt it so: "Our first love, our love of the elements, restored to him his younger self." The natural surfaces of the world conjure up our nostalgia for our pasts: the child is the father of the man. To Piet that the "world was capable at any point of its immense surface of not loving him seemed a mathematical paradox it was torture to contemplate." We contaminate it, not vice-versa. Thus the self, disconnected by its own manufactured poisons from the world's beauty, can contemplate only death, sex, occasional light, occasional dark. And the world, beautiful, cyclical, and unchanging, provides an eternal comfort to and for us, if we could but see it clear, the soul's camera's shutter opening to grasp it. Hawthornian allegory, resting on his conviction of the impenetrability of a dark and mysterious world, cannot abide such sentiments. Updike's allegory remains stillborn and false, and his notions here of Calvinism and the intimations of God's judgment do as well. Sensibilities split. Christian judgment, romantic pleasures, and mystic moments do not jibe.

Couples reminds me finally of *The House of the Seven Gables*, in that in both books structure wars with texture. Hawthorne writes of possible redemption, but his texture, his vision, remains dark, foreboding, unredeemed. Updike implies condemnation of his couples' coupling in his allegorical and cyclical patterns, but his stylistic texture remains bright, full of light and the immediate delight in sex, despite the darker melancholy musing which infects it. In *The Blithedale Romance* Hawthorne undercuts romance to reveal a world of isolation, manipulation, and selfishness. In *Couples* Piet is sacrificed but rises to continue as part of a new couple elsewhere, while the natural world remains beautifully intact.

At one point Updike wrote about "Luther's mighty hymn":

> For still our ancient foe
> Doth seek to work us woe;
> His craft and power are great,
> And arm'd with cruel hate,
> On earth is not his equal.

This immense dirge of praise for the Devil and the world, thunderous, slow, opaquely proud, nourishes a seed in me I never knew was planted . . . branding me with the Cross . . . so distinctly Nordic; an obdurate insistence that at the core of the core there is a right-angled clash to which, of all verbal combinations we can invent, the Apostles Creed offers the most adequate correspondence and response.[13]

That "right-angled clash," laid out and constructed in *Couples*, never materializes. No sense of the Devil and his world exists, except within the shifting moods of Piet and the other characters. If Manicheans disbelieved in the Incarnation, if they believed that Eros led directly to gnosis, then Updike in many ways stands with them. True, language itself can incarnate the mysterious and ambiguous connections between religion and sex: it ceremonializes the moment, lifts it to poetic and metaphoric heights. But if so, then the thin veneer of Christianity should be jettisoned and transcendental celebrations of mystic moments, glorious epiphanies, could or should result. Instead the world remains unchanged and untouched but beautiful and comfortable, and the self, disconnected from it, struggles with a corrosive melancholy solipsism that lies virtually inert, passive, continually brooding over its random flashes of light, its obsession with lost youth, the approach of death, the smell of its own decay. The net closes in and is worshipped; an uneasy comfort plagues the timid soul. Updike chronicles our age and its Manichean division; he reflects it; his fiction reveals its symptoms but does not provide the separate, passionate, personalized vision that our greatest writers do.

"The first breath of adultery is the freest; after it, constraints aping marriage develop." That first impulse unites with a brand-new world, new bright sufaces. These palpable images—the lights, colors, angles—delight Updike. But of course society, social conventions, history trap those impulses, imprison them: we are doomed to repeat ourselves. The self's persistent misery engulfs the whole of it. Hawthorne suggested as much as well; here he and Updike have similar outlooks. And yet it is Updike's poetic appreciation of the benign, "the physical texture of ordinary experience,"[14] that ultimately comforts him. Allegory in both Hawthorne and Updike shatters, the one built upon images and ideas, the other upon images and feelings. They both fudge, slide, equivocate. But Updike's characters remain passive sensibilities, more acted upon than acting, the curse perhaps of contemporary times. Hawthorne's characters assert themselves, in most cases for their own self-destruction, but they grapple with the world in an often fierce manner. That world, however, eventually dooms them; separation is all.

And the doom underscores the Manichean clash. Updike excises doom from his vision of the world. Manichean vision becomes an almost self-imposed, self-centered sensibility at large in a more beautiful universe. In both cases the writer's imagination seems to be not autonomous enough; the world in its "actualities" breaks through and remains impenetrable, whether because too dark or too shimmering with radiance. And each waffles between resolution and reconciliation in some ultimate Christian manner, the constant warfare of Manichean certainties that lead on only to further warfare, and the interpenetration of all things by both matter and spirit that suggests only moral confusion and possible moral anarchy. Is this "restless ambivalence" the true American self with its "protean facility for being everywhere and nowhere, for never being openly caught in unequivocal attitudes, for inhabiting numerous shapes without being identified with any"?[15]

In *A Month of Sundays*, that marvelous meditation on the conflicts of *The Scarlet Letter*, Updike achieves the vision that *Couples* muddled, that *Rabbit, Run* avoided. Sex and spirit, mind and matter, manners and mystery coalesce in this summation of his vision and his style as a writer of fiction. The novel reveals the romantic lineaments of a fable, a palpable moral design. Tom Marshfield is sentenced to a month in the desert for various adulteries. The minister has fallen; he must wrestle with his soul in the wilderness, with the problems Dimmesdale wrestled with before him. The motel he is in is shaped like an omega, as far from alpha, from the scarlet letter, as you can get: the end, ultimate conclusion. The desert air suggests "mythical ether . . . the wilderness is always there, pre-existent and enduring." It embodies a state of soul, the scaffold on which Marshfield (Marsh/field, Dimmes/dale: Manichean mysteries) must rehearse his "personal psychodrama" redolent with puns, cross-references to myths, memories, the Puritans' quest for design and interpretation in signs, symbols: "I suffer from nothing less virulent than the human condition," which shall be played out "upon the baffled chord of self"—the center of the American romance, Hawthorne's territory. The self in extremis; the golden tongue in search of significance; "these sentences have come in no special order. Each of them has hurt." As "these seducing women sought out the scrotal concealed in the sacerdotal"—linguistic trope of the Manichean condition—so will he.

The shape approximates the task. Thirty-one chapters, thirty-one days in most months. And on the seventh day, a sermon; four of them, gradually progressing from the fact of adultery to the self as an example of the function of faith. The obvious allegorical names: Ms. Prynne as "the matrix of us all," the first American Faust, with "your dark and abundant hair." And Professor Chillingworth, his father-in-law, a teacher of ethics who despises the "radical Paulinism" of Barth: ironic switch! Episodes are resurrected, scaffold epiphanies in their own right: Peeping Tom eyeing Ned Bork and Alicia Crick; Tom's seduction of Jane interspersed with

Chillingworth's lectures. Marshfield, writing in the first person, plays fictive author, seeking his own salvation, advising the "gentle reader," both us and the aloof Ms. Prynne: the romancer/seducer at work. The marvelous mingles with the mundane: "Beyond the stairs, there were invisible stairs leading unimaginably upward . . . the sofa felt to be dreaming; it was stuffed with the substance of the spirit." No Robbe-Grillet nullity in so charged a universe. His women—Jane, Alicia, Frankie, Ms. Prynne—strike allegorical poses in his own mind, from ethical married sex to the playfully aesthetic, from the impotency of religious faith to some ultimate wise Sophia; "they seem dolls I can play with," creatures of his own imagination, a benign Coverdale exercising his wit, exorcising his past.

And at the center stands again the Manichean vision: "Imagine me as a circle divided in half, half white and half black. In the white side . . . Karl Barth's prose . . . my own crisp hieratic place within the liturgy and sacraments, a secular sense of order within my middle-class life. . . . This was the Good. I credited God with being on this side. On the other side, the black, which might be labelled the Depressing rather than Evil, lay Mankind . . . my own rank body, most institutional and political trends since 1965. . . ." Bodies are swamps "in which the spirit drowns"; marriage clashes with adultery; feeling good and being good remain distinct from one another; dark is partitioned from light; the mind fumes with its "binomial formulations." Even his two sons are distinct opposites: "A jabber and a taker, a Spartan and a Sybarite: the trunk stands declared in its forking." Christ spawned it: "Before Him, reality was monochromatic: its image is the slab, the monolith, the monotonous pasture. After Him, truth is dual, alternating, riddled."

How to reconcile such polarities becomes Marshfield's quest: his weekly sermons provide the scaffold for "my pantomime of holy agitation . . . impaled upon those impossible texts." At first his sermons appear "so fashionably antinomian" and self-justifying: adultery becomes a sanctuary of truth, a place "stripped of all the false uniforms society has assigned." Marriage exists "to spawn, for each sublimely defiant couple, a galaxy of little paradises." Thus we should embrace adultery: it "is our inherent condition." In the second sermon on miracles he ponders Christ's miracles, viewing them as demonstrations of a power beyond the merely physical world, and clings to "a single mustard seed of faith." The desert symbolizes the place of the soul, God's creation, and even there life abounds;

"no seed is so dry it does not hold the code of life within it." In his fourth and final sermon, he views the self, much as Kruppenbach saw it in *Rabbit, Run*, as a witness to faith. "We can only *profess* to believe," since only Christ believed fully, but that is the minister's ultimate function: "On a boundary of opposing urgencies . . . we so stand as steeples stand, as emblems; it is our station to be visible and to provide men with the opportunity to profess the impossible that makes their lives possible." Self-negation leads to self-fulfillment in the role of believer, not with Dimmesdale's hypocrisy rampant but with full knowledge of the conflict in all things.

A Month of Sundays is no dry tract. It abounds with individual characters, despite their allegorical shrouds, such as the other ministers at the retreat and the various mistresses, and with sexual intrigue. And there is the clash between Marshfield's Barthian profession and the liberalism of Ned Bork, "his limp-wristed theology, a perfectly custardly confection of Jungian-Reichian soma-mysticism swimming in a soupy caramel of Tillichic, Jasperian, Bultmannish blather, all served up in a dime-store dish of his gutless generation's give-away Gemutlichkeit." Dualism does not direct all things to the point of unreality. Bork sleeps with Alicia; he points out the pandering to despair in Marshfield's metaphysics, akin perhaps to Piet Hanema's fear of death which drives/allows him to quaff from more ambrosial chalices of the flesh. Alicia spills the beans to Gerry Harlow about Marshfield and Frankie; nooses tighten. And America is upbraided for its delight in shabby novelty, in transforming Calvinism into a crass money-maker, for becoming brittle in its faith, suffering "religious dislocation," trying "to reverse the divine current and wag the transcendental Dog with the tail of credulity's practical benefits."

But Marshfield presses forward to resolve the Manichean sensibility, "the modern American man . . . not as dogged breadwinner and economic integer, but as romantic minister and phallic knight." Knowing is not enough; analysis kills and creates the void. The actual world must be both adored and resisted. "Generalizations belong to the Devil; particulars to the Lord." The American soul must accept the American body, not divorce the two of them as the Puritans did, as Dimmesdale did. The reunited self must exist in both soul and flesh; grace must emanate from both. Of Jane, Marshfield realizes, "My hate of her, my love of her, meet at the bottom of our rainbow, a circle": beginnings. This emotional realization leads on to a faith that "insists, in the most scandalous and ugliest and least credenced phrase of its creed, that we and our bodies are one. . . . Freud's darkest truism: opposites are one. Light holds within it the possibility of dark. God is the Devil, dreadfully enough. . . . There is something gritty, practical, mortised, functional in our lives, something olfactory and mute, which eludes our minds' binomial formulations." Scrotal in the sacerdotal: the language itself prophesies harmony. Sadness may be more God's than ours ultimately. Ambiguity must be reshouldered, but the profession is assured. And at the last Marshfield's text, his confession, his romance romances Ms. Prynne into bed with him: "What is it, this human contact, this blank-browed thing we do for one another?" Sex, human connection, and the soul remain mysteries, out of our reach. But Marshfield, front and center, has worked the stylistic and visionary resolution of romance that has eluded Updike in his other books. Style, self, sacrifice, seduction reflect one another: omega at last.

Final ambiguities remain. Is Marshfield "saved," or has he just opted for another mistress? His sense of self has shifted; he sees himself more as witness, less as "healer" of spiritually distraught, sexually confused women. The priest's role seems assured. And he realizes the fragile union he has experienced, proclaimed: minister with motel manager, man with woman, writer with reader, tenuous but, as Henry James insisted upon, full here of "felt life." At one point Marshfield remarks, "A common fall, mine, into the abysmal perplexity of the American female. I feel, however, not merely fallen but possessed, and such is demonology that the case needs for cure another woman; and the only woman here, on this frontier, is Ms., you." Ms.: mistress and manuscript. Despite his elation and the language of incarnation, the puns of his deliverance, could everything still be mere delusion, still possessed by demons, trapped in a Manichean world of darker drives? Perhaps, but the acknowledged "gnosis" of witnessing in the sense he describes it transcends such limited prisons at last. If he believes as he states that "this century's atrocious evils have stemmed from the previous century's glorification of the Will," then he at least in his own confession has subdued his will and submitted it to the larger task of witnessing. And the acknowledgment that his face yet remains a stranger's completes the ultimate mystery.

At one point Updike wrote, "The mystery that more puzzled me as a child was the incarnation of my ego—that omnivorous and somehow pre-existent 'I'—in a speck so specifically situated amid the billions of history. Why was I I? The arbitrariness of it astounded me; in comparison, nothing was too marvelous.''[16] Marshfield talks of the simple mystery "that I find myself here and not there. . . . Who has set us here . . . there is a *qui*, a Who . . . we have been placed. As of course we already know in our marrow.'' That mystery unites all others in *A Month of Sundays*. Updike's Marshfield is one of his most fully realized characters, along with Ellellou in *The Coup* and perhaps Bech. They tell their own tales: the "I" takes the spotlight. The romancer with his Manichean vision finds a fragile unity in himself, in his style, in his story. Rabbit, too, shares this spotlight, trapped in his own present tense. There is Updike's triumph as novelist and romancer: surrogate selves working out their own destinies.

The Witches of Eastwick is made to order as an example of Hawthorne's romance. There is the "forbidding, symmetrical face" of the old gothic Lenox mansion, "the haunted plantation" in the remote romantic territory of Eastwick "in this mysterious crabbed state of Rhode Island." "Rhode Island . . . contains odd American vastnesses . . . abandoned homesteads and forsaken mansions, vacant hinterlands . . . heathlike marshes and desolate shores . . . lunar stretches. . . ." In such a place "life like smoke ris[es] twisted into legend."

History provides its necessary demonic ballast; the "witchcraft delusion" permeated old New England states. "Certainly the fact of witchcraft hung in the consciousness of Eastwick." And we all know that "witchcraft, once engendered in a community, has a way of running wild, out of control of those who have called it into being, running so freely as to confound victim and victimizer." And the visible narrator refers to "our town"; he is one of the inhabitants of Eastwick, as Hawthorne was of Salem. As "the rumor of witchcraft stained this corner of Rhode Island," so it stains and saturates our narrator's tale and sets up its own spell in his language.

Long elegaic, hypnotic clauses appear in Updike's early description of Rhode Island, conjuring up that mysterious realm. Images of witchcraft, such as familiars, black cats, and crystal balls, appear in the first pages of the book. "The internal bleeding of . . . melancholy" permeates the whole, and the change of seasons from fall to fall, splendidly conjured up and recreated, provides the fallen cycle of men and women in these Manichean times. Magic appears everywhere; fetishes, changes in weather, spells cast, tennis balls suddenly transformed into snakes, eggs, bats, toads; feathers spit forth from the mouths of harried, spiteful women. And everywhere that mysterious relationship that glowers in all of Hawthorne's fiction, the relationship between mind and matter. We encounter "the threads of sympathy whereby the mind and spirit do move matter," a Hawthornian phrase if ever there was one. Spirits pass through matter like Manichean "sparks of divinity," and individuals court "the beautiful stranger, [the] secret self."

Throughout the book witches and nature transform and destroy. "And magic occurs all around us as nature seeks and finds the inevitable forms, things crystalline and organic falling together." Nature absorbs all things, demands its sacrifices, tortures things into growth, innocently kills. All of nature, including the consciousness of witches, seethes and shifts, "the very granite outcrops around us fluid, the continents bobbing in basalt." Parasites thrive; "matter complicates . . . through accumulating collisions"; and "in attempting creation we take on creation's burden of guilt, of murder and irreversibility," a notion not at all foreign to Hawthorne's vision of the artist as wizard.

The witches, divorcees, sleep around and develop their art. Jane Smart plays the cello; Alexandra Spofford sculpts "bubbies"; Sukie Rougemont writes (terribly) for the Eastwick *Word*. Sukie's lover, the Reverend Ed Parsley, gets blown up by a home-made bomb after he gets involved in a radical group in this Vietnam-haunted era. Sukie moves on to Clyde Gabriel, who murders his wife and hangs himself. But the plot centers around the arrival at the old Lenox place of Darryl Van Horne, self-appointed "dark prince" whose "evil doings" consist of easy sex in hot tubs, strange potions, and uncounted frolics with the three witches, which are observed by his Spanish-speaking servant Fidel and a cat named Thumbkin. At last he marries Jennifer Felicia, the daughter of the dead couple; the three witches cast their spell on her; she dies of cancer; and Darryl disappears with Christopher Gabriel, her homosexual brother. As Alexandra suggests, "He couldn't create, he had no powers of his own that way, all he could do was release what was already there in others." He revealed "a certain contempt for the physical world, a voracious appetite for immaterial souls."

In the guise of his familiar territory of suburban adultery, Updike really inhabits here Hawthorne's allegorical territory. Women absorb the raucous angst of a Janis Joplin song, full of "joyful defiant female despair." They suffer, are descended in spirit from Anne Hutchinson, who was kicked out of nearby Massachusetts Bay by "those old ministers and naysayers and proponents of heroic constipation," they experience visceral torment, enjoy wickedness, are enslaved by society's (men's) expectations of them, and are allied to nature's darker turmoil. Men lead themselves to death, emerging from cruel boyhoods into "one team after another." Adultery suggests damnation but also an escape from the "fussy overlay of Puritania" in old Eastwick: "Martyrs too of a sort were the men and women hastening to adulterous trysts, risking disgrace and divorce for their fix of motel love—all *sacrificing the outer world to the inner,* proclaiming with this priority that *everything solid-seeming and substantial is in fact a dream,* of less account than a merciful rush of feeling" (italics mine). Adultery becomes Updike's witchcraft, the gates into the nether kingdoms of romance, from the rigid confines of suburban decorum to the ritualistic covens of suburban demonology.

Updike's sexual allegory, his luminescent prose, the splendid merger of suburban fact and dark romantic spirit have rarely been so well intermixed in his fiction. *The Witches of Eastwick* achieves what *Couples* did not. Fact and omen interpenetrate one another. Even the Rhode Island names in the book—Benefit, Benevolent and Hope Streets, the Old Stone Bank, to name a few—suggest Hawthorne's allegorical landscape, as if beckoning Updike to his dark task. Guilt transfigures all. "The witches are gone, vanished; we were just an interval in their lives, and they in ours," Updike concludes, as if ridding himself of the events that have transpired. Hawthorne could not awake from the nightmare so easily. The evil days in Eastwick "have left something oblong and invisible and exciting we do not understand," and however readily Updike extricates himself from his dark vision, the lineaments of Hawthorne's shadow remain.

In *A Month of Sundays* the elements of Hawthorne's romance coalesce with Updike's harmonic vision: an allegory of American values, the personal psychodrama at the center, the Manichean ambiguities, the palpable moral design of a self on a quest, the visibly intrusive author weaving the fabric of his vision, the often dreamlike texture. These romantic touchstones are all here in abundance. Grafted onto mood and moral uncertainty in *Couples,* they failed. Within the cinematic prose of *Rabbit, Run* and lurking in the provocative absences in that prose, they glimmered but dissolved. They surfaced again splendidly in *The Coup,* awkwardly and sporadically in *The Centaur,* and sputteringly in *Marry Me,* even though Updike subtitled the novel *A Romance.*

Finally, however, Updike's vision is thoroughly unlike Hawthorne's. The persistence of Hawthorne's devices in *A Month of Sundays* may say more about Updike's "answering" *The Scarlet Letter* than about their own longevity. Manicheism in Updike still lingers more as mood than as stark vision of the world around him; it is far more comfortable, far less unsettling than Hawthorne's haunted mind. But it is the spirit of the age, the contemporary American temperament, that Updike reflects more than he directs. Nostalgia counts too much with him; it permeates his world. Of himself as a boy he wrote, "He saw art . . . as a method of riding a thin pencil line out of Shillington, out of time altogether, into an infinity of unseen and unborn hearts. He pictured this infinity as radiant. How innocent!"[17] That mild reproof in no way undermines his consistent belief still. He may not often penetrate his own shimmering surfaces, and often his characters feel momentarily comfortable within them. Hawthorne felt nowhere at home. His Manicheism led him into darker, endless tunnels; he felt the abyss beneath Rome. Updike's innocence shuns such abysses and leaves us more sentimental than compassionate. But in employing Hawthorne's romance against itself, he may only have proved the enduring American qualities of that vision and its persistent hold.

SEVEN

John Gardner:
Slaying the Dragon

"THE NOVELIST," Frederick Karl suggests in his massive and encyclopedic tome about American fiction since 1940, "should have to struggle against contradictions, as Hawthorne and Melville did."[1] John Gardner, as David Cowart makes clear, recreated again and again "his familiar parable about art's responsibility to deal with those dragons of terrible reality."[2] The artist must at all times "set about 'flooring the ancient abyss with art.' "[3]

Hawthorne's art reproduced the very abyss from which Gardner had set out to escape. Hawthorne's radical dualism reproduced the isolation and disconnection of his characters and of his own contradictory speculations. The polarized allegory of his Manichean romance haunted him and his characters to the point of self-imprisonment and episodic stays against and submission to confusion. John Gardner reproduced the Manichean vision as well (all too simplistically, Karl would suggest: he "is caught in a dualism which sucks out meaning, rather than infusing it"[4]), but his is an attempt to bridge the gap between the poles, to heal the wound that lies between them. His techniques are similar to Hawthorne's—the by now familiar use in American romance of allegorical figures, Manichean polarities, the doom of the past, the episodic tableaux, the sudden epiphanies, the mind haunted by dark inscrutable matter and solipsistic unrelenting dreams—but his hope was to transcend the heart of darkness and resolve, if only in momentary intimations, the conflict at the core of existence.

"Of course, a beautiful affirmation is meaningless if it doesn't recognize all the forces going against it," Gardner maintained. "Faith and despair have always been the two mighty adversaries."[5] Out of this clash of opposites, Gardner built his fiction and his vision. The vision celebrates love,

compassion, community, empathy, and the human choice to choose those
virtues, despite the blackest odds against them in the contemporary world.
The fiction sets up multiple narratives, dialogues, novels within novels,
prisons and magicians—in essence, the multiple perspectives of literary
modernism out of and within which the human choice must be made.
For every Grendel who displays his "ironic set of monster values,"[6]
there remains a James Page, a Fred Clumly, a Henry Soames, a Peter
Mickelsson, who choose otherwise. This is why Gardner celebrated writers
such as John Fowles, perhaps his English equivalent in his own mythic
and cabalistic mix of philosophy and fiction and his awareness of the
amorality of a relativistic, existential age, and John Cheever: "His affir-
mations are sufficiently hard-won to stand up. He qualifies his optimistic
Christian vision with the necessary measure of irony."[7] And, despite
reservations, writers such as Updike, Bellow, Malamud, and Oates—
"joyful terror gradually ebbing toward wonder."[8]

In the massive and complex *The Sunlight Dialogues* (1973) Gardner found
his "system, a governing metaphysical system that I believed. What I've
been doing ever since is pursuing small aspects of the governing system."[9] That system incorporates the Manichean polarities, the compassionate policeman, cartoon figure become human, and the mad anarchist
prophet, human being become raging ideological Babylonian anti-Christ.
The character, himself a Manichean creature, Benson/Boyle, realizes this:
"The opposition came suddenly clear to him—the violent, lawless bearded
man, the violent policeman. It was, he saw with unspeakable clarity, a
picture of his life." Like Hawthorne mining "the soul's disharmony"[10]
in his psychological romances, Gardner set up his confrontation in the
form of a series of dialogues between the man of law and order and the
prophet of Mesapotamian "disorder." Clumly upholds the rules. Hodge
talks of insane dualisms, of life as fate, of a world totally made of matter,
of the Babylonian love of substance and the "coexistence without conflict"[11] between matter and spirit, unlike the Judeo-Christian "idle
speculation" about abstract relationships between soul and flesh. An impersonal universe, suggests Hodge, confronts that "grand American responsibility" for right and wrong.

Clumly's compassion and realization carry the day: "We must all be
vigilant against growing indifferent to people less fortunate. . . . We have
to stay awake, as best we can, and be ready to obey the laws as best as
we're able to see them. That's it. That's the whole thing." And yet

Hodge is by far the more interesting character, the spurious magician, the giddy nihilist. Gardner's attack on the unreliable narrator of many Sixties novels, the artificer as game-player engendering only doubt, pessimism, and further chaos—"immoral" finally in Gardner's terms—ultimately parallels his creation of Taggart Hodge, although the magician delights, however blasphemously, more often than he nihilistically instructs. Perhaps villains are always more interesting. Perhaps this is why Clumly's compassionate vigilance is all, constantly aware of the radical disunities in American culture yet pointing the way toward some kind of awakened, armed reconciliation. Hodge is no callous Westervelt, and yet Hawthorne's attitude toward his character is far less ambiguous than Gardner's, although Gardner's ultimate loyalties are not in doubt here.

The family tree of Gardner's Faulknerian Hodge clan reflects the polarities of *The Sunlight Dialogues*. The Hon. Arthur Hodge Sr., the Congressman, is the old wily patriarch, a Renaissance man of both visionary capabilities and practical "know-how." "If he was an idealist, bookish, he knew trades, too; knew the talk of farmers at the feedmill," enjoyed the "invariable good luck in the conspiracy of outer events." But in his four sons there has occurred "a kind of power failure." Will Sr. is a Batavian attorney, a patcher, a mender; Art Jr. becomes an electrician with Niagara Electric, "a good man, gentle, not a mystical bone in his great square body." Son Taggart, the Sunlight Man, is of course the complete crazed visionary, "beaten by the conspiracy of events," and brother Ben "was a dreamer, a poet, an occasional visiting preacher at country churches from here to good news where. He was blind to the accelerating demolition all around him." Will Sr.'s two sons, Will Jr. and Luke, complete the fragmentation and decline of the Hodge family, for Will Jr. is a Buffalo attorney, a chaser after debtors, "the Congressman through the looking-glass, then, turned inside out, gone dark," and Luke is an ineffectual, romantic visionary, suspended between Uncles Will and Ben, "knowing they were both right but mutually exclusive, as antithetical as the black trees hanging motionless over the motionless water and under the dead, luminescent sky."

The balanced vision between idealism and circumstance, poetic and practical truth of Stony Hill Farm has broken down. Reconciliation has collapsed, leaving poetic insight and practical knowledge as separate, decayed fragments of a once functioning whole. As Reverend Willby laments, "Our civilization is built on work, and to do well in it we must repress our desire to loll about. . . . our puritan ethic in one form or another, is at the heart of the American *problem*." And as Will Jr. realizes, faith is "an outreaching of the mind beyond what it immediately possesses. Self-transcendence. But the reach did not imply the existence of the thing reached for. One knew it even as one reached." Inside the stone walls of Stony Hill Farm, that pastoral keep, "self-contained and self-perpetuating, even as serene—or so it seemed to Will Jr.'s childish eyes—as Heaven itself," lay "a garden for idealism." Outside those walls lies a Manichean world "gone dark."

All Gardner's novels reflect this basic dialectic. The explicit dialogues of *The Sunlight Dialogues* reflect the confrontation between James Chandler and John Horne in *The Resurrection* (1966), the alternating philosophical diary entries of Agathon and Peeker in *The Wreckage of Agathon* (1970), Grendel and the Shaper in *Grendel* (1971), the clash between Henry Soames and George Loomis in *Nickel Mountain* (1973), the teller and the tale in "The King's Indian" (1974), the multiple fictions in *October Light* (1976) and *Freddy's Book* (1980), and the thoroughly Manichean-shaped consciousness of Peter Mickelsson in *Mickelsson's Ghosts* (1982). Alternative realities, juxtapositions, frame stories, flashbacks, contrary riddles, and riddled contraries—Gardner's fictional structures thrive on these modernist techniques. Moral choice fights for survival amid the "trash tradition" of "the detective story, the animated cartoon, the fairy tale, the American country story." And within these marvelous conjurings, "I think that fiction and religion and education ought to be in the business of keeping the kid alive, keeping that noble self alive instead of saying, 'Look, it's all right, we're all punks.' "[12]

Gardner's own background in upstate New York, reflected at its best in such short stories as "Come On Back" and "The Art of Living," grounds him firmly in an American pastoral outlook that has infiltrated and inspired much of the best of American literature and that has certainly been viewed as a particular point of view, an allegorical point of departure, in the American psychological romance. Pastoral art posits a simplified naturalistic setting, a place where one can get down to basics and examine one's own values and sense of self amid the philosophical and often sentimentalized stillness and habitual traditions of a rural landscape. From such a perspective the contemporary world appears as a Manichean nightmare, torn apart, a dark revel on a darkling plain. Gardner combined these states of mind, yet another illustration of his alternative realities battling it out for the character's soul, the reader's heart and mind.

Richard Chase, in an illuminating comment on Hofstadter's "folklore of Populism,"clearly defines the "radical disunities" in American culture in terms which, for the sake of our argument, bring together both the pastoral impulse—restoration, escape, regeneration—and the pastoral form—Theocritus' dialogues, Vergil's confrontations, the encounter with nature. The pastoral impulse can be seen in "what Mr. Hofstadter calls the 'agrarian myth' that ever since the time of Jefferson has haunted the mind . . . of reformers and intellectuals."[13] "This myth involves the idea of a pastoral golden age—a time of plain living, independence, self-sufficiency and closeness to the soil—an idea which has been celebrated in various ways by innumerable American writers. Second, there is the mythology of Calvinism which . . . has always infused Protestantism, even the non-Calvinist sects, with its particular kind of Manichean demonology."[14] The pastoral myth of a golden age has provided American literature, according to Chase, with its surfeit of nostalgic idyll, however elusive, lost, and momentary that idyll may be: "It is restorative . . . it may even bring a moral regeneration. But the pastoral experience is rather an escape from society and the complexities of one's own being"[15] and tends to call up certain elegiac feelings. The Calvinist myth provides American literature with its melodramatic confrontations, reflecting the Manichean dualisms between light and darkness, order and chaos. Both idyll and melodrama create a literature more heavily romantic than novelistic in its fictional narratives. And finally, many American writers "seem content to oppose the disorder and rawness of their culture with a scrupulous art-consciousness, with aesthetic forms—which do, of course, often broaden out into moral significance."[16]

The best of most American literature has always attempted to reconcile pastoral impulse with Manichean confrontation or at least to present the two in a kind of unreconciled head-on encounter, at best capable of achieving some wary kind of equilibrium and at worst resulting in complete alienation and disorder. And certainly the alternative realities in Gardner's fiction, however scintillant with post-modernist artifice (without the accompanying dizzying dance of despair incarnate), reasserts this "timeless, universal struggle of opposites."[17] His governing metaphysical system is complete.

"I agree with Tolstoy that the highest purpose of art is to make people good by choice,"[18] Gardner asserted. In his quixotic, often mean-spirited but penetrating diatribe *On Moral Fiction* (1978), Gardner views fiction as a process of testing values and ideas. These he "tests" in the process of creating characters and situations—the Yankee ideals of James Page, the "monster values" of Grendel, the idealistic ethics of Peter Mickelsson, the human dimensions of Henry Soames. "Ideas as they are embodied in characters and actions"[19] stalk Gardner's fictional landscapes as they do Hawthorne's. Plot moves the story; development is all; a fiction without a plot suggests a failed moral stance; the process has been cut short and undermined. Gardner would have agreed with Robert Caserio, who views plot as purposeful action, "and an act always implies a transformation, a new change, and a significant difference." The modernist distrust of purposeful action, of the self's will to act, Caserio suggests, led to plotless narrative and ultimate negation.[20]

In fiction "the interaction of character is everything." The American romance has always contained characters larger than life, often bordering on certain symbolic types, such as the evil temptress and the evil father-figure. Characters should not be mere "stick figures . . . where plot is kept minimal and controlled by message," for "literature tells archetypal stories in an attempt to understand once more their truth—translate their wisdom for another generation," and the artist is expected to penetrate "what is common in human experience throughout time." Art becomes a process, an evolution of angles of vision on time-honored conflicts, a repository of "eternal verities," and the romantic poet or artist therefore "imitated in finite art the divine created act."[21] This morality of fiction results in a traditional narrative form which reveals the ongoing conflict between two forms of behavior: the Ishmael-Ahab conflict continues, however modified in the very confrontations we have already pointed out, such as Clumly and Hodge, or Jonathan Upchurch and Luther Flint in "The King's Indian."

The pastoral voice with its love of nature and human compassion for one another confronts the mechanistic cry, that darker Manichean belief that the world is mere accident; brute force controls all history, and only outright manipulation will keep things running. The basic pattern of dialogue between the classical/medieval hope for regeneration and redemption, linked to light and often magic, and the modern nihilistic certainty of gloom and despair, linked to darkness and often to black magic, informs the basic narrative structure of Gardner's fiction. These voices set off against one another—the human heart in conflict with itself—set up a counterpoint in his fiction, which slowly works itself out in the process of the confrontation. In *Nickel Mountain* fiction becomes closely involved with birth, death, weddings, those ceremonial rituals which come and go with the seasons. Country rules remain basic, "the rules that a child should have a father, that a wife should have a husband, that a man trying to kill himself should be stopped." Each chapter begins with a particular season, and the rhythms of the earth never change: "Progress, they say. But th'earth don't know about progress." The world is recreated in its basic and natural simplicity: "It was as if one had slipped back into the comfortable world pictured in old engravings. . . . The world would seem small and close when dark came, too—sounds would seem to come from closer at hand and the mountains ten miles away seemed almost on top of you—the trees and hills were like something alive, not threatening, exactly, because Henry had known them all his life, but not friendly, either: hostile, but not in any hurry, conscious that time was on their side."

"Some change, subtle and terrible" and an aura of doom stalk this "burned-over district" of upstate New York, complete with Simon Bale's devil-obsessed religious fundamentalism (matching the stark hostility-friendliness of external nature). But Nickel Mountain—"That was where the real hills were, and the river, cool, deep with echoes of spring water dripping into it and sliding from its banks!"—suggests a particular vantage point, wherein the Manichean confrontation is reconciled. George Loomis, inveterate collector, emotional and physical cripple, harps on "the whole secret of human progress, pure meanness," but Henry Soames, who drives up the mountain often, believes in communion, marries the pregnant Callie, and discovers that "his vision [was] not something apart from the world but the world itself transmuted." If Loomis derides a world of sheer accident, Soames comes to believe in and experience "the holiness of things (his father's phrase), the idea of magical change" rooted firmly in the landscape around him, a "dream unfolding in the mind,"[22] a spell cast by both opposing camps, defining each other by the pattern of dialogue and conflict between them. As Will Hodge suggests, in discussing the crimes of cops or robbers, "it was necessary, merely, that order prevail for those who were left, when the deadly process had run itself down; necessary to rebuild."

Gardner's classic confrontation can be seen in *Grendel*. Grendel represents the voice of brute force, "a mechanical chaos of casual, brute enmity" and rage, doomed to the unrelenting "cold mechanics of the stars," against which all else must be defined. The Shaper, the poet with his harp inventing tales of Gods and men and heroic deeds, represents communion and celebration, however much his words often seem to Grendel mere webs and masks averting the cold reality of existence. Grendel, seduced by harp strings, dies at the hand of the hero, who proclaims, "The world will burn green, sperm build again. My promise . . . by that I kill you." The poet's role may be similar to the magician's, mixing mechanical devices and authentic vision, artifice and heroic ideal: he alone may be capable of healing the split between the garden and the machine, of welding a sturdy reconciliation between Manichean opposites, of making, as Grendel suggests, "the solemnity and grandeur of the universe rise through the slow process of unification in which the diversities of existence are utilized, and nothing, *nothing* is lost."

In Gardner's fiction that "slow process of unification" is most likely to occur in a traditional, pastoral setting. In *Nickel Mountain* the landscape fulfills those traditional pastoral attributes. Man is freer in the country than in the city: "It was different in the country, where a man's life or a family's past was not so quickly swallowed up, where the ordinariness of thinking creatures was obvious only when you thought a minute, not an inescapable conclusion that crushed the soul the way pavement shattered men's arches." He is in a farmer's Eden:

> This side of the trees there were flat acres of winter wheat and peas and hay and stretches of new-plowed ground. It was like a garden, in the gold light of late afternoon; it was exactly what Paradise ought to be like: a tractor humming along, far below him, small, on the seat a boy with a wide straw hat; to the right of the tractor, red and white cows moving slowly down the lane to a big gray barn with clean white trim. With a little imagination a man could put angels in the sky . . . it would be as if he were discovering the place for the first time: a natural garden that had been the same for a thousand thousand years.

The second paragraph of *Nickel Mountain* reveals the psychic landscape of Gardner's fiction and that remote and eerie dreamscape of Hawthornian romance: "Sometimes when he was not in a mood to read he would stand at the window and watch the snow. On windy nights the snow hurtled down through the mountain's darkness and into the blue-white glow of the diner and the pink glitter of the neon sign and away again into the farther darkness and the woods on the other side of the highway. . . . At last, he would sink down on the bed and would lie there solid as a mountain, moving only his nose and lips a little, troubled by dreams." Man and nature seem to encounter one another, quietly, almost in a state of trance but never fully overwhelming each other, as if Robert Frost had walked into a darker wood and stood to listen and watch. Here Henry Soames is described as "solid as a mountain," but that is the closest identity Gardner seeks between man and nature in this dark and remote moment. The diner seems an outpost in a great wood, a clean, well-lighted place inside some great mystery, whose presence can only be suggested by the presence of the great mountain and the falling snow.

The pattern exists as well in *October Light*, in which James and Sally Page launch their battle for personal supremacy. The "radical disunities" continue to collide. The English teacher, Estelle Parks, recalls Wordsworth's "Tintern Abbey," his subdued yet powerful celebration of "a presence that disturbs . . . a sense sublime / Of something far more deeply interfused . . . A motion and a spirit, that impels / All thinking things, all objects of all thought." Ruth Thomas contemplates more modern dilemmas when suddenly she recites Arnold's famous lines: "And we are here as on a darkling plain / Swept with confused alarms of struggle and flight, / Where ignorant armies clash by night." Arnold's dark vision clashes with Wordworth's "light of setting suns . . . and the living air." Later on Ruth recites the poem "The Opossum," which celebrates the crafty designs survivors are heir to. When exhorted by His Son to destroy the opossum because he is a killer, a weary and crafty God replies, " 'Peace and Justice are right' . . . And whispered to the Possum, 'Lie down. Play dead.' " Between polar opposites, strategic retreat may be the only apparent salvation in a chaotic world.

Gardner contrasts the point of view of existence found in *October Light* with that found in *The Smugglers of Lost Soul's Rock*, the novel within that novel: "There are only two kinds of books in the world. . . . There are books that desperately struggle to prove there's some holy, miraculous meaning to it all and desperately deny that everything in the world's mere belts and gears . . . and there are books that say the opposite." *October Light*, with its pastoral setting, opts for the former of these two positions. Locking time, "obscurely magical, a sign of elves working," suggests the same kind of pastoral landscape as in Frost's "Mending Wall." The Vermont village reminds James Page of one of Grandma Moses's paintings, and Norman Rockwell's determination to paint "this safe, sunlit village in Vermont where they were still in the nineteenth century" rests solely on the pastoral impulse to escape the complex illnesses of the modern world, "as if his pictures might check the decay." And yet, despite this sentimentalized pastoralism, reconciliation with the landscape and truth still seem the firm reply to the nihilistic, existentialist maneuverings of the creatures on Lost Soul's Rock. In the passage in the novel entitled "Ed's Song" the recurring and eternal pattern of the seasons is recounted like the most hopeful and holy of rituals, and good poems are as exactly true as a good window-sash or a horse. Page is upbraided by Gardner because of "his excessive Yankee pride in workmanship, his greed, his refusal to stop and simply look, the way Ed Thomas had looked." To "simply look" could be the advice of the dedicated pastoralist. When Page doesn't shoot the bear he confronts, the resolution remains hazy and uncertain, but his heart, like the season which surrounds him, is unlocking slowly.

In *The Resurrection* James Chandler, the dying Associate Professor, experiences a kind of pastoral revelation. He senses "the manyness of things grown familiar and therefore one. . . . he felt such inexpressible joy: He felt intensely what later he would learn words to explain, the interpenetration of the universe and himself. For if he was distinct from all he saw, he was also the sum of it." And in "The King's Indian," in which Jonathan Upchurch, in love not with the "flat and mathematical" landscape of northern Illinois but with the beauty, "dark with timber and bluffs and the slide of big rivers," of southern Illinois, triumphs over Luther Flint's maniacal, mechanical maneuverings, Gardner presents the image of the King's Indian, which suggests both pastoral revelation and mechanical move. The King's Indian is both a move in chess and a state of visionary consciousness: "Human consciousness, in the ordinary case, is the artificial wall we build of perceptions and *conceptions*, a hull of words and accepted opinions that keeps out the vast, consuming sea. . . . A mushroom or one raw emotion (such as love) can blast that wall to smithereens. . . . I become, that instant, the King's Indian: Nothing is waste, nothing unfecund." In much the same way Gardner described his book as both "a celebration of all literature and life" and "a funeral crypt."

What Henry James referred to as American literature's "rich passion for extremes" can be found in Gardner's fiction, and his hope for human communion and love, however fragmentary and diminished, remains undaunted. He was clearly reworking the American fable for our own troubled contemporary times and not merely delighting in structuralist and "post-modernist" techniques for their own artificer's delight. Like Hawthorne, Melville, and Faulkner before him, he seemed intent on dispelling anew the notion of a special American innocence, yet at the same time recognizing the pull and enchantment of the pastoral impulses implicit in that American myth. He was aware of the precariousness in that farther darkness and used his pastoralism as a vantage point from which to observe and recreate the American heart's unrelenting conflict with itself.

Peter Mickelsson, "soul in isolation," suffering from "the great demon" of idealism in *Mickelsson's Ghosts*, Gardner's last novel, envisions the contemporary world and his own consciousness in Manichean polarities and struggles to surmount the spiritual paralysis and philosophical resignation that consciousness creates. He inhabits a Manichean world, savaged by Luther: "The world not only is the devil's, it *is* the devil." Divorce, terrorist sons, teenage prostitutes, his own mental illnesses, the I.R.S., deadly Mormons, ghosts from some incestuous, murderous past, burglars, mobsters, small-town cops, Marxist sociologists plague him relentlessly. Nietzsche's "Satanic hold" will not release him; life and death seem interchangeable, a wasteland of a doomed, self-analyzing spirit; brains and bodies flail at one another. He longs for an ultimate Being, "the perfect resolution of dualism," while bemoaning "the lack of connection between head and heart, the abyss between belief and attitude." He agrees with Goethe that "he who overcomes himself finds freedom" and yet conjures up "a universe of infinitely precious glowing particles, every one of them necessarily *against* every other . . . the tragic law of individuation in space and time, but each and every one lit up by the ruby, emerald, sapphire, and diamond shine of God's consciousness." He seeks to unriddle "the living allegory of the soul," struggling toward Emerson's belief that "every man's life is a solution in hieroglyphic to those inquiries he would put. He acts it as life before he apprehends it as truth." And yet as an academic philosopher hiding out in the Endless Mountains, he pursues comprehension before he acts and locks himself into a

Manichean contemporary and universal world that reduces the possibility of all action to one more clash in a night of necessary ongoing
confrontations.

Mickelsson has internalized Gardner's Manichean fictional structure,
and it threatens to unbalance him completely. He refuses to accept Witt-
genstein's mute, dead world, reduced to linguistic conventions and disembodied signs; and he cannot accept Professor Lawler's self-righteous
ideology of murder for a just cause, the absolutist's faith in external, eternal
values no matter the situation.[23] He acts out of compassion and involves
himself in the death of the fat man with his hoard of cash. Theodosia
and Caleb Sprague, like James's governess's conjurings, both substantial
and dream-creatures—"Here he was, deducing reality from intermingled
dreams and actualities" (Hawthorne would approve!)—haunt him in the
Manichean fashion of a shadowed past, doomed to trap him further and
circumscribe his attempts to escape it and himself. And Gardner's often
uneasy alliance between philosophical dialogue and fictional situation further
entraps Mickelsson in his own battered consciousness.

But Mickelsson acts. He sees Nietzsche "not as the destroyer and absolute doubter he noisily, mockingly proclaimed himself, but as a man
tortured by holiness . . . furious at Christianity for the destruction of
all that was holy and good," deciding that it was "Luther whose Christ
had in the end turned Nietzsche into a self-styled Antichrist, though he
was nothing of the kind." Manichean polarities falter; convoluted paradoxes suggest a growing unity, a course of action. His son Mark appears
and sleeps on his couch. He puts on "his scarlet huntsman's coat," paints
his face red, and goes in pursuit of the apparent love of his life, Jessica
Stark, non-Marxist sociologist. They make love in a pile of coats in a
bedroom beyond the faculty party in session in Jessica's house, while
ghostly visions of people and animals jostle the night air around them,
"pitiful, empty-headed nothings complaining to be born." Manichean
monsters slip beyond the pale, assume metamorphosed shadows, snicker
and look away; they cannot compete—at last—with the "roaring bones
and blood," the clownish, desperate "leap of faith" Mickelsson has made
into the arms of his beloved.

Gardner conjured up a landscape redolent of Hawthorne's, streaked
with sunlight and shadow, "ominous and beckoning" at once, stretching
out into darker swamps where he, for one, like Hawthorne before him,
but from different perspectives—one leaping into faith, the other circling

his doubt in fear of coming upon it once and for all—refused to go, as in *The Sunlight Dialogues:*

> Something about the land, or the York State land as it used to be—the near horizons lifting up their high-angled screens between folded valleys, the days full of clouds forever drifting, ominous and beckoning, sliding past green-gray summits and throwing their strange shapes over the tilted fields, sunny elms inexorably darkened by the march of shadow from the straight-edged slopes. "Standup and seize," the land said; "Or rise and prophesy, cock your ears to the invisible." At the edge of the dark woodlots facing on swamps where no mortal trespasser could ever be expected, there were signs KEEP OUT: THIS MEANS YOU.

And at the same time in moments of epiphany, Gardner, half-romantic poet, wants it all: "substance calling beyond itself to substance," matter communing with mind, riddle leading on to further riddle in the magician's mysterious bag of tricks: "She knew well enough, on days like this, where the truth lay. It was the physical pattern in the carpet, where the blueblack lines intersected the brown and where figures of rose showed their threads; in the broken putty on the windowpanes, in the infinite complexity of lines in the bark of trees, in the dust in the sunbeams: substance calling beyond itself to substance."

Hawthorne could not shake his visions of the abyss and the self in isolation. His affirmation of ultimate separation led him into tragic corners, as the last darker romances teetered on the brink of collapse. Gardner recognized the dark abyss, but he insisted on jumping into the dark, however foolishly and uncertainly to grasp what glimmerings of human compassion and connection remain. His characters overcome their often rigidified philosophical prisons in a way most of Hawthorne's more allegorical creatures could not. The author as poet-priest, as Shaper shaping simultaneously lies and visions, creating images of moral heroism and conjuring up tribal unity in a void, creates his characters in a richly textured, poetic prose that conjures up all the complexities, richnesses, and terrors of contemporary American life. Books could—and should—be written on Gardner's prose style itself, above and beyond the tricks of the artificer at work, the narrative voice at play. The Manichean multiple perspectives are meant to be o'erleapt; the reader is forced to choose, as are the characters. The dilemma is left intact, decisive, the rage between chaos and order, choice and resignation; but Gardner's folk choose, however wrongly and blindly, as do Cheever's and Updike's and, at times, Oates's.

Gardner wished to side with John Napper in his short story, "John Napper Sailing Through the Universe," who declares, "Let there be light, a splendid garden." His pastoral perspective and recreations of the landscapes of upstate New York, Pennsylvania, and Vermont clearly indicate that urge for restoration and reconciliation in the human spirit. At the same time he shared the modern view that, as in "The King's Indian," "there is no purity or innocence in theaters, or in forests, or in oceans— and no wickedness either. Only survival, only cunning and secrecy." The elimination of Calvinistic wickedness in that statement is the pastoral Gardner unregenerate. His attempts to strike a balance, or better yet to reconcile these two opposite points of view (and he does seem intent on reconciling them within some pastoral landscape, however circumscribed and momentary), place him firmly within the mainstream of the American psychological romance. His untimely death, however, removed from it a major American romancer.

EIGHT

Joyce Carol Oates: Contending Spirits

JOYCE CAROL OATES's Manichean vision of contemporary America threatens to overwhelm any literary form she uses to try to encompass it. Emotions override reason; monologue buries meaning; individual characters dissolve beneath the full force of their feelings, insights, and omnivorous yearnings. Even her apparent method of creation suggests the power these characters and emotional forces have upon her: "When I'm with people I often fall into a kind of waking sleep, a day-dreaming about the people, the strangers, who are to be the "characters" in the story or novel I will be writing. . . . At times my head seems crowded; there is a kind of pressure inside it, almost a frightening physical sense of confusion, fullness, dizziness. . . . 'My characters' really dictate themselves to me. I am not free of them, really. . . . They have the autonomy of characters in a dream."[1] It is as if exorcism replaces fiction. Confession overpowers its literary container.

Dark dualistic design stalks Oates's haunted mind as starkly as it did Hawthorne's, but with more sheer emotional power and force: "In the novels I have written, I have tried to give a shape to certain obsessions of mid-century Americans—a confusion of love and money, of the categories of public and private experience, of demonic urge I sense all around me, an urge to violence as the answer to all problems, an urge to self-annihilation, suicide, the ultimate experience and the ultimate surrender."[2] Dualism becomes a dominant demonic force that, if outrun, suggests both an ultimate freedom and ultimate self-destruction. As G.F. Waller suggests, Oates tears through that very American sensibility with its often uneasy alliance between the mystical and the material, "the dislocation between dream and materialism in America."[3] In fact, "to assert the primacy of the unquantifiable seems necessarily to end in the

Manicheism which has constantly characterized American experience."[4]
"All the books published under my name in the past ten years," Oates
asserts, "have been formalized, complex propositions about the nature
of personality and its relationship to a specific culture (contemporary
America)."[5] Obsessed with the Western myth of the self, the ego,
Oates presses that fiction to its limits, seeking necessarily some wider
space beyond, some other ultimate reality beyond the materialized, self-
conscious self in contemporary America.

Violence alone seems capable of breaking through the boundaries of
the Western ego. Only a palpable, forceful wrenching can shatter such
historical self-images. "Violence is always an affirmation," Oates insists,[6] and in her remarks on Dostoevski she seems to reveal her own
method for writing fiction: "It seems likely that the acts of violence—
the sheer consummation of murderous impulses designed to 'change one's
life'—are the bases upon which the novels are written; the ideological
dialogues come second."[7] Oates sounds similar to the more tradition-
ally Catholic O'Connor in her insistence on the primacy of violence to
break through outmoded habits, stale rites of Western consciousness. In
fact, in writing about O'Connor she insists that one "can be delivered
from the trance of self only by violence."[8] Passion alone can liberate and
save, no matter how it is expressed, how it erupts through and within
social experience. "What are we except passion," Oates states, "and how
are we to survive when this passion breaks its dikes and flows out into
nature?"[9] How, indeed! And yet without the overflow of passion, there
is nothing: "Nihilism is overcome by the breaking-down of the dikes
between human beings, the flowing forth of passion."[10] A very thin
line, then, between liberation and destruction, creation and collapse.

The self battles an incomprehensible world, whether etched in numbing poverty—an experience from Oates's own family background—or
steeped in the sheer pervasiveness of American wealth and material goods.
And it needs that incomprehensible world to battle against. Oates suggests, in writing about D.H. Lawrence, that "when the Other is obliterated, the individual is also obliterated. . . . He . . . exhibits a deep un-
shakable faith in the inexplicable processes of life—or fate, or time, or
accident—against which the individual must assert himself in a continued
struggle."[11] Emotion battles reason, overwhelming the limited nar-
rowness of rational thought and design. As Waller suggests, "The paranoid
search for material security is the external sign of inner restlessness born

of the dream of an America permanent only in its changes and chances.''[12] Such conflict permeates the very being of man, that terrible opposition which Oates discusses in regard to Schopenhauer between "the will and the idea, the blind primitive force of will, or life, and the enlightened, would-be autonomous force of the intellect. The struggle is dramatic and endless. . . . man splits in two, drawn by the erotic in one direction and by the principles of the mind in another, unable to synthesize the two.''[13] Manichean dualism lacerates man's self-consciousness. The will seeks its own triumphant isolation and in so doing generates its own self-destruction. The Christian idea of losing the self, of propelling one's self beyond dualistic design in order to find it, becomes the apocalyptic equilibrium of annihilation, liberation, and surrender. As Walter Sullivan asserts, "The modern hero, placed irrevocably beyond good and evil, must create himself. The necessity for self-creation is at once his doom and his only avenue to freedom; he must transcend his own society and in the process he will destroy himself.''[14]

"I feel that my own place is to dramatize the nightmares of my time," Oates explains, "and (hopefully) to show how some individuals find a way out, awaken, come alive, move into the future.''[15] The nightmares of women as victims, urban slums, and isolated selves in most cases overwhelm the possibility of an individual's awakening. Passion almost precludes knowledge, nearly obscures self-recognition in its ferocity and tumble. If, as Oates suggests, "all literature deals with a contest of wills,''[16] what we have in her huge novels has a kinship with Poe, with his enclosed worlds and the rage within, the vampiric wills battling one another to the point of life and death. Imps of the perverse stalk her fictions, as they clutter Hugh Petrie's blurred consciousness in *The Assassins* (1975). Reality—whatever it is—emerges in gothic garb, lurid and passionate in its stare, as in *Mysteries of Winterthurn*. "Gothicism, whatever it is, is not a literary tradition so much as a fairly realistic assessment of modern life,''[17] Oates insists, and, in insisting, reveals the Manichean manic tone and style of her art. If the gothic can be defined as an awareness of another interior or spiritual realm, usually demonic and terrible in its essence and conscious of human decay and irrationality, then certainly Oates's fiction, however naturalistic in appearance, is essentially gothic. Add to this her eye for the grotesque, a form of modern gothic literature in which the "normal" is elusive and the misshapen and isolated are central to the character, plot, and setting, and you approach the fierce center of her haunted mind. Her comments on Dostoevski reveal the added dimensions of power in her own work: "Dostoevski's imagination is such that he conceives the kernel of his drama as a conflict within the parts of one self. . . . his psychological insights deal mainly with the self-lacerating effects of egoism and its corollary, the wish for destruction and death."[18] We are left admiring "the splendid unpredictability of the writer as writer, who can *leave nothing unsaid*, whose imagination is so nervously rich that characters and ideas multiply themselves as if by their own volition."[19]

How can an artist with such a vision harness such a torrential flow? Oates's earlier novels, discussed in detail by other critics, rely essentially on third-person narrative. That particular form has led several critics to misinterpret her essential vision and to claim her as kin to Dreiser or, in some outrageous cases, William Dean Howells! Some more perceptive interpreters recognized the truth of the matter: "Oates' early fiction is clearly in the dominant American fictional tradition of romance, derived from Hawthorne and beyond. . . . It insists predominantly upon atmosphere and action, and upon a constant use of allegorical, mythical, and symbolic devices to point the reader beyond the surface action."[20] As Oates acknowledges, "It *is* a good time to be an imaginative writer. Most writers today are free of the necessity of telling a story in a conventional manner; now we are able to use fantasy and surrealism and even mythic and fairy-tale elements in our art."[21] One critic even goes so far to suggest that *them*, her award-winning novel, is in fact a parody of naturalism.[22]

In any case, with the earlier exception of *Expensive People* (1968), by the time of *The Assassins* and *Childwold* (1976) Oates had begun to experiment with more open-ended fiction, fiction recounted from the point of view of the characters themselves. The first-person interior monologue replaces the third-person more objective narrative angle of vision. Mystery enters the more romantic mode of the confession; the self imposes its own order upon the world around it more readily or at least more visibly, trapped within certain egos, certain minds, and the naturalistic or more realistic perspectives surrender to the "up-front" obsessions of these characters. Reality—the character's angle of vision—constantly threatens to fragment and shatter, always outracing the mind's abilities to comprehend it: "Reality is constantly turning into something else; simplicity breaks up into fragments, baffling us; nothing stays, nothing is permanent; characters who are defined in one way break loose and assume deeper, vaster dimensions. . . . what is intended to be a parable or prophecy . . . becomes a great mystic work in which all man's acts, whether 'good' or 'evil,' are held finally to be of little account."[23]

Such a vision consistently threatens the patterns Oates the artist intends to create, and in several cases shatters the work itself. When consciousness consumes itself and the palpable physical world is swallowed up within the bloated blur of that babbling consciousness, as in *The Assassins* and *Angel of Light* (1981), Oates's later novels become monotonous, tedious, and inert. They fail under their own convoluted weight. When she has a firmer grasp on some wider reality, some more palpable design, where her characters' self-consciousness is in league with some "other" world, some suggestion of an "other" realm—contemporary America, myth, religion, whatever—as in the novella *The Triumph of the Spider Monkey* (1976) and *Son of the Morning* (1978), her novels succeed. And when—at last!—the Manichean vision emerges solidly within the romantic form it seems destined to inhabit, as in the magnificent *Bellefleur* (1980), Oates not only achieves her masterpiece—so far—but masters in full force her authentic voice.

Bobbie Gotteson, the handsome maniac who plays guitar, wishes for a screen test, and desires only "to be a face on a billboard," inverts standard Christian and American values in his frenzied confession in *The Triumph of the Spider Monkey* with almost as much fervor and perverse pleasure as Richard Everett, who subverts the suburban values of *Expensive People*. He is the mad isolato, a grotesque creature whose name ironically mimics his isolation and whose very existence indicts and at the same time appears to be an extention of the values that come under attack. His "gnosis" emerges in his strong will, his apparent ability (so he thinks) to bend others to his psychic powers: "I felt my powers rise and flow over, like light if light could turn into water, fountains of water." It follows then that "God is a Maniac like me," even though finally "I was out-guessed by the God of Night." And all the time he explains that his insanity is merely a pose, a way of keeping his inviolate self intact: "And so I pretended madness, to save myself from disaster. Yet I was always sane. I am like you: a progression of states of mind, forms of sanity that keep moving and eluding definition. I was always sane and had practiced insanity." In this essential image of himself, the Manichean vision of the book takes root.

Gotteson makes quite clear, like Nathaniel Vickery after him, that his true self exists in the realm of the spirit. The body disgusts him. When murder takes over, the hacking of nine women, "my body took over, and when bodies take over the spirit sails over the horizon." This irreconcilable split, fiercely schizophrenic and at the same time reflecting the American society of which he considers himself a part—heading west, longing for a career as a songwriter and singer in the style of "Sloe-Eyed Gypsy, American"—rages throughout the book. Hate and pity emerge from one another. His own rage fuels his music, as if the latter could in some way soothe the former. Thoughts come as convulsions; ideas appear to be spasms. His handsome body momentarily hides a mad spirit. His career in films becomes a pornographic circus, the height of his art being "Seventeen Mannequins and a Guy," in which he sexually assaults and then dismembers with a machete seven female dummies. Events slide into hallucinations and vice-versa. Prison for him represents the inside of experience; everything else exists outside, and, as in America in the Seventies, "the Outside styles approximated the Inside spirit." All death for Bobbie is suicide, even if it be murder. Even the assassination of President Kennedy enrages him: *It made me want to kill someone.* Whether he is the norm or the subversion of the norm, he can no longer tell, muddying the impenetrable Manichean waters of his consciousness: "I couldn't come from anything normal or good. . . . But since everything in the world comes from the world and is normal and good, I must be somehow normal and good."

Oates structures the novel along traditional Christian lines. The first of twenty chapters is entitled "Nativity," the final chapter, "Redemption." Out of darkness into light he is born, although he is found in Locker 79-C in the main waiting room of the Trailways Bus Terminal on Canal Street in New York City. Each chapter, like an emblematic episode in a romance, provides a glimpse of Gotteson's life. Each appears in a series of "jumpshots, athletic tricks of the camera, montage-freezings," as "An Unfilmed Love Scene," "Unrehearsed Interview," "How the Maniac Gotteson Travelled West," "Why I Hacked," and "Gotteson's Pilot-Film": the detritus of modern media—news items, psychological explanations, scenes from a lost script. Each functions as a kind of failed epiphany, a microcosm of Gotteson's mind and the state of the materialistic world around him that values sex, Hollywood careers, and the superficiality of all things.

Several people throughout his life call him a monkey because of his dark hair, his inhuman exploits, his athletic and sexual abilities. The final Manichean triumph: spider monkey overrides the human beings to the point where Gotteson declares only half in jest, "I told them I was in essence a Spider Monkey, in my soul, with a looping furry cunning tail scrunched up inside my trousers." Oates's vision is complete. The Manichean trap clamps shut.

The novel as confession approximates the realm of the romance. An individual self wrestling with particular problems projects himself upon the world around him. The reader views an almost allegorical realm surrounding that central self. Gotteson appears doomed from the start: the world on the "outside" and the "inside" allows no escape, no place for any possibility of self-transcendence or recognition. Rather, a Manichean realm presses relentlessly against him, driving him inward, outward, beyond the pale. As a boy he is buggered by blacks in New Jersey; his therapist calls him an ugly monkey and declares he'll kill someone someday; his own rage is driven inward with no place to go. Interior violence broods and festers. A prison dentist gives him no Novocain while lambasting his appearance and his status as a prisoner; Melva, the aged mistress who picks him up, promises him screen tests and recording sessions but only delivers more sex, while he chauffeurs her around Hollywood. Prison warps him. His "old man" there, Danny Minxs, buggers him in front of the other inmates as punishment and power play to subdue him, rails against women, infects Bobbie with his own "psychic powers," and deserts him on their way west. The world of El Portal, a Hollywood estate overlooking the sea, promises only more parties and sex, and Melva and her crew egg him on to climb up on the house like a trained monkey. He falls; they laugh; Melva offers him a stooge role in a television comedy. There is nowhere to turn in a progressively sadistic world.

Gotteson's quest goes nowhere except into the darker realm of murder, and even then it seems to him the machete is acting by itself. "It sliced up more people. . . . this frightened me because my soul blacked out at such times and abandoned me to whatever was going on." Time "collapsed into itself." A sense of doom and dark shadows hovers everywhere.

Gothic romance lies at the heart of Gotteson's compulsive, obsessive behavior, as if the confessional novel, mirroring more the internal world of emotions than the external world of social conventions, had entered the realm of the romance in the dark terms of some of Hawthorne's self-obsessed characters. One critic suggested that Hawthorne's characters resembled Poe's, except that Hawthorne's appeared in his own third-person narration, while many of Poe's demonic creatures relied upon the first-person confession to reveal their lurid tales.[24] Oates demonstrates her ability to conjure up Poe's world in word and deed here.

All the elements of romance are here, submerged in Gotteson's first-person confession: the withdrawn settings, the episodic, dreamlike nature of the plot, the mix of light and dark, the self at the center of the narrative, the visible author at work—and the ongoing unravelling of various compulsions, obsessions, guilts. And if ever a vision was founded on Manichean polarities, this certainly has its palpable designs on us.

If pity had not claimed him, Gotteson explains, "my life would not be this disjointed confession, but a series of haunting melodies joined to lyric language." The language of the book, while not exactly lyric, certainly embodies the hypnotic spell of most romances. Here it begins:

Noise, vibrations, murmuring nosey crowd of bastards with nothing else to do but gawk—grunting sweating bastard in a uniform reaching in and grabbing me out of the darkness and delivering me to light—
—to lights, that is—
Holding me up to those lights. *A baby! A baby still alive!*
Time: 6:05 PM. Date: February 14, 1944.

Sensations precede thought. The style lurches forward, filled with repetitions, as if consciousness were trying to grasp what was going on— "light—lights—lights—." Ellipses break the flow, increase that sense of grappling with circumstance and event. Italics preach astonishment at what is happening. Long hypnotic paragraphs shatter, stumble onto sudden short sentences. The jerkiness of the rhetoric again reveals the teetering consciousness trying to maintain control and pursue understanding. Facts seem cursory, beside the point, almost ironically tossed in. The date of Gotteson's birth is the least important item here, other than the fact that it connects him and his future life with specific, however shadowy, American reality and historical moment.

Oates shares Faulkner's power, but her style only superficially resembles his. Faulkner never abandons his sense of place, the habits and notions of a peculiarly southern mind: a Balzacian reality lurks within the circuitous rush of rhetoric. In Oates regions blur. Mind and matter tremble, fuse, separate. Language attaches itself to the direct emotions and states of mind of a particular character. The outside world, however recreated with a Dreiserian thirst for details, remains vague, curiously distant, remote. In her less successful novels, as we shall see, it entirely evaporates, leaving the reader within a convoluted rhetoric that swallows itself and dissolves everything within and beyond it. Dream precedes history in Oates's vision: "We seek the absolute dream. We are forced back continually to an acquiescence in all that is hallucinatory and wasteful."[25] Finally Oates shatters the hypnotic circuitousness of a Faulkner by breaking the line, injecting gasps, italics, curiously random facts and figures. This exaggerates the character's isolation, his distance from any known world, his Manichean entrapment within himself.

Melville, Oates has written, sought not the equilibrium of opposites, the balanced art of alternative positions—his famous "contraries"—but a nihilistic destruction of tension. Of *The Confidence-Man* she writes, "The underlying motif of the novel is not just the tension of antipodal forces but rather the fact of no tension—of a final nihilism."[26] Evil does not triumph over good; the struggle between good and evil is eradicated. "For a writer whose aim is to penetrate into a 'basic truth,' the sustainment of any two points of view will suggest, in the end, the mockery of assigning to one of two antithetical views a positiveness worthy of one's faith—worthy of one's life. The quest ends, ideally, in the negation and not in the compromise or resolution of tension in Melville's irreconcilable world of opposites; it is at once a transcendence and an annihilation."[27]

At the conclusion of *The Triumph of the Spider Monkey*, Gotteson remains by the side of his final dying victim. He has already foreshadowed his murder of Doreen B., his last murder, by referring to it as "that revelation." As his anger slowly leaves him, reflecting the blood leaving her body, he thinks, "I began to panic that she would die before she could explain." Death mirrors a purity, a place of not-female and not-male, of the not-human (in contrast to the all-too-grisly humanity of his own experience), an almost religious place which Gotteson has sought but never found. His murders he describes as his victims' suicides: he releases them from the horror he has lived. As Doreen dies, she utters, "I can see into it . . . ." Gotteson's violent act becomes for him a final act of self-definition and self-destruction. He realizes suddenly that he is one whole person, a horror in his own right: "He is Gotteson the Spider Monkey and nobody else is Gotteson and Gotteson cannot get born into being anyone else, Gotteson is Gotteson is Gotteson forever.'' The splintered fragments of his confession coalesce in this chilling shock of recognition. Manichean dualisms shatter and leave behind "Gotteson Inside, Gotteson Outside . . . all's one Gotteson Gotteson Gotteson unrepeatable. There you are." He screams for an ambulance: "It isn't too late, help me!"

Transcendence and annihilation erupt simultaneously. It is at once "a penitential act. A Negative Act. An undoing-of-Magic Act." In a sense he has earned his final humanity, however terrible it is. He is capable of anything. The self becomes an act of horror. He is us. It is not here a nihilistic act. Gotteson seems to recognize what has happened, what a creature he is: he calls for help. We can see the final cry as an act of both despair and liberation. But he at once recognizes both, as no one else in the book has or can. Manicheism may not have been so much transcended as ineradicably fused, the same kind of horrifying interpenetration of opposites that frightened Hawthorne. In any case it seems to be the point that Oates longs for in her fictions, the pinnacle of her vision, freighted at once with deliverance and disintegration. In such a violent landscape, however, both inside and outside, it is indeed the spider monkey's triumph.

Selfhood and the physical world are always threatened by submergence in the manic sensationalism of Oates's style. When this happens, voices wail in a void and turn tedious and unrelated to anything but their own garrulous chatter. The physical world evaporates, blurs; everything dissolves; emotions turn vaporous; vertigo takes over. In such instances Oates sounds as though she were hyperventilating, awash in a babble of ellipses and dashes, a Jamesian "talking head" gone mad. Frenzied fragments don't so much dance as congeal, echoes reverberate off other echoes, and a rhetorical stupor prevails. Such is the case in *Angel of Light* and *The Assassins*.

As a point of contrast, here is the opening of Updike's *Rabbit Run*: "Boys are playing basketball around a telephone pole with a blackboard bolted to it. Legs, shouts. The scrape and snap of Keds on loose alley pebbles seems to catapult their voices high into the moist March air blue above the wires." Images prevail, hard and pure, so much so that the observing self is practically submerged in the physical reality of the world.

In *The Assassins* in a similar scene the opposite is true: "Basketball court, midwinter. Boys running loose. Like dogs, like colts, like deer.

Black boys—of high school age mainly—a single white boy, no more than thirteen—shouting and darting from side to side—the basketball bouncing at odd unpredictable angles from the uneven surface of cracked asphalt—yells, screams, shouts of joy—disappointment—sudden rage—and then joy again, and again the pounding of feet." Here the sensations of the event take over. The concrete images, many of them tumbled upon one another, are submerged in the sheer rush of the event. So much is piled on that the event itself is heavily submerged in the experienced sensations of it.

This paragraph suggests the general nature of the style in *The Assassins*. Manicheism reigns: dreaming and waking, light and dark, God and the Devil, truth and lies. "The Petries have chosen improbable mates, they've been guided more by romance than by reason [revealing] *a bizarre inclination toward the precarious, the forbidden, the wobbling, the dizzy.*" But as Friedman suggests, the novel registers only "the complete isolation of the individual in his personality."[28]

Hugh, the grotesque cartoonist, babbles relentlessly about art, death, jokes. His own impotence shatters his fragile ego, although the reader is aware of such impotence by the sheer repetitious breathlessness of his ponderous probing. Yvonne Radek, poor orphan, widow of the dead Andrew, falls numb, exudes a glacial calm, imagines her own murder at the hands of a crazed ax-man. Stephen pursues religious mysticism, a bodiless, timeless trance that reduces the world and everyone in it to unimportant ciphers, distant presences. All in their own way remain detached, self-conscious, paranoid, obsessed, and each detests the body. They are all Manicheans, prisoners of an ineradicable, feverish self-consciousness that worships a tenuous self-control, a querulous celebration of "the intellect and the precise measurements, its setting-up of empires, word by word by word, which nothing could demolish." All this babble turns in upon itself, making the novel almost unreadable, a sterile vacuum of stupefied stuttering.

We can see what Oates is up to, a theme that will emerge triumphant in *Bellefleur*. The original Petrie—"petrified," Hugh calls his older brother Andrew—fled England in the 1600s and became "a deranged Puritan minster—famous for the transactions viciousness can make with civilization." He was "a zealous preacher of the Word, a nonconforming, stubborn, querulous hero who braved the Atlantic Ocean with other maniacs." Andrew is the modern-day Petrie, a right-wing political theorist who quits politics to write his supreme opus, praising legalism over anarchy, a masterful public speaker and public presence who casts his giant shadow across the lives of Hugh, Yvonne, and Stephen, the remaining triptych of the novel, maimed by the Petrie "curse." Andrew is aware of the problem: "The Puritans were capable of extraordinary acts of courage . . . because they were so certain of themselves, their own conscience. They were fanatics. . . . Their only problem was that they were deluded, as we know: they thought it was God directing them, but in fact it was history." This is Hawthorne's territory, the god of romance battling with the history of the novel.

In Andrew's time the Word has degenerated into words. Puritan self-control and God-obsessive people have "petrified." "An abstract tower of words" casts its distorted shadow over the entire book. Creation becomes concept; image becomes idea: "The words are always the same words but changed, turned upside down, reversed, they are mirror images of one another and we are mirror images of one another." Oates has fallen into the very abyss she warns us of: her "attack" on consciousness, on words, on intellect sinks under the weight of these characters' consciousness, their omnivorous, emasculating words. The image of the Petrie family is there—America in microcosm, Puritan certainty shattered and dispersed—but it gets lost in the monotonous monologues of the Petrie survivors. It is not that the characters scrutinized are too abnormal to identify with (as one critic suggests, a "ranting psychotic, a suicidal public figure, a frigid schizoid, a drifting mystic"[29]); it is their unrelieved talk that does them in.

Oates has a significant point. Consciousness itself is the ultimate assassin. Ego kills. Even Andrew, in love with motion and power, sinks into depressive stasis and in doing so at last contrives his own suicide to look like an assassination. Consciousness prides itself on conjuring up its own apocalyptic demise, caught up in "the romance of disaster, sheer catastrophe . . . to want to believe suddenly and irrevocably that all was lost." Hugh attempts suicide; Yvonne hallucinates about her own dismemberment; Stephen, like Alice through the looking glass, drifts away from language into abject silence. The end of the novel reveals "the Devil whom you cast down a thousand years into that bottomless hole." The beast arises; apocalypse now: "I am the way, the tooth the might." But Stephen is correct to repudiate such babble; he remains willing to accommodate himself to anything, a glimpse of resurrection and perseverance.

"One must be connected to the world," Andrew Petrie tells Stephen, "but how?—how? They don't tell us." When Oates is disconnected from the world, her vision blurs. Rhetoric clamors but rings hollow. No amount of screaming will help. All rings false.

In *Son of the Morning* (the title is taken from the *Book of the Prophet Isaiah*, 14:12-15, and refers to the devil), Oates succeeds once again with the form of the confessional novel, sustained and enlarged by the distinctive elements of romance. The book's three chapters and epilogue parallel the Christian pattern once again: "The Incarnation," "The Witness," "Last Things," and "The Sepulcher." The text itself represents Nathanael Vickery's testament, his "desperate prayer" to God, "an utterance of faith, of infinite faith," looking back on his failed career as a charismatic preacher, presently waiting for God's presence to show itself anew, left waiting forever in his own private sepulcher: "Yet there was, there is, no *we*: there is only an *I*." Recounting his life he recounts his vision and like the romancer envisions a world as a self-projection of that vision.

Vickery's quest reflects Wesley Kort's analysis of religiously pluralistic American society.[30] Kort suggests that for religious pluralism to exist, people must agree to a common nonreligious life, a public domain where no one religion may dominate. Consequently, society constructs this nonreligious domain; it becomes the unifying influence upon, the identifying mark of that society; and it relies upon the language of logic, of rational, empirical verification, to uphold it. As a result the depersonalization of society's members must triumph, leaving no place for the personal or the religious. Therefore a split results in American society between the private and the public, between immanent mystery and solvable problem, retreat and work, the "religious-withdrawn" and the "nonreligious engaged." Kort sees many confessional novels (he cites several of Updike's) as opportunities to attempt to heal this basic American division, "a torn world in which two goods are separated from one another, in which two self-enclosed worlds are unrelated."[31] The problem itself is Manichean. So too is Oates's "solution."

One other important organizational and structural device holds *Son of the Morning* together. In his lifetime Vickery experiences seven visions, "seven revelations of extraordinary magnitude . . . seven small crucifixions." These visions not only reveal Nathan's character development and the mad escalation of his faith; they also establish a decisive pattern throughout the novel and give it the kind of organic shape that *The*

Assassins lacks. And they suggest the scaffold epiphanies that organize Hawthorne's romances.

Nathan progresses—or regresses, as the case may be—from a vision of radiance and light at the age of five, fondling snakes in a fundamentalist church service, to a sixth vision in which he envisions himself as God, the two of them inseparable, to the seventh and final vision of utter collapse and withdrawal at the age of thirty-four (a year older than Christ at his death) on—Oates's marvelous touch—August 8, 1974, the day Richard Nixon resigned from the presidency. At eight he enters a trance when his father rejects his "Christ-madness"; at twelve he bites off a chicken's head to humble his aspiring pride; at nineteen he knifes out an eye during a sermon as penance for the reassertion of pride and lust. At twenty-seven he perceives an overwhelming oneness wherein he himself is above sin and Christ is eclipsed. These epiphanies focus the self-escalation of the book, both structurally and thematically.

And what is Nathan's vision? Pure Manicheism reigns supreme again. Christ had no body; he was just a spirit. The spirit of the Lord is not bound up in the flesh in any manner or form; the Devil rules flesh, distorting our vision to accommodate it: "The Devil wants us to think that Jesus Christ was really a man and that he really died. . . . Before my fleshly being came into the world, *I* was." The senses, the will: these incorporate sin. "The only reality is the interior and invisible." Grace becomes the "cessation of all duality," for there can be none when only spirit is genuine. Vickery's vision eradicates Christ, "a mere image of God," and hurries toward destruction of that thin membrane between the fullness of an invisible spirit and the consequent emptiness if that spirit should withdraw. His horror during that final vision is to recognize "the odd ineffable *reality* of what was outside him." God shatters, "broken and separated into parts, into individuals, into people, 'men' and 'women' and 'children.' " It is a vision he cannot bear.

Of course Nathan's vision reflects the outer world of his narrative, or more particularly that outer world reflects his vision of it. His grandparents, by whom he was raised, reflect the Manichean design: Opal hungers for the spirit of the fundamentalist Christian; Dr. Thaddeus, a man of science, views the universe in strictly materialistic terms: "There is no spiritual world, only a materialistic world in which soul and mind are evolved with the body, grow old with the body, ail with the body, and finally die with the body's death. There is nothing permanent." His refuge resides in stoicism: "Better the vanquishment of all desire and all strife. The cessation of instinct itself." We inhabit only "a universe of change, flowing about us, flooding against us, bearing us away. Only the present moment is real."

The plot of the novel erupts along Manichean lines. The Vickerys' daughter is raped while returning from a church service; she becomes Nathan's mother. William Japheth Sproul III, Princeton graduate in a family of divines, becomes Nathan's disciple, but his eagerness and devotion suggest homosexual compulsion. He tries to murder Vickery, then commits suicide. Nathan's own lusts for the daughter of his eventual boss, the Reverend Marian Miles Boloff, drive him toward his outrageous faith in the spirit. And of course his spiritual faith appears to unbelievers as a "gospel of hate! Of regressive disdain for human relationships!"

Oates's America bristles with Manichean urges. Americans "are hungry for a true prophet, for a *true* evangelistic voice." Imagine Pentecostals thriving in Boston in 1965! And "in the early seventies it seemed as if everyone was hungry for this teaching. Salvation had nothing to do with social responsibility or action of any kind; it had nothing to do with human relationships." Middle-class youth turn from drugs to their own self-absorbed Christ. The landscape is ready in this "Age of Non-belief . . . materialistic, skeptical, blinded, atheistic. . . . Satan was the secret god of America." Which came first, Nathan's vision or the America he inhabits? And does his destruction suggest some wider apocalypse?

The elements of romance clearly haunt Nathan Vickery's confession: the allegorical characters inhabiting the design of flesh and spirit; the hypnotic style of the seven revelations, beautifully rendered by Oates at her rhetorical best; the episodic, dreamlike visitations and emblematic scenes; the emotional tenor and power of certain compulsions, obsessions, and guilts that seem to dictate the characters' every move. And in that strange opening scene in which Ashton Vickery contemplates shooting a pack of wild dogs ravaging the countryside (Manicheism at full cry) we get the strange, eerie setting of romance: "Only a peculiar glowering light that was like moonlight, like mist. . . . Like sleep, it was; like the dreamless sleep of the depths of the night. Perhaps he was sleeping?—dreaming? . . . and the pallid, dissolving Chautauqua Mountains and the oppressive sky itself . . . mesmerizing . . . drawn . . . into the vast silence, thinking that this had happened before: many times: and would happen many times again . . . everything he touched was an extension of himself." Nathan, now William, is left in his private sepulcher, waiting for a God who will not return, almost as if Oates were waiting for that full-blown romantic vision and form to come forth once and for all, out into the open, complete. In *Bellefleur* it finally does.

In *The Assassins* one of the characters comments, "Fairy tales are exactly analogous to life as it is lived in the family." In *Bellefleur* that astute observation becomes structure. Romance embodies Oates's Manichean vision in that splendid opening paragraph: "It was many years ago in that dark, chaotic, unfathomable pool of time before Germaine's birth . . . on a night in late September stirred by innumerable frenzied winds, like spirits contending with one another . . . that Mahalaleel came to Bellefleur Manor on the western shore of the great Lake Noir. . . ." The opening suggests *Absalom, Absalom!* in its pacing and poetic accretions. Time is distant; space is distant; the "neutral territory" all but announces its dominance. And spirits are already contending with one another, intimations of Leah and Gideon's marriage—"their love was too ravenous to be contained by their mortal bodies." Lake Noir suggests Poe; the name Mahalaleel suggests strange spirits, magic omens, haunted demons.

Bellefleur spawns "disturbing labyrinthian tales. . . . The living and the dead. Braided together. Woven together. An immense tapestry taking in centuries . . . a dizzying profusion of plots . . . calculations, aspirations, dreams—some of them . . . quite mad . . . stories, tales, anecdotes set in the mountains, which no one quite believed and could not quite disregard." Oates shares the "simple frank astonishment at the pathways others' lives took" with her huge canvas of characters, the sheer torrent of tales and tellers: dwarfs, beasts, feuds, mass murders, mystics, doomed romances, transformations, disappearances, ghosts, prophecies, rapes, celebrations: the Bellefleur clan as all of American history, of the American psyche. Many brood on strange obsessions, linked to objects of their rapt devotions: Leah and her huge spider Love, Noel's vial of poison, Jedediah's submission to Mt. Blanc, Raphael's mystic awe for Mink Pond, Samuel's disappearance into the Turquoise Room, "the room of contamination." Strange attachments, mystical unions, obsessed alliances create a fairytale world, a nightmare realm, in which objects assume emblematic powers. The world speaks in omens; events double, spawn unforeseen consequences, spill over into inner tormented souls. Here is the American-Manichean "ethos" raised to its romantic heights, its metamorphic triumph.

Worlds split, mirror one another. The palpable physical world of Oates's Adirondack region prompts astonishment: "What maddened mind, deranged by an unspeakable lust, had imagined all this into being?" In such a world chronological order collapses; Bellefleurs show only contempt at such linear notions of time and consequence: "Everything shifts, changes, grows fluid, transparent." And at the same time the turmoil of the mysterious interior world—the true world of Hawthorne's romance—continues and thrives unabated, "a universe simultaneous with this universe . . . a shadow-world, a mirror-world." Both are beautifully balanced; neither eradicates the other, though the demonic inner world colors the exterior landscape around Lake Noir. Of *The Brothers Karamazov* Oates speaks of "a double of itself contained in its most brilliant of pages, a kind of shadow or antinovel whose tragedy mocks the positive accomplishments of the larger, Christian work."[32] She could as well be describing *Bellefleur*, though here the world of gothic romance overshadows the Christian parallels and dimensions. Her characters pass in and out through "slits in the fabric of time," inhabiting that "dark, chaotic, unfathomable pool" of romance, spaces between exterior and interior worlds, one reflecting the other, a territory not so much neutral as nightmarishly realized.

Parallels abound to parallel these worlds. In the first eight chapters Oates shifts between present and past times, between the birth of Germaine in the present and Jedediah's retreat to the mountains in 1806 and 1809. Jedediah withdraws because he is drawn to the young wife, Germaine, of his younger brother Louis. In the present, Leah awaits the birth of her daughter Germaine. In 1825 Germaine alone survives the mass murder of the original Bellefleur, Jean-Pierre, her husband Louis, and their three children, and eventually marries the "reformed" mystic Jedediah: they generate the Bellefleur family tree, the somber, sexless survivor and the religious fanatic. And of the three surviving Bellefleurs after the destruction of the Manor and everyone within it, two are ancient women; the other is Germaine, age four.

Bellefleur represents both a historical family, interwoven with American history, a state of soul, the exterior world of ambition, action, the "lust of acquisition," the pursuit of money and power, and the interior world of consciousness, reflection, the lust for solitude and retreat, the pursuit

of some uncontaminated place or the sweetness of pure revenge. It suggests Emerson's mystic materialism or materialistic mysticism, that curious
American amalgam.

History reveals the abuse of Indians, tenant farmers, blacks, and fruit-
pickers, the acquisition of land, empire-building, frontier violence, family feuds, regional fracases. The official attitude of the Bellefleur clan in
this regard "was one of robust jocularity. . . . Nothing so important it
can't be laughed away. Shouted away." These early men suggest Faulkner's
southerners in their "passion for gambling . . . their reckless, inventive
challenges, and for their courtesy and grace in defeat." "Only in motion
is there life," Gideon declares in his pursuit of cars, horses, women, planes.
"The notion of *thinking*, of withdrawing oneself from action in order
to systematically *think*, struck him as not only unmanly but implausible:
for how could one force oneself to think, merely *think*, when the world
awaited!"

Jean-Pierre's arrival in America parallels American legends and myths.
He envisions "forests of prodigious beauty . . . streams visibly crowded
with salmon and trout, a virgin wilderness ripe for exploitation," diamonds
and rubies and sapphires and great blocks of jade in the soil, and silver
and gold deposits of a lushness never seen before on earth. "We are all
Americans now," declares Raphael, Jedediah's son, a millionaire ten times
over—who will have his skin stripped and made into the covering of a
drum after his death, whose vast lands Leah plots to regain in present
time, a prophecy she feels resides within daughter Germaine's strange
psychic powers. And for these Americans, the first Jean-Pierre, banished
from France, "repudiated by his own father . . . the past simply ceased
to exist." American myth is symbolized by the Bellefleur coat of arms,
"a falcon volant, a snake draped about its neck": power, exploitation,
isolation, the triumph of the self in pastless natural paradise, acquiring
"in the 1770's, some 2,889,500 acres of wilderness land for seven and
a half pence an acre." Hawthorne's Pyncheons. Faulkner's Sutpen.

But there is the shadow-world, the state of soul, the Manichean
Bellefleur curse, "an unfortunate combination of passion and melancholy . . . a propensity for energy and passion that might be countered
at any time by a terrifying bleakness, a queer emptiness of vision": man
deprived of history in a dark uncertain wilderness of his own making,
the demonic side of the American Adam, the gothic loneliness. "Indeed,
the spirit of contention was sometimes thought to be the essential curse

of the Bellefleurs—for isn't it out of contention that all evils spring?"
"Spirits contending with one another": the solitude of Jedediah's withdrawal to the mountains, Vernon's metaphysical poetry, Raphael's pond,
the passionate brutality of Leah and Gideon's marriage. This is a world
where death constantly threatens, where a God of Destruction broods
and watches, a world of grudges and revenge. "For revenge . . . makes
war against what is fixed. It is always revolutionary. It cannot exert itself
but must *be* exerted; and exerted only through violence, by a selfless individual who is willing to die in the service of his mission." Gideon crashes
his plane into Bellefleur Manor, killing them all on Germaine's fourth
birthday, at once a supreme Bellefleurian act of pride, tragedy, revenge,
suicide, and self-righteous self-destruction.

Oates's haunted mind has at last produced the romance she has seemed
on the verge of producing from the beginning. Bellefleur Manor, like
the Pyncheon House or Sutpen's Hundred, symbolizes the entire Bellefleur
saga, "with its innumerable walls and towers and turrets and minarets,
like a castle composed in a feverish sleep, when the imagination leapt
over itself, mad to outdo itself, growing more frantic and greedy." Time
twists and coils in that psychic inner realm of the romance, as Oates assures
us in her author's note: "*Bellefleur* is a region, a state of the soul, and
it does exist; and there, sacrosanct, its laws are utterly logical." Shades
of Hawthorne's prefaces, apologizing, defending his fictional creation.
Some tales soar; others dissipate. Style can turn both monotonous and
riveting, can be "overwrought and exaggerated and unhealthy." But it
is the sheer scope and power of Oates's *Bellefleur* that triumphs. At this
point in her prodigious career it is her masterpiece. And as such it reflects,
comments upon, extends, and achieves the kind of romance Hawthorne
would have celebrated. Form and content, vision and voice match as splendidly as in Faulkner's *Absalom, Absalom!* Exorcism assumes romantic em-
bodiment. At one point in the book, Oates quotes at length from Wordsworth's *The Prelude*, entranced herself, one would guess, by "something
far more deeply interfused. . . . A motion and a spirit, that impels / All
thinking things, all objects of all thought, / And rolls through all things.
. . ." Her spirit shares Hawthorne's darker compulsions and angle of
vision. And in *Bellefleur* it "impels" her darker vision of the soul with
an artistic integrity and authority that astounds.

NINE

Joan Didion:
Witnessing the Abyss

AT THE CENTER of Joan Didion's art, a black hole of dread yawns, the kind she describes in *Democracy* (1984): "Time was no longer just quickening but collapsing, falling in on itself, the way a disintegrating star contracts into a black hole." Everything vanishes into it, pulled down toward an even murkier center by the relentless gravitational forces of spiritual paralysis, a paranoia chilled to the point of numbness, a dazed but absolute sense of isolation that will not scare. Blood corrupts: "The heart of darkness lay not in some error of social organization but in man's own blood."[1] All else seems masquerade, history an illusion, a projection of man's "interior wilderness." Ambiguity stalks everything except the realization of "that dread of meaninglessness which was man's fate."[2] Dread fosters only "extreme and doomed commitments" to one's own defensive paralysis, one's style, the stubborn urge to self-sacrifice and immobility. It is small wonder that Didion's fiction reveals this vision over and over again, since for her "a novel is nothing if it is not the expression of an individual voice, of a single view of experience."[3]

Didion's staring into the abyss borders on such a numbed, trancelike state that it almost eradicates the devices and methods of traditional fiction altogether. It is as if Hawthorne's shadow were cast into a pit so deep that no possible fictional technique could ever hope to resurrect and explore it. California freeways, Central American wastelands, and nihilistic states of mind threaten to obliterate any "neutral territory" at once and leave the reader so disconcerted and disconnected that episodes appear and vanish without any scaffold upon which to stage them. Fictional narrative seems to evaporate, leaving only shards of language and glimpses of eternal chaos behind. First impressions, however, give way to deeper scrutiny, and from such a perspective the Hawthornian techniques reveal themselves more clearly: the brooding of the author or character over the meaning of existence, the use of language casting its spell like some religious litany, the cinematic fragments resolving themselves into the episodic tableaux of American romance, the polarization of characters reflecting Manichean mandates, the radical dualism between a self and a world that consistently thwart and undermine one another. Fashionable veils exist to be lifted and discarded, and beneath them the skull beneath the skin leers as icily and as relentlessly as any of Hawthorne's shadowy fiends.

Didion's is essentially a romantic consciousness, teetering riskily on the edge of a glorified abyss, "an essentially romantic ethic" which she defines as the belief "that salvation lay in extreme and doomed commitments, promises made and somehow kept outside the range of normal social experience."[4] These border on Hawthornian obsessions, if not in substance at least in scope, and they reduce society around them to a projection of them. At the same time the Manichean conflicts in her fiction—the West versus the East, men versus women, the self versus society—threaten to evaporate, dissolve into that state of paralysis that her heroines inhabit. Beyond conflict lies a dark frozen turf of the soul, that "mood of wary somnambulism," as she describes it in *Salvador* (1983), an immobility stunned by the conscious contradictions of contemporary American society and its moral burdens.

All order and connections shiver and wilt within such a numbed vision. Any connection threatens to vanish on closer inspection; cause and effect wither under such cold scrutiny: "All connections were equally meaningful, and equally senseless." Didion confronts "an authentically senseless chain of correspondences."[5] Is it she, laboring under "a stroke-like aphasia, and a crippling inability to make even the most routine connections?"[6] Is it the modern world? "I remember mainly images, indelible but difficult to connect."[7] In either case, disconnection spawns vertigo; "disorder was its own point."[8] Dread and the "endemic apprehension of danger," as she describes it in *Salvador*, ride the wake of a primal chaos. To write from such a perspective, again as it appears in *Salvador*, is "to plunge directly into a state in which no ground is solid, no depth of field reliable, no perception so definite that it might not dissolve into its reverse."

Where to from here? Since "a certain external reality remains, and resists interpretation,"[9] and since all significance remains ultimately elusive, Didion's sense of disaster propels her into the orbit of religious mystery. She writes of "secular communions," of "regional mysteries," of the forever elusive and interior depths of human motive. Mind and matter blur and spin. She has entered Hawthorne's black territory of the soul, a Manichean mystery of self trapped not only in a mysterious world but, worse, within the cosmic disharmonies and labyrinthine spheres of itself. Yet even here a moral universe of ultimate good and evil cannot be shaken; however paralyzed, they are never uncertain. As Alfred Kazin explains, "All is symbol, every character is a *statement* that evil reigns."[10] And as Katherine Henderson elaborates, "Like the heroes of Hawthorne and Melville, Didion's heroines inhabit a world in which good and evil are not merely social or political, but part of the impenetrable universe itself."[11]

From Didion's perspective the outside world becomes an allegory of the soul; places symbolize a state of mind, whether in the desert pleasures of Las Vegas, the apocalyptic fires and winds of southern California, or the naive romanticism of youth in New York City. Society and history entrap, become costume dramas for lost souls. Physical objects glimmer with omenlike auras, talismans of secret ceremonies. "Fiction has certain irreducible ambiguities . . . in most ways hostile to ideology,"[12] Didion believes; these haunt her haunted mind. Ideology seems so much patronizing, posturing cant. Menace underlies all things.

The romantic sensibility harbors loss the way cowards cling to grief. And for Didion that ancient Edenic archetype thrives in her vision of Sacramento and the great Central Valley of California, "a place in which a boom mentality and a sense of Chekhovian loss meet in uneasy suspension."[13] As in Faulkner's fiction, doom, decay, and corruption stalk favored agricultural lands. Old agrarian cultures shatter before the fiery assaults of a postwar boom. As one critic has suggested, Didion's California of 1946 suggests Faulkner's Mississippi of 1865.[14]

Myths haunt Didion as they did Hawthorne. His cold eye, cast upon transcendental aspirations and Emersonian new selves, becomes her vision of America's mythic West, freed ostensibly from the corruptions of the past, the East, history, the complications of old worlds, a *tabula rasa* erected in shimmering desert. Myth asserts that self can thrive on its own mobility, a free and private agent in a void of opportunity, but at the same time it masks a "socially suicidal" belief which leads only to the repetition of human greed, callousness, and anomie. Business success does not furnish the spiritual grace that latter-day Puritans are convinced it can. The Pyncheons fail here, too.

How much of Didion's vision remains an essentially "female" one remains open to endless debate, but she does describe what in her terms it is like to be a woman, burdened with "that sense of living one's deepest life underwater, that dark involvement with blood and birth and death."[15] Drowning apotheosizes paralysis. She feels power only when striding huge dams in the desert, in awe of the turbines: supreme power and remoteness from the human ego. Mother and child seldom thrive. Lily's Knight and Julie are selfish and materialistic; Maria's Kate is retarded; Charlotte's Marin and Grace's Gerardo stagger belligerently and unenlightenedly into revolution and sex; Inez's Jessie and Adlai sink into drugs and political posturing. And Didion's women seem trapped between Apollonian and Dionysian men:[16] Everett and Ryder, Les Goodwin and Ivan Costello, Leonard and Warren, Harry Victor and Jack Lovett. Victimization becomes a woman's vision and, curiously enough, self-protection.

Didion's romance becomes paralyzed prophecy, a self nearly destroyed by the world around it, by its own dark dreams. Easy sex satisfies Manichean urges, as radical dualisms tumble into a void and lead to some great cosmic dread. Nihilism stalks every page, and out of it Didion stretches for a palpable metaphorical design in her fiction, a design that must acknowledge the inveterate lack of one. Ordinary experience, the present realities of the social novel, evaporate within the presence of such an all-encompassing, hard-edged, relentless vision of vacuity.

How can an author literally make something out of nothing? How does Didion, in Mark Shorer's estimation, achieve such a performance? Is there, perhaps, more a triumph of style than of insight?[17] "I was influenced by Hemingway when I was 13, 14, 15," Didion explains. "I learned a lot about how . . . a short sentence worked in a paragraph, how a long sentence worked . . . how every word had to matter." *Vogue* taught her to write long and publish short.[18] But she also admits her own impervious perfectionism, the kind that "can take the form of spending most of a week writing and rewriting and not writing a single paragraph."[19] Clearly one first recognizes the terse, spare prose of her fiction and journalism, the tight sense of dread that suggests Emily Dickinson, the insidious underlying menace suggested by the discipline and self-control Harold Pinter wields in his plays. As suggested in *Salvador*, she writes "of grace not simply under pressure but under siege."

The visibility of her verbal performance rests on the photographic recreation of her images. Concrete images, actions, snippets of conversation appear like pure ikons, with the flat, sharp lines that iconography celebrates. It is as if the physically visible world were unaided by reflection or consciousness, presented in its sharply detailed surfaces. In three of her novels, *Play It As It Lays* (1970), *A Book of Common Prayer* (1977), and *Democracy*, Didion admits that images haunted her first, as in many ways they did Faulkner. The story followed as a way of getting at the significance of these images—a woman in a Las Vegas hotel, a woman at the airport,[20] Jack Lovett's staring at Inez Victor on the runway on March 26, 1975—, of trying to penetrate and explore them fully. Much of her fiction seems mesmerized by Sixties "chic"—the clothes, the right fashions, the right hotels, the easy sex and money, as if in some cases the real villains were doubleknit suits and vinyl siding—but the heart of it is built upon the same scaffold epiphanies, those emblematic episodes, that Hawthorne cherished. Each scene becomes a posing on the scaffold, the self in extremis.

The prose and the images reveal Didion's obsessive deliberateness, her excessive control of language in an almost procedural or surgical lucidity. Pressure builds from that damned precision; "the ability to think for one's self depends upon one's mastery of the language."[21] Self without language for Didion is inconceivable; it swallows itself and spouts back only what a decadent and corrupt society feeds it. Each word carries "totemic weight,"[22] each acts its own momentary stay against confusion. Dread batters at the door of the consciousness; the tight skein of language barely prevents it from entering and overwhelming the keep, "a perilous triumph of being over nothingness."[23]

And yet such control contains a spare lyric quality that achieves a biblical cadence and richness in its repetitions, parallels, and doublings. Liturgy faces dread. Litany ritualizes each passing moment and allows it to pass intact. Her "histrionically desolate"[24] style achieves a luminosity because of this ancient shape, because of Didion's "acute sensitivity to cadence, the rising and falling rhythms of words."[25] Such religious rites "help to ward off evil" in the manner of Didion's liking the words of the Episcopal service, the delight in saying them "over and over in my mind."[26] The self marks off its ceremonies in the void, as if Didion were embroidering her spare prose in the manner of Hawthorne's flaming letter.

Cinematic juxtaposition provides the shock and drive of Didion's prose. It is the characteristic technique of her art. As she herself explains, "This particular juxtaposition of the spoken and the unspeakable was eerie and unsettling."[27] It undercuts cause and effect, destroys any seeming surface continuity, and engages both the conscious and the unconscious mind in a continuing struggle, a Manichean match that in most cases suggests the paralysis and terror her heroines embody. Didion has clearly learned her cinematic lessons from Hemingway's prose and Robbe-Grillet's menacingly soulless universe of ominous objects. The emphasis on physical action, the absence by and large of reflection, the objective, economical style, the disconnected episodes with the ellipses between, the montage of murder and motherhood, the carefully controlled point of view with the camera's precision in a graphically condensed Jamesian manner: these indicate the influence of film technique both on the contemporary novel and on Didion's work. For Didion, as in films, montage becomes metaphor; the arrangement of episodes reveals the state of mind of her heroines, of her contemporary world. The abstract and concrete meet head on in her ordering of images, her expert cutting from scene to scene, the discontinuous juxtapositions of a shattered world.

Didion's style, perhaps because of her inveterate celebration of ambiguity, achieves a delicate balance between a need for form and a fear of form, the divisive edge between dream and dread that Tony Tanner describes in his vision of American literature.[28] In their need for form, Didion's heroines choose paralysis as a kind of defense; they hold steady to the litany of language and life to ritualize the emptiness in their lives and thus not only to endure but in some cases actually to prevail, however wounded and imprisoned. In its fear of form the self succumbs to victimization; style is imprisoned in the "hard" cinematic scenes of *Play It As It Lays*, for example, and choice is impossible. Careful repetition breeds both truculence and trance. In both instances style shapes the territory but surpasses mere technique in revealing a contemporary state of soul that registers a shock of recognition.

In her four works of fiction Didion has searched for a particular form to embody her style and vision. In *Run River* (1963) the historical or chronological family saga encapsulates Lily's numbness and morbid sensitivities. *Play It As It Lays* suggests the cinematic style of Updike's *Rab-*

bit, Run: both heroine and reader are trapped in a seemingly merciless present. In *A Book of Common Prayer* one character attempts to witness the significance of another in the prophetic, all-involving pursuit of the best of Faulkner's romances. Didion chooses the same method in *Democracy*, with herself as witness. In each case Didion employs flashbacks to reveal the weight of the past, the doom that haunts her creatures, thus suggesting further parallels to the romantic territory of Hawthorne's fictions. And throughout, a tumbling into the pit of dread is never far off. It is her teetering on the brink that chills and fascinates. And that accounts for her power as a writer.

The basic Manichean confrontation in *Run River* exists between the state of Didion's main character, Lily Knight McClellan, and the very nature of the family chronicle. On the one hand Lily believes that "all the connections had been broken"; on the other hand, the very nature of the family novel involves "the complexities, the down-right complicity, of family love." The former threatens at all times to undercut the latter, reducing historical sweep and involvement to an individualized yet allegorical state of paralysis in a Lily who "would concentrate upon the details while the essence eluded her."

The historical sweep is there, the "closed perfect circle"[29] of the Central Valley, of the Knights and McClellans: Eden and the family seemingly immortally entrenched. Lily Knight marries Everett McClellan, an orderly but blank personality; his sister commits suicide; Lily's father and his mistress die in an auto accident. Neat patterns work themselves out, as Everett shoots the sly opportunist with the "studied smile," Ryder Channing, who has slept with Everett's sister, then his wife; and then he shoots himself. These tight balances of personalities and family disintegration, the collapse of an incestuous order in an agrarian paradise, undercut Didion's more modern belief in "a history of accidents: of moving on and of accidents," despite the thematic import of such human accidents and human frailties undercutting the mythic American redemption out west. The cutting clean from history does not redeem the characters as much as the pride and blindness of such a faith destroy them. The suicides and the abortion reveal a tale of blood and loss that creates fine novelistic patterns of plot, but these very patterns can find no place for Lily's excruciating sense of malaise and disorientation.

Lily remains an enigma, at once "morbidly sensitive" and clinging to every genteel cultural and social cliché she can; a Daddy's girl, "no

good around people," and even a "deaf mute" with "scared eyes" that
lure men to her bed as easily and as unthinkingly as if she were perform-
ing any ordinary, unimportant daily ritual. She remains a fascinating blank,
a precursor to Maria Wyeth, Charlotte Douglas, and Inez Victor, full
of imagined disasters, presenting a precarious composure to the world,
a maimed consciousness spawned in this closed Edenic valley world where
hops and the river are everything.

At the heart of Lily's suffering lies the recognition that "nothing we
did matters to me. Nothing touched Everett and nothing touched me.
. . . It did not seem to matter any more who had first resented whom,
or for what. It did not seem to matter what either of them did any more:
it could begin out of nothing." Everett notices the moment he kills Channing that a dead sameness underscores all things: "Channing pitching
forward over the log, his flashlight rolling into the water: they were events
of equal importance." It is as if both Lily and Everett are stillborn, empty
husks masquerading as human beings. And yet the historical sequence
of the novel, so artfully devised out of flashbacks which are sandwiched
between the present moment of Everett's murder of Ryder Channing
and Everett's suicide (August 1959 in sections One and Three, 1938-1959
in the middle section), contradicts such assertions. If historical sequence
is so important, how can such characters remain so virtually untouched
by it, strange creatures stranded in a relentless chronology of waste?

Lily, Everett, and Ryder Channing are described as characters who
"seemed afflicted with memory." As Lily wonders, "Was there ever
in anyone's life span a point free in time, devoid of memory, a point
when choice was any more than the sum of all the choices gone before?"
But memory does not bear down upon her consciousness so much as her
awareness of her own apparent blankness does, "whoever she was now."
History does not so much leave its mark as evaporate in the stone-cold
glare of Lily's paralyzed state. Something affects her deeply, but history
it is not. All events pass before and around her with that dazed sameness
that recognizes no distinctions, feels no real pain or joy.

Snakes haunt Didion's failed Eden, and corruption bubbles in the blood
of those Valley families who think of themselves as the Elect, but history
leaves no mark, as sex does its scar. Memory reflects only the strange
paralysis that has always been there since before time began, the broken
connections of a vacuum so apparent that it seeks out only its own further isolation, not the complexities of any family saga. Form and content

fail to merge, although Didion's first novel is skillful, powerful in parts, and reveals that developing sense of dread that nearly explodes and immobilizes her famous second book.

So skillfully cinematic and contrived is *Play It As It Lays* that no one has really noticed how monochromatic it is, how close it comes to stopping dead in its tracks, steeped in the unbroken circuit of exhaustion, spiritual paralysis, dread, and vacuous persistence. Maria Wyeth's mindlessness suggests both conscious surrender and collapse. The two become so much a part of one another that one cannot really distinguish them. No need to ask what makes Iago evil; Maria has lived the motiveless or multi-motivated malignancy. And why has she? Well, why not? A chic flippancy almost sinks the ship, but Didion's superbly crafted fragments and juxtapositions, her way of submerging plot in the separate and disconnected pieces the reader must pursue, and her making the novel a flashback for the institutionalized Maria to recreate in order to find out what has happened, push the fractured narrative into the realm of ultimate mystery and the darker self-projections of romance.

Maria chooses to avoid connections: "I am working very hard at not thinking about how everything goes. I . . . keep my mind in the now." Not exactly; she reveals certain facts without any possible theories to shore them up against her ruin, viewing "the pursuit of reasons" as a task her careful sanity cannot handle. If she thinks "none of it adds up," Didion's juxtapositions will attempt to prove otherwise, and the reader will become a participant in the puzzle, another consciousness and point of view amid these tangles of modernist and post-modernist art.

Maria is the recognizable Didion persona. Dread threatens: "Her life had been a single sexual encounter, one dreamed fuck, no beginnings or endings, no point beyond itself." All patterns crumble: "In the whole world there was not as much sedation as there was instantaneous peril." Apocalypse looms, and a relentless Calvinistic-Manichean ethos prevails: "Maria did not particularly believe in rewards, only in punishments, swift and personal." Unpardonable sins haunt her. The abortion appalls and derails her, reappearing constantly in her dreams. Yet she survives, she hangs on: "After everything I remain Harry and Francine Wyeth's daughter and Benny Austin's godchild. . . . You call it as you see it, and stay in the action. . . . I know what 'nothing' means, and keep on playing." Perhaps the desert spa has worked mysteriously with its "restorative power of desolation." Perhaps her father's sorry optimism—"What came in on the next roll would always be better than what went out on the last"—has seen her through, even despite the wasteland aura of Silver Wells, Nevada.

Evil stalks the California landscape. Good seems knowable only by its absence. Didion has created a slick cinematic hell in which snakes lurk under rocks ready to strike and one can only go with the flow in all its relative, arbitrary meanderings:[30] "Life itself was a crap game . . . [but] overturning a rock was apt to reveal a rattlesnake." How do you know when to play and when to pass? Silver Wells reveals no answer to this inherent contradiction in Harry Wyeth's cynical outlook, despite his continued and irascible hope. Gang bangs, abortions, retarded children, lazy sexual intrigue, the anesthetization of driving on the freeway, BZ's homosexuality and suicide, Helene's selfishness, Carter's remoteness and kindness, Maria's mother's death: these snakes are cruelly recognized, coral or king.

And California epitomizes this state of soul: "The water in the pool was always 85 degrees." Desert heat flattens the mind: "The stillness and clarity of the air seemed to rob everything of its perspective, seemed to alter all perception of depth." Maria inhabits "the hard white empty core of the world," both within and without. Physical landscape and psychological mindscape merge and reflect one another. The territory of romance thrives in such a haunted place. Maria "was watching the dead still center of the world, the quintessential intersection of nothing."

Maria is well versed in cinematic terms and devices. She speaks of scenarios, cuts, images in a freeze frame, set-ups, almost in the manner of Carter, the director, who offers "some scenes" at the beginning of the book as a way of knowing Maria but admits that he can find no order, no pattern. On the one hand these film techniques constantly distance her from her own life by conscious choice; on the other they suggest an unreal realm of theatre and Hollywood dialogues that disconnect her from herself all too completely, all too habitually. Is this merely the case of a would-be actress having taken her threadbare career too seriously in all its techniques and jargon? Didion's emblematic episodes break through the slick cinematic surfaces and at the same time the mindless snippets of conversation reveal how anesthetized and habitualized her characters have become. The style both reveals and embalms them, presents and imprisons. They remain cinematic selves, trapped in "life-styles," tied so completely to certain acceptable outward display and social performance that without them they are nothing. Interior selves, if there are any, evaporate. They become what Maria chooses to become: "Her mind was a blank tape, imprinted daily with snatches of things overheard, fragments of dealers' patter, the beginnings of jokes and odd lines of song lyrics."

Maria survives, emerges slowly from the California paralysis of consciousness, but is still its victim. Like Rabbit in Updike's *Rabbit, Run* she exists in a perpetual present, redeemed by her looking back to present the facts as she knows them, even though she acknowledges, "I mean maybe I was holding all the aces, but what was the game?" The beginning of some awareness on her part—"You are all making me sick," she declares at one point—comes early: "What she was sorry about seemed at once too deep and too evanescent for any words she knew, seemed so vastly more complicated than the immediate fact that it was perhaps better left unraveled." And yet is this recognition or evasion? The precarious balance continues to teeter.

Acute notions of good and evil survive and fuel Maria's choice of stupor and her surrender to it. Hell remains a cinematic image, almost the cinematic style itself, but Didion's moral perspective does not lapse. For Didion's vision, however, the form of *Play It As It Lays* suggests a dead end. The state of soul is so complete, so much a product and process of her California landscape and of Maria Wyeth's own fears and despairs as a woman and an actress, so much a reflection and creation of the hard cinematic style itself with which Didion conjures up her "hard white empty core of the world," that the book achieves a kind of paralysis in its own right. Jettisoning Darwinian logic, that pursuit of reasons and connections, Maria arrives at some still sad point in time that leads nowhere. The snake consumes its own tail. Manichean conflicts evaporate, as the Manichean imprisonment in the world nearly triumphs. "Only certain facts" will finally not cure Maria Wyeth; they may only establish her final victimhood. And yet the key is in her surviving, no matter the psychic cost. And yet again she winds up playing solitaire in the sun, watching a hummingbird. She is even playing her possible recuperation as it lays and in doing so awaits only another rock, another snake, another roll of the dice. But this time even Silver Wells no longer exists.

If Lily Knight remains buried in a historical novel, the kind that does not do her angst justice, and if Maria Wyeth seems too "up front" in her cinematic novel, raising questions about the author's own aesthetic distance, in *A Book of Common Prayer* Didion finds the perfect means to preserve both her vision of paralysis and an aesthetic distance that presents and tries to penetrate it. Grace Tabor Strasser-Mendana plays Ishmael to Charlotte Douglas's Ahab, Carraway to Gatsby, Rosa Coldfield to Faulkner's Sutpen. Charlotte lives the dazed and numbing consciousness of a Didion heroine; Grace attempts to witness the significance of it, thus placing *A Book of Common Prayer* in that significant range of American literature which includes the person of action and the person of reflection, the doer and the pursuer of wider meanings.[31] Design hurries to catch up with the designer; speculation pursues image. And thus the reader becomes participant as well in Grace's attempts to fathom the nearly fathomless personality of the elusive and enigmatic Charlotte Douglas.

The facts themselves are strange. Charlotte flees from two husbands, just walks away from them, in much the same manner as Maria Wyeth, leaving, then circling back, then abandoning them again. Leonard Douglas, the calm, rational lawyer, is involved in running guns to would-be revolutionaries. Warren Bogart pursues Charlotte relentlessly, full of lust, a corrosive wit, too much liquor, and terminal cancer. Daughter Marin, whom Charlotte pretends is her loving and wonderful child, rigs bombs for a pseudo-revolutionary group in California and is in hiding, a casualty of the Sixties. The F.B.I. pursues Charlotte; she flees the country with a baby she knows will die, and it does; she stumbles blithely into sexual liaisons with Grace's brother Victor and revolutionary son Gerardo, with no inkling of the political consequences of the cyclical upheavals in Boca Grande. In the background brother Victor vies with brother Antonio for the presidency of the country, while Gerardo traffics with Bebe Chicago, a notorious homosexual conspirator who is vaguely connected with Leonard Douglas—perhaps. The facts alone reveal the inevitable breakdown and corruption of older, more stable values: the family, American life, individual identity, loyalties, suburban mores, California pieties.

Through it all Charlotte maintains publicly that all is well. She and Marin are "inseparable"; so too are she and Warren and she and Leonard. She tells personal anecdotes in which "every memory was 'lyrical,' every denouement 'hilarious,' and sometimes 'ironic' as well," anecdotes that have nothing to do with the truth, as if she existed in a permanent daze, erasing what went before, walking away from complicated situations as if not thinking about them would extricate her from them permanently.

Grace begins to suspect that there was "a certain interior logic in her inability to remember much."

Certainly Charlotte's personality remains as strange as the facts of her circumstances. Her life becomes a series of "revisions and erasures." She talks as if she had no specific history of her own. For Grace Charlotte's character only "shimmer[s]"; it never comes together in any conscious way. "So entirely underwater did Charlotte live her life" that even her promiscuity suggests only her own "reflexively seductive" manner. "Charlotte had no idea that anyone else had ever been afflicted by what she called the 'separateness'. . . . I think I have never known anyone who led quite so unexamined a life." Oblivion becomes her allegorical emblem, and the genteel cliché-ridden language she uses fails to mask it. Some shock of recognition occurs. For thirty-four hours she administers inoculations during a cholera epidemic in Boca Grande and is appalled when further vaccine is destroyed by would-be revolutionary soldiers: "I think I loved Charlotte in that moment as a parent loves the child who has just fallen from a bicycle, met a pervert, lost a prize, come up in any way against the hardness of the world," Grace comments. And perhaps Charlotte's refusal to leave the country, a decision which is tantamount to committing suicide, has something to do with her finally deciding not to run anywhere else, despite the incipient declaration of her own death: "I walked away from places all my life and I'm not going to walk away from here." Such a determination seems the most positive act of her checkered career and at the same time reveals those "revisions and erasures" that lead only to a final paralysis.

Charlotte also represents a certain female vision: "She had tried only to rid herself of her dreams, and those dreams seemed to deal only with sexual surrender and infant death, commonplaces of the female obsessional life. We all have the same dreams." This suggests similar obsessions in Lily Knight and, in particular, in Maria Wyeth. The idea of sex scarring "the female with the male's totem" adds to this distinctly female vision of the world in Didion's eyes.

But Charlotte occupies a larger, more mythic landscape as well. As "la norteamericana" she stalks the airport of Boca Grande as a symbol of the American spirit and faith. Didion makes this clear: "As a child of the western United States she had been provided as well with faith in the value of certain frontiers on which her family had lived . . . of thrift, industry and the judicial system, of progress and education, and in the generally upward spiral of history. . . . She was immaculate of history, innocent of politics. There were startling vacuums in her store of common knowledge. . . . She understood that something was always going on in the world but believed that it would turn out all right. She believed the world to be peopled with others like herself."

Once again Didion indicts the American myth, the Western faith in self-renewal and ultimate progress, suggesting that Charlotte's "blankness" may be the result of such "innocence," such ignorance of other places, of darker emptier landscapes. The American myth has warped her; her self-withdrawal and self-indulgence lead inevitably to social suicide, to child revolutionaries in destructive times. Her daughter attended an Episcopal day school whose aim included " 'the development of a realistic but optimistic attitude,' and it was characteristic of Charlotte that whenever the phrase 'realistic but optimistic' appeared in the school communique she read it as 'realistic and optimistic.' " Her solipsism, her noninterest in Boca Grande politics, confirms in her own mind that she can in no way become involved in them: mind cancels out matter. She goes daily to the airport, blindly, waiting for a plane she has no knowledge of. Escape beckons as a constant. Her own vacuous presence can become a political liability; her innocence can—and does—betray her into political involvement, and in fact it finally kills her. The illusions of family, the future, of historical progress, evaporate in Boca Grande; the American Adam/Eve falls again, unknowingly this time, unwittingly, and ancient religious rites, the secret ceremonies of human motive and growth/decline, destroy her.

Grace Tabor Strasser-Mendana prides herself on her inability to uphold illusions: "Unlike Charlotte I learned early to keep death in my line of sight, keep it under surveillance, keep it on cleared ground and away from any brush where it might coil unnoticed." Death and wisdom in the image of the serpent: ancient gnosis: Charlotte's Manichean opposite— at first. Grace harbors no romantic fantasies. She is the clear-thinking, cold-eyed rationalist, as opposed to Charlotte, "the outsider of romantic sensibility." Thus she likes and craves the flat hard light of Boca Grande, the exposure of unpleasant truths: "How flat it is, how harsh and still. How dead white at noon." And yet she too has lost a child to the mesmerizing influences of revolutionary conspiracies and easy sex.

Boca Grande symbolizes Grace's state of soul. Here once again is Didion's "amniotic stillness," the dead center of the world, "the equatorial view" where everything "is relentlessly 'the same,' " where contrasts are swallowed and vanish, "the very cervix of the world," the place of ultimate "weightless isolation." Boca Grande suggests Didion's El Salvador, where "the place remains marked by the meanness and discontinuity of all frontier history, by a certain frontier proximity to the cultural zero." "The colorful Latin juxtaposition of *guerilleros* and colonels" suggests change, but that is only superficial. "The bush and the sea do not reflect the light but absorb it, suck it in, then glow morbidly." One thinks of Melville's demonic blankness and bleached-out nothingness. "A banana palm is no more or less 'alive' than its rot." The Carribbean essence, "volatile with conflicting pieties and intimations of sexual perfidy," a Manichean stew of perpetual conflict, evaporates in this no-man's-land of the soul. *Guerilleros* are merely pawns. Power operates above and around them in cyclical, almost seasonal patterns. The labyrinthine struggles of family feuds, political corruption, and economic injustice crumble before the ineradicable sameness and desolate, cold-eyed vision of inevitable doom and decay that Grace espouses. The rot in her body reflects the rot of Boca Grande, as the present appears "to sink as tracelessly as the past." Hawthorne's "neutral territory" becomes this static, paralyzed land, where "there are no real points in knowing one way or another."

Grace's faith in logic, rational process, and cause and effect has been shaken but not destroyed: "I am an anthropologist who lost faith in her own method. . . . I did not know why I did or did not do anything at all." Biochemistry offers deliverance: "Fear of the dark is an arrangement of fifteen amino acids." If Charlotte sees herself mired in a tale of passion, Grace sees only delusion, herself "a student of delusion, a prudent traveler. . . . The world will reveal itself." Meaning can be discerned: "As usual I favor a mechanical view." Systematic study will save us: "The most reliable part of what I know, derives from my training in human behavior." Thus for Charlotte, "I will be her witness. . . . My own letter from Boca Grande shall be my witness to Charlotte Douglas." Thus has she legitimized her voice as a narrator: "We are uneasy about a story until we know who is telling it. . . . 'the narrator' plays no motive role in this narrative, nor would I want to." Her relentless logic will reveal the truth of the matter as she pursues Charlotte's tale, although she admits early in the book that she will do so "only insofar as the meaning of that sojourn continues to elude me."

Elude her it does. Logic leads nowhere: "I also recognize the equivocal nature of even the most empirical evidence." Charlotte disturbs her; the fact that "maybe there is no motive role in this narrative" disturbs her even more. She begins to draw parallels between herself and Charlotte: "It occurred to me that my attempt to grow roses and a lawn at the equator was a delusion worthy of Charlotte Douglas." She shares Charlotte's obsessional female dreams. She, too, has lost a child. She suddenly recognizes that she knows less about her husband than she thought, despite her conviction of inevitable and eternal corruption: "I prided myself on listening and sewing and I had never even heard or seen that Edgar played the same games Gerardo played." Her visions of corruption begin to reflect and parallel Charlotte's dazed erasures of innocence. She admits finally, "I am more like Charlotte than I thought I was." Perhaps she has lived too long at the equator. If she once declared, "I revised my impressions to coincide with reality. Charlotte did the reverse," at the end of her witnessing she is no longer so certain: "I have not been the witness I wanted to be."

Grace moves from measurement to mystery, from the testimony of an "objective," logical spectator to the prophecy of an involved, mystified participant in Charlotte's story. The apparent Manichean conflicts between corruption and innocence, North American ignorance and Central American shrewdness, passion and delusion slowly erode, as Grace tells her tale. If Charlotte's decision to remain in Boca Grande reveals some recognition on her part about human limitations, the boundaries of necessity beyond her romantic fantasies, and the awareness of some kind of ineradicable evil in the world (even if it be her own suicidal stance and final paralysis, a culmination of all that is Charlotte, as it is all that is not), then Grace experiences a kind of opposite recognition, a sense of ultimate mystery and awe in the face of human character and motive, a decided doubt about the ability of logic, scientific theories and necessary conceptual schemes to explain the realities of another human being.

Grace begins as a novelist and ends as a romancer: testimony gives way to prophecy, for she has witnessed as a prophet has, recreating and reproducing a life in all its ambiguities and intimations, not as the fact-oriented prosecutor of some crime. The two women share a sense of personal growth and awareness, however ultimately ambiguous in the finally unknowable Charlotte Douglas and ultimately mysterious in the final witnessing of Grace Strasser-Mendana.

Grace believes that "the consciousness of the human organism is car-ried in its grammar." It is Didion speaking of the romance as an extension of self, as a particular, limited point of view. Never has her style been more liturgical, more full-bodied in its use of doublings, juxtapositions, repetitions, the cadences literally of *the* Book of Common Prayer. Certain lines act as a kind of Greek choral response throughout the book, turning up again and again at different times from different perspectives, adding up to a kind of litany of despair: "How could I leave you . . . somebody cuts you . . . I've never been afraid of the dark. . . ." The repetitiveness at once reveals Grace's forcing herself to come closer to the "heart" of Charlotte's story, and at the same time becomes a kind of defensive mechanism in its own right, prayers in the dark, lines to paper over the abyss that will never disgorge its secrets:

> There had been words about it.
> There had been words between Leonard and Warren about it in the room at the Ochsner Clinic but she could barely remember the words.
> There had been words in the room at the Ochsner Clinic and there had been peonies.

> We could have been doing this all our lives, Warren said.
> We should be doing this all our lives, Warren said.
> We should have done this all our lives, we should do this all our lives.
> The verb form made a difference. . . .

> I have noticed that it is never enough to be right.
> I have noticed that it is necessary to be better.

Words become chants. Chants both mesmerize and particularize, consoling the lost soul in the music of calm repetition to block out thought, forcing the lost soul to penetrate the specific details of the moment by trying to enunciate the exact thought or image, and to encourage, therefore, the creation of significant patterns of experience and understanding. Words and peonies, interchangeable to Charlotte. Verb forms tyrannize and evaporate in memory. But the morality of a better consciousness pursues Grace, despite the flat hard light of her corrupted vision of reality. Perception itself, the heart of modernist art, represents the closest any man or woman can come to the "truth." Facts, personalities, mythic patterns, landscapes, conceptual schemes: each leads on only to further mystery and wonder, the ambiguous legacy of Hawthorne's romance.

One of the most remarkable things about *Democracy* is that Didion essentially plays herself. She has become the Grace Tabor Strasser-Mendana of the book. "Call me the author," she proclaims in the second chapter. Shades of Melville's Ishmael! And like Grace she moves from what begins as "an essentially reportorial technique" to the more involved and mystified role of the romancer: "What I had . . . was a study in provincial manners, in the acute tyrannies of class and privilege by which people assert themselves against the tropics; Honolulu during World War Two, martial law, submariners and fliers." What she becomes is the romancer hypnotized by the emblematic encounter between Jack Lovett and Inez Victor, a moment fraught with mystery and peril, filled with inscrutabilities and elusive secrets. The image comes upon her in all its hypnagogic fascination: "Still: there is a certain hour between afternoon and evening when the sun strikes horizontally between the trees and that island and that situation are all I see. Some days at this time one aspect of the situation will seem to me to yield the point, other days another. I see Inez Christian Victor in the spring of 1975 . . . I see Jack Lovett watching her. . . ."

As to Melville's Pierre, images come to Didion the narrator "palpable to the senses, but inscrutable to the soul." She finds it "difficult to maintain definite convictions," as she abandons, scuttles, and jettisons images, ideas, and events in the process to clarify her focus and zero in on the dark heart of the matter.

And that dark heart remains the inscrutability of human motive, the "emotional solitude" and "detachment" of Jack Lovett, his seemingly total self-control and near-demonic will "devoid of ethical content altogether"; the "secretiveness" of Inez and Jack together: "They were equally evanescent, in some way emotionally invisible; unattached, wary to the point of opacity, and finally elusive." And Inez's daughter Jessie, another of Didion's doomed daughters, shares that "certain incandescent inscrutability, a kind of luminous gravity." Here is Hawthorne's heart of darkness, the mysterious isolated soul at the elusive core of things.

The visitor to Salvador learns to concentrate only on the stray detail, the ironic encounter, "to the exclusion of past or future concerns, as in a prolonged amnesiac fugue." Likewise the seemingly indifferent Inez never looks back, smolders with anger, remains passively detached and virtually impenetrable, the hallmark of Didion's dazed heroines. For her the "major cost of public life," of living life in the celebrity camera's eye, is memory, and normal life beyond the camera's range remains "remote." "Then trot out the smile and move easily through the cabin, babe, OK?" her husband's adviser Billy Dillon tells her, as Inez "had come to view most occasions as photo opportunities." She moves in the amnesiac's world of role-playing moments; celebrity has stolen whatever soul she had. She moves with the wariness of a somnambulist, not through dooms of love but through the vacuous, meaningless, photographable world of the celebrity.

And Didion pursues her relentlessly in her reportorial guise, looking for clues, for moral guidelines. She achieves only "this novel of fitful glimpses," that romantic structure of scaffold epiphanies, of Inez dancing on the St. Regis roof, of Jack looking at her, of the murder scene. Like Inez she searches for "correspondences . . . as if they were messages intended specifically for her, evidence of a narrative she had not suspected. She seemed to find these tenuous connections extraordinary." She searches for "a higher predictability, a more complex pattern discernible only *after the fact*" (italics mine). "Find the beast in the jungle, the figure in the carpet. . . . The reason why." Which leads her to that dark inscrutability of the human condition, the heart of Hawthorne's romance. And as in *Salvador* "even the most apparently straightforward event takes on . . . elusive shadows, like a fragment of retrieved legend." She enters Grace's romantic realm, becomes the prophetic witness of some ultimate mystery: "It has not been the novel I set out to write, nor am I exactly the person who set out to write it."

Narrative itself shatters and teeters, a calculated mix of post-modernist self-consciousness and the romancer's grappling with impenetrability, akin to Hawthorne's "multiple devices" and self-generating allegorical contradictions. "The heart of narrative" may be "a certain calculated ellipsis," but Didion describes her lack of faith in coherence, in cause and effect, in inevitability. It is the spell she wants: "Look down and that prolonged spell . . . snaps, and recovery requires that we practice magic. We keep our attention fixed on the wire," a remarkable feat requiring

"certain objects, talismans, props," the stuff of the romancer's incantation to keep the mystery intact. Words, images, encounters she returns
to again and again, part pursuit, part self-hypnosis, the territory of the
dark romance.

All the romancer's "tools" are on view in *Democracy*. The book opens
at dawn "during those Pacific tests": the beginning of the apocalyptic
nuclear age in the remote Pacific. In the spring of 1975 the collapse and
evacuation of Saigon are under way: "The world that night was full of
people flying from place to place." It is a "lurid phantasmagoria of air
lifts and marines on the roof and stranded personnel and tarmacs littered
with shoes and broken toys." No longer a "neutral territory" surely,
but romance's remote region of the spirit.

Language creates its other-worldly spell on the very first page in its
triadic litany: ". . . something to see. Something to behold. Something
that could almost make you think you saw God, he said." In the first
full paragraph words such as "never," "pink," "wet," "smelling like
flowers," "air," "gardenias" are repeated like some religious chant to
keep the mind intact, the senses together, the mystery pursued. The biblical
repetitions soothe and trouble, as if Didion were searching for an ultimate
source and at the same time recognizing the disruptions in her, in time,
that prevent ultimate revelation: "I read such reports over and over again,
pinned in the repetitions and dislocations of the breaking story as if in
the beam of a runaway train." Early on she tells us, "This is a hard story
to tell." And actual history—of Saigon, Honolulu, nuclear explosions,
uprisings in Jakarta—buttresses her narrative, anchors it in apocalyptic
contemporary times, as Hawthorne's recreation of his witchcraft-haunted
past anchored his.

Lovett manages to rescue Jessie from a collapsing Saigon, but the tale
leaves us with failed rescues, ultimate isolations, Inez's "penance" with
the refugees in Kuala Lumpur, the murder of a daughter and possibly
her lover by her father. Again this is the world of Manichean romance,
a tale of a thoroughly corrupt realm like some dark prison in which glimmerings of spirit, of possible moral actions, result in murder, abandonment, and flight. Manicheism has always revealed that deep urge to flee
the world. The twins, Jessie and Adlai, like mother and father, recreate
the dark doubling of such romances. And obsession mirrors possession
in the characters of Lovett, the self as cause of the ultimate deal, and

Inez, the self as function of some dark design of lust and surrender.

At one point Didion suggests that there are "similarities in style, and presumably in ideas of democracy (the hypothesis being that the way a writer constructed a sentence reflected the way that writer thought)." "Consider the political implications of both the reliance on and the distrust of abstract words, consider the social organization implicit in the use of the autobiographical third person." She quotes George Orwell, who reminds her of Hemingway, in relation to their reliance upon and distrust of abstract words, and goes on to quote Henry Adams (whose own novel *Democracy* displayed the corruption of the America of his era), who "struck a note that would reverberate in Norman Mailer," both of whom relied upon the autobiographical third person in *The Education of Henry Adams* and *The Armies of the Night*, to name only two particular instances. Style and thoughts about democracy do reflect one another and reveal the essential allegorical lineaments of the tale.

The Christians, the ironically named family of *Democracy*, display with relish the "colonial impulse." They are "prosperous and self-absorbed . . . sufficiently good-looking and . . . confident and . . . innocent." In short, they are typical Americans, the stuff of legend, and Americans in *Democracy* are slowly "learning lessons in Southeast Asia." In the face of death and grief the American business class serves crackers and keeps up a cocktail-party banter of light conversation and aplomb. Life and death are referred to as not an either/or situation. Congressmen remain radio actors, and the use of drugs becomes "adolescent substance abuse." Innocence, however corrupt, insists on euphemism. As in *Salvador*, Americans rely on appearances, on "dreamwork," on "mirage." "American diction in this situation tends toward the studied casual, the can-do, as if sheer cool and Bailey bridges could shape the place up." Language becomes the art of persuasion, the act of advertising and ultimate success. Billy Dillon guides all of Harry Victor's and Inez's actions in the persistent camera's eye.

But corruption confounds such disguise. Slowly, carefully Didion peals away the American rhetoric and exposes the rot beneath, the labyrinthine business duels between Wendell Omura, Dwight Christian, and Jack Lovett. Democracy is exposed, at least in its American guise, as riddled with corruption, international commerce, shadowy agencies in cahoots with the likes of Jack Lovett, media celebrity, the inherent apocalypse of the nuclear age, the thin layer of American belief in its own "innocence" and "can-do" faith. Didion applies her moral scalpel to such hideously diseased flesh.

And the characters play their assigned allegorical roles, beyond the murkier, impenetrable depths of Jack, Inez, Jessie, and the thwarted "stubborn loneliness" of Inez's mother, Carol Christian. Harry Victor displays the "obtuse confidence" of the politician constantly on the make. He mirrors Secretary of State Thomas Enders's belief, in *Salvador*, that every disaster and collapse is in some way an example of "nascent democratic institutions." Paul Christian, Inez's father, becomes the "romantic outcast," the self-described victim of the Christian family's implacable business deals. He attacks the company, Christcorp, and murders his daughter and Wendell Omura in a self-declared crusade akin to Paul Hammer's in Cheever's *Bullet Park*, a moral act to puncture the complacency of corruption. His brother Dwight stands for the cold, ruthless businessman, the one who will wheel and deal wherever it takes him, who in discussing his niece's funeral service does not want the Twenty-third Psalm used in it: "Passive crap, the Lord is my shepherd. . . . No sheep in this family." And Janet Christian, stung by her mother's abandoning her and Inez, remains imprisoned within the "veneer of provincial gentility," only to die at her father's hand. The allegory is completed by Inez's American faith in the "record of individual triumphs over a hostile environment," that belief in a special "American exemption" from the dark places of human evil and history that places Didion in the same thematic categories as Hawthorne, Melville, Mailer, and Oates. The American exemption provides the mythic certainties that underlie the "untouchable" Christian family, but it does not and cannot save them from ultimate disaster, the basic inscrutability of human motives, and the collapsing towers of history's apocalyptic spectacle.

Didion's developing "gnosis" is the romancer's stock in trade. Her vision of the self, her carefully drawn polarities, especially in *A Book of Common Prayer* and *Democracy*, the allegorical dualisms of her characters and her landscapes, the sense of the past as a doom that cannot be escaped, the force of the psychological obsessions, compulsions, and guilts that drive her characters, the dreamlike/nightmarish place of her tales, however physically recognizable, and the splendid visionary style, part litany, part cinematic juxtaposition, suggest the still unexhausted wellspring from which Hawthorne created his romances. Whether located in the Western mind, the American spirit, a religious vision, personal psychologies, historical eras with the sense of centers not holding, in the sense of old values broken and scattering, these certain "Hawthornian" traits continue to persist in contemporary American fiction. Hawthorne was the first to deal with them in his American romances. And for whatever complex and ultimately mysterious reasons, he still casts a long, long shadow.

TEN

Hawthorne and the Sixties: Careening on the Utmost Verge

WHAT WOULD Hawthorne have made of the "literary disruptions"[1] in the more experimental and daring fictions of the Sixties and Seventies? How would he have viewed such writers as John Barth, Thomas Pynchon, John Hawkes, Jerzy Kosinski, Kurt Vonnegut, Donald Barthelme, Robert Coover, to lump these names simplistically, for the sake of argument, as the awkwardly phrased "post-modernists"?

In his book on the writers of the Sixties, Raymond Olderman makes a strong case for linking them to the traditions of the American romance and seeing them as an extension of that tradition. They too mix fact and fiction in their "explosion of the ordinary by the fabulous." They too use "two-dimensional characters . . . and a continued hint of the mythic, allegorical, and symbolistic." They create fables, self-conscious tales about the nature of modern society, revealing "the fear of some mystery within fact itself that holds power over us."[2]

These contemporary fables differ, however, from Hawthorne's kind of romance. For one thing these writers generally employ blatant artifice in their yarn-spinning, calling attention to letters answering letters, creating narratives to be shattered and undercut, inventing games, constructing cartoons, reveling in comic-strip slapstick to display the sheer buoyant artificiality of their fiction. Such self-consciousness betrays a mannerist art in which surface action replaces reflection, the result perhaps of cinematic techniques applied to fiction. Characters appear victimized by their environment, produced by savage historical forces bearing down upon them, reduced to cartoon folk, the automatons of a behaviorist outlook and psychology. However funny, however battered, these figures reveal none of the psychological complexities of Hawthorne's characters. They react to a mad consumerism and preen and strut like television-commercial creatures, whether figures of fun or of villainy. At times the authors seem more interested in constructing their vision of a savage apocalyptic capitalism, of a sensual desire run amuck, of sheer brutal survival instincts and cliché-ridden babble than in creating more complex characters. Stick figures inhabit a terrifying landscape, puppets strung up to visions of evil militarists, collectivist societies, corrupt politics.

The post-modernist emphasis on fragmentation as form recreates a primal chaos, an open-ended arbitrary universe in which nearly every value is upended and sabotaged. "Conspiracy is both Deity and Demon"[3] in this thoroughly Manichean world, the world of Hawkes's landscapes of dream and desire, of Pynchon's blitzes and Kosinski's stark realm of survival of the fittest, of Coover's outrageously funny all-American anti-heroes. People are powerless. The individual is mauled by social mechanics. Demonic visions reign supreme, beautifully, artfully done but more one-dimensional in their blackness than are Hawthorne's ambiguously resonant dark designs. Pynchon's sprocket holes, Kosinski's steps, and Vonnegut's cartoon-chapters disrupt, probe, shatter, and maim the reader's quest for connections. The visions seem so unrelievedly dark, so much the wasteland terror of Eliot's world, that one wonders if Ihab Hassan may not be right when he suggests that the post-modernists as harbingers of blight display "a radical literary imagination in the interest of essentially conservative feelings,"[4] if they are not latter-day Puritans wreaking their vengeance on a society so materialistic that their fiction will completely reproduce the density and claustrophobia of all that materialism.

The age of irony produces its black comedies. Satire, farce, parody, the picaresque, the grotesque: all are in league to distance the reader from these dark visions, in effect to make him feel superior to the stick figures that parade and are quashed before his eyes. A radical doubt disrupts all moral design. People exist only in the roles society screws them into. In attacking the trap of social convention and history, many of these writers seem to imitate that trap, creating self-enclosed, shimmering fictions that evaporate when the last page is turned. Nothing is learned. And irony protects us all, the last wedge of defense, the new sentimentality of our self-conscious materialism.

Clearly these writers produce a Manichean vision more "pure" than

Hawthorne's, and for that reason their fictions, however brilliant the vision, the prose, and the artifice, seem simpler, less "real" than Hawthorne's romances. All reality remains elusive; consequently, illusion follows delusion only to reveal further levels of false self-justification or the Freudian dark depths of sadomasochistic dreams, a lust for sex and death as the final conflagration. Olderman's connections are valuable and point clearly to the antirealistic structures of these fables as an extension of American romance, but just as clearly these fables in their dark simplicities and fragmented texts, in their Manichean starkness, do not—no matter the brilliant artifice—approach Hawthorne's moral and philosophical designs. Poe stands as godfather to these fierce fictions, especially those of Pynchon, Barth, Hawkes, and Kosinski. The spritely humor of Vonnegut, Barthelme, and Coover suggests a sourer Twain, an Ambrose Bierce in contemporary togs. The precarious balance of a Hawthorne, Faulkner, O'Connor, Gardner, Cheever vanishes. And it is that uneasy balance that may be Hawthorne's lasting legacy to the tradition of romance, that "careening on the utmost verge of a precipitous absurdity, and the skill lies in coming as close as possible, without actually tumbling over."[5]

For Hawthorne facts remained stolid, physically visible realities, the tombs of the spirit that had to be overcome, transcended. "The world has sucked me within its vortex; and I could not get back to my solitude again even if I would."[6] The attempt as a romancer was to vault that vortex, to escape becoming "covered with earthly dust . . . by rude encounters with the multitude,"[7] not to submit totally and recreate it: "How much mud and mire many pools of unclean water, how many slippery footsteps and perchance heavy tumbles, might be avoided, if we could but tread six inches above the crust of this world. Physically, we cannot do this; our bodies cannot; but it seems to me that our hearts and minds may keep themselves above moral mud-puddles, and other discomforts of the soul's pathway; and so enjoy the sunshine."[8] Surely the tension in Hawthorne's art emerges from just this confrontation, although his fascination with "moral mud-puddles" held him firm, and once he got his feet wet, he could never get into the sunshine to dry off.

Words too seemed to thwart Hawthorne, reproducing "all sorts of external things, leaving the soul's life and action to explain itself in its own way . . . [used] merely for explaining outward acts."[9] They solidified all too quickly, entrapping "spiritual realities" in the very bulk and heft that trapped them in the physically visible world of nature.

Writing to Sophia as the ardent lover: "Words come like an earthly wall betwixt us. Then our minds are compelled to stand apart and make signals of our meaning."[10] Common ardent-lover remarks, and yet words like facts "compel" minds to stand apart and become only "signals," a code to break. The physical and the spiritual remain at Manichean odds; too much remains "an earth-born vision."[11] Ideas put into words run through Hawthorne's tales "like an iron rod . . . this circumstance gives the narrative a character of monotony."[12] Beyond lurks some phantasmagorical "real self," some ultimate, inviolate mystery, some soul devised of romantic aspiration in some purer state. No wonder facts and scenes, the darker the better, pressed in upon his doubly blasted allegories: at once damned by the very darkness of their vision and doomed as successful allegorical structures.

Hawthorne's invention of the American romance was both an escape from and a submission to his sense of history. He escaped into a dimmer past, where his home-feelings allowed him to undercut the bold factual realities of his earth-bound existence. That "slumbrous withdrawing of myself from the external world"[13] had to take place before his imagination could break free from the world around him. How he wanted "to make the mere words absolutely disappear into the thought,"[14] as the "real" material world disappeared into a dimmer, more shadowy past. The haunted mind conjured up spells triggered in part by the moral physical darkness of the material world, embodied in his sense of the past as shadowy veil, the aura of romance. Facts killed; the imagination, unfettered in gloomier realms, created. To Bridge he wrote: "I would advise you not to stick too accurately to the bare fact, either in your descriptions or narrations; else your hand will be cramped, and the result will be a want of freedom, that will deprive you of a higher truth than that which you strive to attain. Allow your fancy pretty free license, and omit no heightening touches merely because they did not chance to happen before your eyes. If they did not happen, they at least ought—which is all that concerns you. This is the secret of all entertaining travellers."[15] And, one would add, of successful romancers as well. Matters of fact must be linked to the imaginative; both battle for recognition.

And finally, in the realm of romance even facts themselves become suspect: "Every day of my life makes me feel more and more how seldom a fact is accurately stated; how, almost invariably, when a story has passed through the mind of a third person, it becomes, so far as regards the impression that it makes in further repetitions, little better than a falsehood, and this, too, though the narrator be the most truth seeking person in existence. How marvelous the tendency is! . . . Is truth a fantasy which we are to pursue forever and never grasp?''[16] The romancer in full bloom. Faulkner would heartily approve.

Thus Hawthorne subverted historical realities for his own purposes, envisioning a world in the guise of a Manichean morality play, noble if intolerant early heroes against present-day lesser folk, sunk in dissipation and materialistic folly, revolutionary inspirations frozen into social roles and conventions as Christian parable hardened into dogma, the "new" American self in conflict with the frail old human self, guilt-ridden, prideful, sinful: in short, the human condition of the Fall recounted over and over again. The darker, grimmer, lumpier romances, *The Blithedale Romance* and *The Marble Faun*, broke beneath the weight of sin and egoism, caught up in power plays, perched on the edge of the abyss, undercutting the romancer's art almost entirely, fact become word become gloomy legacy become inert fiction or mechanical, novelistic maze. The moral and/or aesthetic equilibrium, the link in the dark design, could not hold, and if the essence of the romance became the embroidery on the "A," the labyrinthine quest for multiple meanings without a final signification, an ultimate freedom and an ultimate dread, then Manichean darkness—as in post-modernist fables—finally won. Perhaps that is why so many contemporary critics have been interested in Hawthorne's last two romances, particularly in the apparent dreamlike shape-shiftings of the faun's mythic tale.

But of course Hawthorne also submitted his romances to history. He used history, or at least the guise of history, to authenticate his own private vision. He "finds" the scarlet letter, "locates" the Pyncheon manse, mentions Brook Farm, lived in Rome: these "facts" he employs to ground his fantasies, to shape and color them. They are the ballast of his fictions, the necessary clay and soil of his neutral territories, talismans of witchcraft, the objects necessary to cast the spell. Duyckinck early admired the linking of seen to unseen, of fact to imagination, when, in fact, it was just as likely that Hawthorne was linking them in the opposite manner, linking his vision to fact to make it appear historically "true" or at least as the stuff of legends passed down from generation to generation. It is this essentially conservative stance that separates Hawthorne from the post-modernists, for whom the fabulous nature of all fact is a matter of imaginative belief.

Hawthorne may also have been conscious of the sexual overtones that existed in the nineteenth century in regard to the literary work of male and female authors. As Ann Douglas suggests, popular fiction in the nineteenth century existed for the most part in "the realm of 'feminine' fantasy," whereas "the realm of 'masculine' reality" was history.[17] We know of Hawthorne's aversion to the "damn'd scribbling women" of his era. His idea of authenticating his romances with elaborate historical settings and backgrounds may have been his way of dissociating himself and his art even further from the likes of Susan Warner and Lucy Larcom.

Hawthorne would probably have understood and sympathized with the fuss over nonfiction novels and "history as a novel, the novel as history" in the Sixties. He could not have freed himself so readily from "the facts" as the fabulators appeared to do, nor would he have succumbed so readily to them as Norman Mailer and Truman Capote seemed to wish to do, or at least to look as though they were doing. So mesmerized was Mailer by the historical convolutions of the Sixties, the sheer apocalyptic fervor of them, that in describing what a novel should be he describes almost exactly what Hawthorne's definition of the romance asserts, namely, that "the novel must replace history at precisely that point where experience is sufficiently emotional, spiritual, psychical, moral, existential, or supernatural . . . that world of strange lights and intuitive speculation."[18] Mailer's novel, though he doesn't seem to realize it, is Hawthorne's romance.

In the first paragraph of The House of the Seven Gables, Hawthorne establishes the historical "authenticity" of his setting, at the same time throwing the shadows of the past around it, at once locating the scene of his romance on firm ground and disconnecting the reader from the ordinary events of the everyday world of the novel:

> Half-way down a by-street of one of our New England towns stands a rusty wooden house, with seven acutely peaked gables, facing towards various points of the compass, and a huge, clustered chimney in the midst. The street is Pyncheon Street; the house is the old Pyncheon House; and an elm-tree, of wide circumference, rooted before the door, is familiar to every town-born child by the title

of the Pyncheon Elm. On my occasional visits to the town aforesaid, I seldom failed to turn down Pyncheon Street, for the sake of passing through the shadow of these two antiquities,—the great elm-tree and the weather-beaten edifice.

The writer creates his spell. He has visited the house. Tree and house are "huge, clustered," "wide," "great." The name Pyncheon is repeated four times as if chanted, conjuring up both a name and a place, as if there were something magical in them, fraught with significance. The house is "old," "rusty," "weather-beaten," and in the second paragraph it affects the romancer "like a human countenance." And to get there one must walk halfway down a bystreet off the beaten path, "passing through the shadow of these two antiquities." The writer is drawn to the spot, the shadow, the face of the old house. And in appearing himself, he displays that attraction to the reader, connects the house, the tree, the past, old New England, and finally "a human countenance." The reader watches the writer make these connections, a man solving a mystery, conjuring up a sacred spot.

Cheever accomplishes the same thing at the beginning of *Bullet Park*: "Paint me a small railroad station then, ten minutes before dark. Beyond the platform are the waters of the Wekonsett River. . . . The setting seems in some way to be at the heart of the matter . . . this is your country—unique, mysterious and vast." The remoteness, the shadowy atmosphere, the setting as "heart of the matter": here romance begins, as it does in the first paragraph of both Wapshot books. Other examples exist in the same tradition. Here is the opening of *Set This House on Fire*: "Sambuco. . . . Aloof upon its precipice, remote and beautifully difficult of access, it is a model of invulnerability . . . ." The first two paragraphs of the novel give Sambuco's guidebook history: the facts are established. And then Styron the romancer creates his landscape. And Oates's *Bellefleur*: "It was many years ago in that dark, chaotic, unfathomable pool of time before Germaine's birth . . . on a night in late September stirred by innumerable frenzied winds, like spirits contending with one another. . . ." The remote setting, the shadows of the past, and the Manichean vision are revealed almost at once.

How different is the opening of Thomas Pynchon's monumental *Gravity's Rainbow*: "A screaming comes across the sky. It has happened before, but there is nothing to compare it to now. It is too late. The Evacuation still proceeds, but it's all theatre. There are no lights inside the cars. No light anywhere . . . it's night. He's afraid of the way the glass will fall— soon—it will be a spectacle: the fall of a crystal palace. But coming down in total blackout, without one glint of light, only great invisible crashing.'' The reader is plunged immediately into a dramatic scene, a cinematic spectacle in its play of light and shadow, a theatre of conspiracy and collapse. We don't know who "he" is. The passage is disconcerting, disconnected; chaos and turmoil thrive on the verge of some apocalyptic event. The author designs the scene but he is nowhere seen. Disconnection and fear replace Hawthorne's spell of connection and hypnotic fascination. Things are shattered and will shatter. All is darkness, including the reader's sense of exactly what is going on. This is almost an "anti-spell," a disorienting presentation, an almost total Manichean darkness without light. The author remains an objective, hidden observer, commenting ironically on the theatrical spectacle of the scene, distant and removed from his character's fear amidst the impending shattering of glass, the end of an era, a crystal palace "coming down in total blackout."

A similar sense of disconnection occurs at the beginning of *Slaughterhouse-Five*, though Vonnegut's lighter touch, his comic distance, almost undercut the darker incidents of his remembering: "All this happened, more or less. The war parts, anyway, are pretty much true. One guy I knew really was shot in Dresden for taking a teapot that wasn't his. Another guy I knew really *did* threaten to have his personal enemies killed by hired gunmen after the war. And so on. I've changed all the names." Even the act of recounting, of telling, is served up with suspicion, the fable doubted from the very beginning, "more or less." Trivia and horror mingle with one another: murder and teapots, followed by Vonnegut's throwaway line about changing all the names. The author visibly detaches himself from his material, as if that is the only way he can confront it. Irony and distance replace Hawthorne's creation of a mesmeric spell. Facts shift and remain unreliable because the narrator is unreliable, for whatever reasons. How unlike the dreamlike openings to John Gardner's *Nickel Mountain* and *The Sunlight Dialogues*. How more like John Hawkes's opening to *Virginie*—"Mine is an impossible story. My journal burns"—or Robert Coover's to *The Public Burning*: "On June 24, 1950, less than five years after the end of World War II, the Korean War begins, American boys are again sent off in uniforms to die for Liberty, and a few weeks later, two New York City Jews, Julius and Ethel Rosenberg, are arrested

by the FBI . . . and it is on the night of their fourteenth wedding an-
niversary, Thursday, June 18, 1953." (And yet Coover considered calling his encyclopedic novel, *An Historic Romance,* described Uncle Sam
as reminding him of "Handsome Frank Pierce, puzzling over the
metaphysical obscurities in the books of his friend Nat Hawthorne," and
at the very beginning of the book referred to one of the pronouncements
of "the Divine Hawthorne": " 'There is a fatality, a feeling so irresisti-
ble and inevitable that it has the force of doom . . . !' ")

How like, too, Joseph Heller's splendid opening to *Something Happened,*
the title itself almost a post-modernist proclamation of elusive facts, illusory realities, a sense of something ominous but not exactly what: "I
get the willies when I see closed doors. . . . the sight of a closed door
is sometimes enough to make me dread that something horrible is happening behind it, something that is going to affect me adversely . . . I
can almost smell the disaster mounting invisibly. . . . Something must
have happened to me sometime." The ironies, the dread, the disconnected
thoughts leading to a premonition of disaster, the uncertainty about just
what has happened or is happening: post-modernist fable certainly, but
not Hawthornian romance. An extension of the romance—the self at the
center, the disconnection from an ordinary world, a mysterious dread
or isolation, the sense of complete Manichean trap—but without Hawthorne's use of historical placement or his sense of the unending, ever-
present New England past of legends, generational morality plays, and
quest for allegorical significances, however "mud-puddled."

Contemporary fiction reflects the Hawthornian split between novel
and romance. Saul Bellow, Philip Roth, John Updike, and Paul Theroux,
to name a few, write novels of character, using fairly straightforward
historical and chronological narrative structures, despite the several
flashbacks and juxtapositions they may create within them. Pynchon,
Coover, Hawkes, and Doctorow, for example, write fables of vision in
which characters are subordinated to the author's more public visions
of society in general, of a world in arbitrary flux, a wasteland, a realm
of ultimate conspiracy. These writers use the fragmented narrative to
recreate their sense of disconnection and turmoil. The latter lies in
Hawthorne's shadow more than the former, however distorted, however
flattened.

And yet we find in Roth's opening of *The Ghost Writer* significant
hints of romance: "It was the last daylight hour of a December after-

noon more than twenty years ago . . . when I arrived at his hideaway to meet the great man. . . . my impression was that E.I. Lonoff looked more like the local superintendent of schools than the region's most original storyteller since Melville and Hawthorne.'' We can recognize the fictional "region" created here, with a tip of the hat to its creator.

Paul Theroux has been heralded as a literary realist in most critical circles. "He has mastered the encounter, the scene, the techniques of blending past and present,'' Frederick Karl suggests, and his observations are chiefly those of a "bemused witness.''[19] There are, however, several recognizable traits of the American romance that one can locate beneath or within the precise fictional realism of his novels: the descriptions of ambiguous American innocence, the Manichean confrontations, the conjuring up of dreams and possession, the exotic settings in unusual and remote places, the shadowed past emerging in gothic details, the intimations of allegorical or at least symmetrical structures in regard to characters and situations. Beyond the gothic vision of such novels as *Girls at Play* (1969) and *The Black House* (1974) and the carefully crafted observations of manners and social conventions in his short stories and in such novels as *The Family Arsenal* (1976) and *Doctor Slaughter* (1984), lies a far greater realm, the more mysterious and ultimately enigmatic moral issues that confront Jack Flowers in *Saint Jack* (1973) and Charles Fox in *The Mosquito Coast* (1982). It is as if romantic elements were submerged in novels of manners, similar perhaps to the psychologically realistic surface of an Updike novel but striking chords and creating scenes that Hawthorne could respond to. Nowhere is this more apparent than in *The Mosquito Coast* (1982).

Charlie Fox, the fourteen-year-old narrator of *The Mosquito Coast* exorcises his fascination for and the burden of his father, an adolescent ritual in which the son recognizes that the father is no longer a god. His sharp poetic eye and reportorial skills miss nothing: the shame, envy, awkward speculation, and eager eye conspire to reveal the truth, slowly and in glimpses: "I was ashamed of Father, who didn't care what anyone thought. And I envied him for being so free. . . . Selfishness had made him clever. He wanted things his way. . . . He thought of himself first!'' It is Charlie who, amidst the wreckage of his father's relentless schemes, begins to see the realities of paradise ("I saw cruelty in the hanging vines and selfishness in their root systems'') at the same time holding onto the glorified image of his father, despite younger brother Jerry's insistence

that he is crazy, despite the mounting horror of his deeds. Slowly disillu-
sion sets in: "It was like the slow death in dreams of being trapped and
trying to scream without a voice box." It is like seeing Honduras from
a distance, before the cruel reality of the place sets in: "The view from
the ship had been like a picture, but now we were inside that picture."
The town at night suggests "magic—the halos on old lampposts . . . the
snuffle of traffic," but in the morning the town "was cracked and
discolored and mobbed by people actually screaming above the braying
car horns. There was no magic now." Charlie's maturation destroys his
childhood faith.

Allie Fox inhabits Theroux's novel like a striding colossus with feet
of clay. He is Yankee ingenuity run amock who believes that "man is
God," that God created an imperfect world that he must set to rights:
"Nature is crooked. I wanted right angles and straight lines." He howls
and rages about an America of junk food and drug addicts, a place of
scavengers and savages. He will be the God to salvage his survival, usurp-
ing the deity's role, pulling his family out of Massachusetts and floating
them into the jungles of Honduras to erect his own Xanadu, his sur-
vivalist's camp. Fox turns self-reliance into obsession. "From will power
alone, so it seemed, he had made the pleasant valley appear." Becoming
his own derelict god, a robber baron of his sons' souls, he lusts for do-
minion everywhere on his own inventor's terms, a modern Ahab seeking further wilderness to conquer and cultivate: "I want a real backwater.
Solitary. Uninhabited. An empty corner. That's why we're here! If it's
on a map, I can't use it." Mammoth ego stalks ultimate emptiness to
enjoy its full expanded powers; a rampant imperialistic nihilism lurks within
the crazed compulsion to invent, reinvent, move on to darker corners.
He lies, murders, drags his family up river, destroys a missionary's plane,
and blows up his generator. From fire he produces ice; from his own
fiery self-certainty—the mad center of the American myth—he produces
destruction and devastation.

Romantic elements surface within this Manichean confrontation between the Foxes, between the idealized father and the mad inventor—
"I'm Doctor Frankenstein!"—"I'm the last man!"—within the psychologically realistic disillusionment of adolescence. The Mosquito Coast
itself becomes the "edge of the precipice," the ultimate void, that stark
landscape of psychological confrontation and showdown. To Allie it sug-

gests that America is everywhere: his ultimate obsession chills. That "allegorical" setting reflects the allegory of Father and Mother, the wild man and the angel in Charlie's perspective. The children build their own camp, the Acre, away from Allie's jungle sanctuary, Jeronimo. Theroux's use of doubling widens the resonances of plot. The Maywits, the family at Jeronimo named by Father (their real name is Roper, but they're too timid to tell Allie otherwise) appear to Charlie as "our reflections—shrunken shadows of us." Mr. Maywit tells Fox about the Duppy: "Everyone got a Duppy. They is the same as yourself. But they is you other self. They got bodies of they own." The condition of the Maywits prophesies the future condition of the Foxes. At the same time, Charlie views Allie's icebox invention, Fat Boy, as a reflection of his father. Inventor and invention reflect one another: "This was Father's head, the mechanical part of his brain and the complications of his mind, as strong and huge and mysterious." And again: "I had seen Father's mind, a version of it—its riddle and slant and its hugeness—and it had scared me." Hawthorne's villain-heroes would understand the riddle and the mystery. And before Allie Fox dies, his head is all that remains alive, and then that too is ravaged, appropriately by vultures on the beach who peck away his tongue.

By far the most elaborate vision within the novel is that of the crucified scarecrow. One night in Massachusetts Charlie wakes and sees "men with torches marching at midnight across the valley fields. . . . In the fiery light of the circle of torches, I saw the cross raised up with a man on it." Searching for his father he thinks that the scarecrow is both a hallucination of his father and is in fact his father, "as if it was something I had imagined, an evil thought that had sprung out of my head." The son's immolation of the father: a gothic dream of Hawthornian romance suggesting the public disgrace and collapse of "my kinsman, Major Molineux." That image continues to haunt Charlie: "It had been upraised like a demon and struck terror into me." The three evil soldiers of fortune who come to take possession of Jeronimo look like scarecrows, and "we had gotten used to Father looking like a live scarecrow, the wild man of the woods, and hollering." As they approach the "coastal hell" of the Mosquito Coast, Fox's image of the entire world as ultimate desolation, Fox utters a nearly final epitaph: " 'Vultures,' he said, and then the terrible sentence, 'Christ is a scarecrow!' "

Allie Fox, facing down a derelict world, proclaims his Manichean faith: "That's a consequence of perfection in this world—the opposing wrath of imperfection." That wrath, of course, is his own, which comes back to destroy him. Knowing no past, viewing the present only in terms of exploitation and escape, conjuring up a future of perfect control and order which can never be, which he himself would be unable to tolerate because there would be no place in it for his self-righteous wrath and his inventor's compulsions to go, he inhabits a nihilistic no-man's-land, a place finally that his family cannot follow him into. Charlie realizes the distinctions: "Yet for me the past was the only real thing, it was my hope. . . . The future spoke to Father, but for me it was silent and blind and dark." It is at once a very un-American, a very human thing to admit.

The Mosquito Coast displays Theroux at his best. The novel resonates with the foundation elements of psychological romance, the "American" heart of Hawthorne's vision. Even its Aylmer at the center of things suggests Theroux's attachment to the great American themes. Demons and dreams and edges of precipices reveal the dark crux of a Hawthornesque world, and Allie Fox's Manichean madness illuminates that continuing fictional tradition.

Hawthorne's American romance is still with us, alive and well in its various forms and persuasions, as is the Manichean vision that created it. Paradox bred not unity but spiritual warfare unresolved, resolution hinted at only in the unending battle and the ongoing confrontation. This may indicate the very liveliness of American culture and of its literature, for resolution may breed stagnation and an ultimate complacency. The Manichean vision can lead to paralysis, as it does in several of Norman Mailer's fictions, a place where demon and deity are so equal to one another that only a stand-off remains. But for the most part conflict, in American literature at least, breeds our special "brand" of fiction, that romantic view of the world which reveals our own uncertainties and dreads, a continuing moral quest amidst fierce polarities that will not cohere. When and if they mingle, they collide and confuse, leaving darker designs in their wake.

Perhaps this results from the American myth that raises the individual self to the *sine qua non* of moral focus. The individual must exercise what he takes to be his free will. Ultimate human value demands that he choose. But in choosing he may choose evil, and in doing so may commit an action which is both good, because of the act of choice, and evil, because of what he has chosen. This basic paradox and contradiction, deeply imbedded in Western thought, spawns the Manichean clash of opposites and interpenetration of opposing forces, exaggerated in an American wilderness where the self must ultimately confront itself.

In "The Minister's Black Veil" (1836) Hawthorne spins the tale of a Calvinist clergyman who covers his eyes with black crepe and walks among his congregation as a visible emblem of Calvinist sin. He rejects the one woman who loves him and thus compounds his sin in the very act of transforming himself into a visible emblem of it. Such duplicity haunts the townspeople and himself; they are victims of their Manichean vision of a dark imprisoning world and a consciousness that knows only isolation, solitude, self-abasement and sorrow. They see nothing but that vision which traps and engulfs them.

In the story the veil, symbolizing that Manichean vision, achieves demonic powers. It possesses the people and the minister and becomes the dark idol of their devil-worship, though they insist on the guise of Christian consciousness and obeisance. What happens to that veil, how it is transformed into a demonic object of veneration and power, suggests what happens to the romance in Hawthorne's hands: it too reproduces the demonic powers of the very Manichean vision it was initially designed to transcend. The author's text becomes one more black veil, the penetration of which leads only to other veils and darker mysteries. At bottom fiction becomes the amulet, as R.P. Blackmur has suggested, to ward off a totally veil-less experience which, in Manichean terms, can only be death itself.[20] And the romancer is left to confront the saddest of all prisons, his own heart.

This dark vision lies at the heart of the American romance in its sheer bold attempts to escape from and/or submit to the world of fact that threatens and surrounds it. Perhaps this is why so many great American writers have been drawn to it, to Hawthorne's art. Such darkness may veil a vision of America too big and too terrible to contemplate and at the same time may mirror the dark interior of such an enlightened progressive democracy that fails to grapple publicly with its own doubts and deceptions. In any case the black veil has fascinated the best of our writers, and Hawthorne first drew attention to its ambiguous and mesmerizing implications.

Hawthorne was the first American writer to seize this vision in all its moral complexities, uneasy as he was with it (unlike Poe, for instance), and to create a form that suited it. The long shadow cast from that creative act haunts us still and will continue to do so as long as American fiction lasts.

NOTES

ONE: Hawthorne's Shadow

1. *Hawthorne's Lost Notebook, 1835-1841*, introduction by Hyatt H. Waggoner (University Park: Pennsylvania State Univ. Press, 1978), p. 35. Hereafter cited as *Lost Notebook*.

2. Ibid., p. 12.

3. Alexis de Tocqueville, *Democracy in America*, quoted by Edgar A. Dryden, *Melville's Thematics of Form: The Great Art of Telling the Truth* (Baltimore: Johns Hopkins Press, 1968), p. 18.

4. William Barrett, *The Illusion of Technique* (New York: Anchor Press/Doubleday, 1978), p. 216.

5. Harold Bloom, *The Visionary Company: A Reading of English Romantic Poetry*, quoted by Bainard Cowan, *Exiled Waters: Moby-Dick and the Crisis of Allegory* (Baton Rouge: Louisiana State Univ. Press, 1982), p. 68.

6. George Widengren, *Mani and Manichaeism* (London: Weidenfeld and Nicolson, 1965), p. 62.

7. Leo Marx, *The Machine in the Garden* (New York: Oxford Univ. Press, 1964), p. 343.

8. Daniel Hoffman, *Form and Fable in American Fiction* (New York: Norton, 1961), p. 153.

9. Ibid., p. 159.

10. Peter Brooks, "The Melodramatic Imagination," quoted by Richard Poirier, *Norman Mailer* (New York: Viking, 1972), p. 62.

11. Michael Davitt Bell, *The Development of American Romance: The Sacrifice of Relation* (Chicago: Univ. of Chicago Press, 1980), p. 10. Hereafter cited as *American Romance*.

12. Daniel J. Schneider, *Symbolism: The Manichean Vision: A Study of the Art of James, Conrad, Woolf and Stevens* (Lincoln: Univ. of Nebraska Press, 1975), p. 29.

13. Richard Chase, *The American Novel and Its Tradition* (New York: Doubleday Anchor, 1957), p. 7.

14. John Updike, "Hawthorne's Creed," *Hugging the Shore: Essays and Criticism* (New York: Knopf, 1983), pp. 77, 78. Updike goes on to suggest: "Where the two incompatible realms of Hawthorne's universe impinge, something leaks through; there is a *stain*. A sensation of blasphemous overlapping, of some vast substance chemically betraying itself, is central to the Gothic tradition of which Hawthorne's tales are lovely late blooms."

15. Duyckinck in a letter to his wife, Aug. 9, 1850, cited by James K. Mellow, *Nathaniel Hawthorne and His Times* (Boston: Houghton Mifflin, 1980), p. 333.

16. Wylie Sypher, *Loss of the Self in Modern Literature and Art* (New York: Vintage Books, 1962), p. 21.

17. *Lost Notebook*, p. 19.

18. Ibid., p. 18.

19. Sharon Cameron, *The Corporeal Self: Allegories of the Body in Melville and Hawthorne* (Baltimore: Johns Hopkins Univ. Press, 1981), p. 123.

20. Ibid., p. 126.

21. For a fuller analysis see John Irwin, *American Hieroglyphics* (New Haven: Yale Univ. Press, 1980).

22. F.O. Matthiessen, *American Renaissance* (London: Oxford Univ. Press, 1941), p. 276.

23. W.H. Harvey, *Character and the Novel* (Ithaca: Cornell Univ. Press, 1965), p. 145.

24. For further analyses of the romance, see Edgar A. Dryden, *Nathaniel Hawthorne: The Poetics of Enchantment* (Ithaca: Cornell Univ. Press, 1977); Richard H. Brodhead, *Hawthorne, Melville, and the Novel* (Chicago: Univ. of Chicago Press, 1976); John E. Becker, *Hawthorne's Historical Allegory: An Examination of the American Conscience* (Port Washington, N.Y.: Kennikat Press, 1971); Ursula Brumm, *American Thought and Religious Typology* (New Brunswick: Rutgers Univ. Press, 1970); Angus Fletcher, *Allegory: The Theory of a Symbolic Mode* (Ithaca: Cornell Univ. Press, 1964); Edwin M. Eigner, *The Metaphysical Novel in England and America: Dickens, Bulwer, Melville, and Hawthorne* (Berkeley: Univ. of California Press, 1978); Richard Swigg, *Lawrence, Hardy and American Literature* (New York: Oxford Univ. Press, 1972); Cameron, *Corporeal Self*; Rita K. Gollin, *Nathaniel Hawthorne and the Truth of Dreams* (Baton Rouge: Louisiana State Univ. Press, 1979); Flannery O'Connor, "On Her Own Work," in *Mystery and Manners*, selected and edited by Sally and Robert Fitzgerald (New York: Farrar, Straus and Giroux, 1961), p. 118; John F. Lynen, *The Design of the Present: Essays on Time and Form in American Literature* (New Haven: Yale Univ. Press, 1969); Patricia A. Carlson, *Hawthorne's Functional Settings* (Amsterdam: Rodopi, 1977), p. 53; Joel Porte, *The Romance in America: Studies in Cooper, Poe, Hawthorne, Melville, and James* (Middletown: Wesleyan Univ. Press, 1969).

25. Porte, *Romance in America*, p. 95.

26. Horace Walpole, "Preface to the Second Edition," *The Castle of Otranto, Three Gothic Novels*, ed. E.F. Bleiler (New York: Dover, 1966), p. 21.

27. Donald A. Ringe, *Charles Brockden Brown* (New York: Twayne, 1966), p. 16.

28. Norman S. Grabo, *The Coincidental Art of Charles Brockden Brown* (Chapel Hill: Univ. of North Carolina Press, 1981), p. 167.

29. David Lee Clark, *Charles Brockden Brown: Pioneer Voice of America* (Durham: Duke Univ. Press, 1952), p. 169.

30. Donald A. Ringe, *American Gothic: Imagination and Reason in Nineteenth-Century Fiction* (Lexington: Univ. Press of Kentucky, 1982), p. 13.

31. Ibid., p. 57.

32. Ibid., p. 41.

33. Bell, *American Romance*, p. 35.

34. Ibid., p. 136.

TWO: Melville to Mailer

1. Edwin Haviland Miller, *Melville* (New York: George Braziller, 1975), p. 180.

2. Ibid., pp. 221-22.

3. Ibid., p. 191.

4. Ibid., p. 42.

5. Donald Pizer, "Introduction," *The Literary Criticism of Frank Norris*, ed. Pizer (Austin: Univ. of Texas Press, 1964), p. 69.

6. H. Bruce Franklin, *The Wake of the Gods: Melville's Mythology* (Stanford: Stanford Univ. Press, 1963), pp. 13, 180.

7. Kingsley Widmer, *The Ways of Nihilism: A Study of Herman Melville's Short Novels* (Los Angeles: California State Colleges, 1970), p. 75.

8. Robert J. Begiebing, *Acts of Regeneration: Allegory and Archetype in the Works of Norman Mailer* (Columbia: Univ. of Missouri Press, 1980), p. 152.

9. Norman Mailer, "Hip, Hell, and the Navigator," in *Advertisements for Myself* (New York: Putnam's, 1969), p. 351.

10. Richard Poirier, *Norman Mailer* (New York: Viking, 1972), pp. 162, 158.

11. Joyce Carol Oates, "Melville and the Tragedy of Nihilism," in *The Edge of Impossibility: Tragic Forms in Literature* (New York: Vanguard, 1972), p. 73.

12. Joyce Carol Oates, "Norman Mailer: The Teleology of the Unconscious," in *New Heaven, New Earth: The Visionary Experience in Literature* (New York: Vanguard, 1974), p. 200.

13. William Barrett, *The Illusion of Technique* (New York: Anchor Press/Doubleday, 1978), p. 115.

14. Stanley J. Gutman, *Mankind in Barbary: The Individual and Society in the Novels of Norman Mailer* (Hanover: Univ. Press of New England, 1975), p. 79.

15. Robert Solotaroff, *Down Mailer's Way* (Urbana: Univ. of Illinois Press, 1979), p. 117.

16. Barry H. Leeds, *The Structured Vision of Norman Mailer* (New York: New York Univ. Press, 1969), p. 146.

17. Solotaroff, *Down Mailer's Way*, p. 88.

18. Widmer, *Ways of Nihilism*, p. 129.

19. Cowan, *Exiled Waters*, p. 69.

20. Millicent Bell, "Pierre Bayle and *Moby-Dick*," *PMLA* 66 (1951): 640.

21. Harold P. Simonson, *Radical Discontinuities: American Romanticism and Christian Consciousness* (Rutherford, N.J.: Fairleigh Dickinson Univ. Press, 1983), p. 166.

22. Franklin, *Wake of the Gods*, p. 77.

23. This is the title of Franklin's chapter on *Moby-Dick*.

24. Miller, *Melville*, p. 289.

25. Cowan, *Exiled Waters*, pp. 19-20.

26. Ibid., p. 20.

27. Miller, *Melville*, p. 262.

28. Widmer, *Ways of Nihilism*, p. 73.

29. Alfred Kazin, *Bright Book of Life: American Novelists and Storytellers from Hemingway to Mailer* (Boston: Atlantic-Little, Brown, 1973), p. 154.

30. Tony Tanner, "On the Parapet," in *Will the Real Norman Mailer Please Stand Up*, ed. Laura Adams (Port Washington, N.Y.: Kennikat Press, 1974), p. 143.

31. Norman Mailer, "The White Negro," in *Advertisements for Myself*, p. 316.

32. Letter to the author from Jack Abbott, May 29, 1983.

33. Poirier, *Norman Mailer*, p. 114.

34. For an excellent discussion of the bestial universe, the primordial force field, and the "deifying movement of the present," see Richard D. Finholt, " 'Otherwise How

Explain?' Norman Mailer's New Cosmology," *Modern Fiction Studies* 17 (Autumn 1971): 375-86.

35. John Stark, *"Barbary Shore*: The Basis of Mailer's Best Work," *Modern Fiction Studies* 17 (Autumn 1971): 403-13.

36. Ibid., 407.

37. George Alfred Schrader, "Norman Mailer and the Despair of Defiance," in *Norman Mailer: A Collection of Critical Essays*, ed. Leo Braudy (Englewood Cliffs, N.J.: Prentice-Hall, 1972), p. 93.

38. Solotaroff, *Down Mailer's Way*, pp. 107, 98.

39. Jean Radford, *Norman Mailer: A Critical Study* (New York: Barnes and Noble, 1975), p. 163.

40. Frederick R. Karl, *American Fictions, 1940-1980* (New York: Harper and Row, 1983), pp. 522, 523.

41. Ibid., p. 523.

42. Solotaroff, *Down Mailer's Way*, p. 173.

43. Gutman, *Mankind in Barbary*, p. 80.

44. Richard Brodhead, "Hawthorne, Melville, and the Fiction of Prophecy," in *Nathaniel Hawthorne: New Critical Essays*, ed. A. Robert Lee (New York: Barnes and Noble, 1982), p. 241.

45. Ibid., p. 237.

46. Peter Brooks, "The Melodramatic Imagination," *Partisan Review* 2 (1972): 209-11, *passim*, quoted by Poirier, *Norman Mailer*, pp. 59-60.

47. Leo Braudy, "Introduction: Norman Mailer: The Pride of Vulnerability," in Braudy, *Norman Mailer*, p. 15.

48. Leo Bersani, "Interpretation of Dreams," in Braudy, *Norman Mailer*, pp. 122-24.

49. Radford, *Norman Mailer*, p. 174.

50. Poirier, *Norman Mailer*, p. 158.

51. Flannery O'Connor, "Novelist and Believer," in Fitzgerald, *Mystery and Manners*, p. 168.

52. Walter Clemons, "A Novelist Builds a Pyramid," *Vanity Fair* 46, no. 5 (May 1983): 60.

53. Harold Bloom, "Norman in Egypt," *New York Review of Books* 30, no. 7 (April 28, 1983): 3-6.

54. See Irwin, *American Hieroglyphics*, especially pp. 145-46.

THREE: Harold Frederic

1. James W. Tuttleton, *The Novel of Manners in America* (New York: Norton, 1972).

2. Ibid., p. 74.

3. Edwin H. Cady, *The Light of Common Day: Realism in American Fiction* (Bloomington: Indiana Univ. Press, 1971), p. 134.

4. Patricia Marks, " 'A Magic in His Way': Hawthorne's Posthumous Reputation in *Life*, 1883-1910," unpublished paper, Valdosta State College, Valdosta, Ga.

5. Jane P. Tompkins, "Masterpiece Theatre: The Politics of Hawthorne's Literary Reputation," unpublished paper, Temple University, Philadelphia, p. 39.

6. Cady, *Light of Common Day*, p. 134.

7. Ibid.

8. Ibid., p. 135.

9. Charles Child Walcutt, "Harold Frederic and American Naturalism," *American Literature* 11 (March 1939): 22.

10. George W. Johnson, "Harold Frederic's Young Goodman Ware: The Ambiguities of a Realistic Romance," *Modern Fiction Studies* 8 (Winter 1962-1963): 361.

11. Donald Pizer, "Introduction," *The Literary Criticism of Frank Norris*, ed. Pizer (Austin: Univ. of Texas Press, 1964), p. 69. My thanks to Bob Morace of Daemen College for bringing this to my attention.

12. Frank Norris, "A Plea for Romantic Fiction," *Boston Evening Transcript*, Dec. 18, 1901, p. 14, quoted by Pizer, *Literary Criticism of Frank Norris*, p. 75.

13. Frank Norris, "Zola as a Romantic Writer," *Wave* 15 (June 27, 1896): 3, quoted by Pizer, *Literary Criticism of Frank Norris*, p. 72.

14. Harold Frederic, *The Damnation of Theron Ware* (New York: Holt, Rinehart and Winston, 1967), p. 28.

15. Johnson, "Harold Frederic's Young Goodman Ware," p. 371.

16. Larzer Ziff, *The American 1890's* (New York: Viking Press, 1966), p. 212.

17. Johnson, "Harold Frederic's Young Goodman Ware," p. 372.

18. Stanton Garner, *Harold Frederic* (Minneapolis: Univ. of Minnesota Press, 1969), p. 45.

19. Ibid., p. 133.

20. *The Spectator* 76 (1896): 486, quoted by Austin Briggs, *The Novels of Harold Frederic* (Ithaca: Cornell Univ. Press, 1969), p. 132.

21. Johnson, "Harold Frederic's Young Goodman Ware," p. 362.

22. Garner, *Harold Frederic*, p. 8.

23. Briggs, *Novels of Harold Frederic*, p. 133.

24. *The Critic* 25 (1896): 310, quoted in ibid., p. 130.

25. Briggs, *Novels of Harold Frederic*, p. 133.

26. Johnson, "Harold Frederic's Young Goodman Ware," p. 373.

27. Garner, *Harold Frederic*, p. 36.

28. Nathaniel Hawthorne, "The Haunted Mind" in *Selected Tales and Sketches*, 3rd ed., ed. Hyatt H. Waggoner (New York: Holt Rinehart and Winston, 1970), p. 412. Theron Ware in effect can control or select nothing, since he often seems incapable of any aesthetic or moral judgment. He is in many ways the victim of the "New Thought," the Soulsby strategy of relativism in all things, and is undermined by it. Further observations on this idea can be found in George Spangler's article, "Theron Ware and the Perils of Relativism," *Canadian Review of American Studies* 5 (1974): 36-46.

29. Tom Sullivan, "Standing Pat," unpublished paper, Wheaton College, Norton, Mass.

30. Ziff, *American 1890's*, p. 214.

31. Johnson, "Harold Frederic's Young Goodman Ware," p. 374.

32. Garner, *Harold Frederic*, p. 33.

33. Johnson, "Harold Frederic's Young Goodman Ware," p. 373.

FOUR: Faulkner, McCullers, O'Connor, Styron

1. C.P. Snow, *Sunday Times*, Dec. 27, 1953, quoted in David Lodge, *The Novelist at the Crossroads and Other Essays on Fiction and Criticism* (Ithaca: Cornell Univ. Press, 1971), p. 18.

2. Panthea Reid Broughton, *William Faulkner: The Abstract and the Actual* (Baton Rouge: Louisiana State Univ. Press, 1974), p. 174.

3. Roger Shattuck, quoted in Arthur F. Kinney, *Faulkner's Narrative Poetics: Style as Vision* (Amherst: Univ. of Massachusetts Press, 1978), p. 111.

4. Ibid., p. 4.

5. W.J. Cash, *The Mind of the South* (New York: Vintage, 1941), p. 387.

6. Hyatt H. Waggoner, *William Faulkner: From Jefferson to the World* (Lexington: Univ. of Kentucky Press, 1959), p. 266.

7. William Faulkner, *Chicago Tribune*, July 16, 1927, quoted in *William Faulkner*, ed. James B. Meriwether (New York: Random House, 1964), p. 198.

8. Carson McCullers, quoted in Mark Schorer, "McCullers and Capote: Basic Patterns," in *The Creative Present: Notes on Contemporary American Fiction*, ed. Nona Balakien and Charles Simmons (New York: Doubleday, 1963), p. 85.

9. Tennessee Williams, "Introduction: This Book," in Carson McCullers, *Reflections in a Golden Eye* (New York: Bantam, 1950), p. xiv.

10. Northrop Frye, *The Secular Scripture: A Study of the Structure of Romance* (Cambridge: Harvard Univ. Press, 1976), p. 165.

11. Ibid., p. 109.

12. Ibid., p. 125.

13. Simeon M. Smith, Jr., "Carson McCullers: A Critical Introduction," Ph.D. dissertation, Univ. of Pennsylvania, 1964, pp. 196, 33.

14. Ibid., p. 196.

15. Ibid., p. 23.

16. Flannery O'Connor to William Sessions, Sept. 13, 1960, in *Letters of Flannery O'Connor: The Habit of Being*, ed. Sally Fitzgerald (New York: Farrar Straus Giroux, 1979), p. 407.

17. Flannery O'Connor to John Hawkes, Nov. 28, 1961, *Letters*, p. 457.

18. Flannery O'Connor, "Some Aspects of the Grotesque in Southern Fiction," in Fitzgerald, *Mystery and Manners*, p. 39.

19. Flannery O'Connor, quoted in Margaret Inman Meades, "*Flannery O'Connor*, 'Literary Witch,' " *Colorado Quarterly* 10: 384, quoted in Thomas M. Lorch, "Flannery O'Connor: Christian Allegorist," *Critique: Studies in Modern Fiction* 10, no. 2 (1968): 71-72.

20. O'Connor, "Some Aspects of the Grotesque," p. 46.

21. Flannery O'Connor, "The Teaching of Literature," in Fitzgerald, *Mystery and Manners*, p. 124.

22. Flannery O'Connor, "The Nature and Aim of Fiction," in ibid., p. 68.

23. Flannery O'Connor, "The Catholic Novelist in the Protestant South," in ibid., p. 197.

24. Flannery O'Connor, "The Fiction Writer and His Country," in ibid., p. 33.

25. Frederick Asals, *Flannery O'Connor: The Imagination of Extremity* (Athens: Univ. of Georgia Press, 1982), p. 206.

26. Flannery O'Connor, "On Her Own Work," in Fitzgerald, *Mystery and Manners*, p. 118.

27. Flannery O'Connor, "Introduction to 'A Memoir of Mary Ann,' " in ibid., p. 227. Hereafter cited as "Mary Ann."

28. Ibid.

29. Ibid.

30. Ibid., p. 219.

31. Asals, *Flannery O'Connor*, p. 163.

32. Leon V. Driskell and Joan T. Brittain, *The Eternal Crossroads: The Art of Flannery O'Connor* (Lexington: Univ. Press of Kentucky, 1971), p. 17.

33. See especially Josephine Hendin, *The World of Flannery O'Connor* (Bloomington: Indiana Univ. Press, 1970); Carol Shloss, *Flannery O'Connor's Dark Comedies: The Limits of Inference* (Baton Rouge: Louisiana State Univ. Press, 1980); and Suzanne Morrow Paulson, "Apocalypse of Self, Resurrection of the Double: Flannery O'Connor's *The Violent Bear It Away*," *Literature and Psychology* 30, nos. 3 and 4 (1980): 100-111. Hendin sees O'Connor's rage as totally undermining any orthodox Christian vision; Schloss sees only a "portrayal of monomania" (p. 90) with O'Connor never clearly defining what is holy and what is foolish; and Paulson views only the psychic determinism of "an odyssey toward madness" (p. 100).

34. Flannery O'Connor, "The Church and the Fiction Writer," in Fitzgerald, *Mystery and Manners*, p. 148.

35. O'Connor, "On Her Own Work," p. 112.

36. Joyce Carol Oates, "The Visionary Art of Flannery O'Connor," in *New Heaven, New Earth*, p. 150.

37. Flannery O'Connor, "Catholic Novelists and Their Readers," in Fitzgerald, *Mystery and Manners*, p. 175.

38. Thomas M. Carlson, "Flannery O'Connor: The Manichean Dilemma," *Sewanee Review* 77, no. 2 (April-June 1979): 272-73.

39. Interview with William Styron, in *Writers at Work: The Paris Review Interviews*, ed. Malcolm Cowley (New York: Viking, 1958), p. 275.

40. William Styron, "Recollections of a Once Timid Novelist," *Hartford Courant Magazine*, Jan. 3, 1982, p. 8.

41. John Gardner, "A Novel of Evil," *New York Times Book Review* 84, no. 21 (May 27, 1979): 17.

42. Interview with William Styron by the author, July 15, 1969.

43. Ibid.

44. William Styron, "The Prevalance of Wonders," *Nation* 176 (May 2, 1953): 371.

45. Norman Mailer, *Esquire* 60 (July 1963): 64.

46. Jonathan Baumbach, "Paradise Lost: The Novels of William Styron," *South Atlantic Quarterly* 63 (Spring 1964): 215.

47. Gardner, "A Novel of Evil," p. 16.

48. O'Connor, "Mary Ann," p. 227.

49. Joyce Carol Oates, "Norman Mailer: The Teleology of the Unconscious," pp. 191-92, 200.

FIVE: John Cheever

1. John Cheever, interview with the author, June 3, 1975. Cited below as 1975 interview.

2. John Cheever, *The Leaves, the Lion-Fish and the Bear* (Los Angeles: Sylvester and Orphanos, 1980), p. 16.

3. Elizabeth Hardwick, quoted in Michiko Kakutami, "In a Cheever-Like Setting, John Cheever Gets MacDowell Medal," *New York Times*, Sept. 11, 1979, p. C7.

4. John Updike, "On Such a Beautiful Green Little Planet," *New Yorker*, April 5, 1982, p. 190. See also Karl, *American Fictions, 1940-1980*, especially pp. 49-50.

5. "The Talk of the Town," *New Yorker*, July 12, 1982.

6. 1975 interview. For a thorough and graciously written exploration of Cheever's philosophical and religious themes and intimations, see George W. Hunt, *John Cheever: The Hobgoblin Company of Love* (Grand Rapids, Mich.: William B. Eerdmans, 1983).

7. John Cheever, "The President of the Argentine," in manuscript in my possession.

8. 1975 interview.

9. Ibid.

10. John Cheever, quoted in Jesse Kornbluth, "The Cheever Chronicle," *New York Times*, Oct. 21, 1979, p. 29.

11. Ibid., p. 103.

12. John Cheever, quoted in Samuel Coale, *John Cheever* (New York: Frederick Ungar, 1977), p. 3. Interview with the author, June 3, 1975.

13. Daniel Hoffman, *Form and Fable in American Fiction* (New York: Oxford Univ. Press, 1961), p. 173.

14. Beatrice Greene, "Icarus at St. Botolphs: A Descent to 'Unwanted Otherness,' " *Style* 5 (1971): 123, 120.

15. John W. Aldridge, "John Cheever and the Soft Sell of Disaster" in *Time to Murder and Create* (New York: David McKay, 1966).

SIX: John Updike

1. John Gardner, *On Moral Fiction* (New York: Basic Books, 1978), p. 98.

2. David Lodge, "Post-Pill Paradise Lost: John Updike's *Couples*," in *The Novelist at the Crossroads and Other Essays on Fiction and Criticism* (Ithaca: Cornell Univ. Press, 1971), p. 243.

3. John B. Vickery, "The Centaur: Myth, History, and Narrative," *Modern Fiction Studies: John Updike* 20, no. 1 (Spring 1974): 61.

4. John Updike, "On Hawthorne's Mind," *New York Review of Books*, Mar. 19, 1981, pp. 41, 42.

5. Quoted in George W. Hunt, S.J., *John Updike and the Three Great Secret Things: Sex, Religion, and Art* (Grand Rapids, Mich.: William B. Eerdmans, 1980), p. 126.

6. John Updike, "More Love in the Western World: *Love Declared* by Denis de Rougemont," in *Assorted Prose* (New York: Knopf, 1965), pp. 284-85.

7. Updike, "More Love," p. 299.

8. John Updike, "The Dogwood Tree: A Boyhood," *Assorted Prose*, p. 172.

9. Ibid., p. 186.

10. Updike, "More Love," p. 199.

11. Robert Detweiler, *John Updike* (New York: Twayne, 1972), p. 165.

12. Hunt, *John Updike*, p. 140.

13. Updike, "Dogwood Tree," p. 181.

14. Lodge, "Post-Pill Paradise Lost," p. 243.

15. Richard Swigg, *Lawrence, Hardy and American Literature* (New York: Oxford Univ. Press, 1972), p. 319.

16. Updike, "Dogwood Tree," p. 182.

17. Ibid., p. 185.

SEVEN: John Gardner

1. Frederick R. Karl, *American Fictions, 1940-1980* (New York: Harper and Row, 1983), p. 593.

2. David Cowart, *Arches and Light: The Fiction of John Gardner* (Carbondale: Southern Illinois Univ. Press, 1983), p. 139.

3. John Gardner, "Nicholas Vergette 1923-1974," in Cowart, p. 1.

4. Karl, p. 64.

5. John Gardner, interviewed by Joe David Bellamy and Pat Ensworth, in Joe David Bellamy, *The New Fiction: Interviews with Innovative American Writers* (Urbana: Univ. of Illinois Press, 1974), pp. 185, 187.

6. John Gardner, "Backstage with Esquire," *Esquire* 76 (Oct. 1971): 56, quoted in Helen B. Ellis and Warren U. Ober, "*Grendel* and Blake: 'The Contraries of Existence,' " in *John Gardner: Critical Perspectives*, ed. Robert A. Morace and Kathryn Van Spanckeren (Carbondale: Southern Illinois Univ. Press, 1982), p. 47.

7. Gardner, *On Moral Fiction*, p. 97. For a full discussion of Gardner as a moral artist and slayer of dragons, see Cowart, *Arches and Light*.

8. John Gardner, "The Strange Real World," *New York Times Book Review*, July 20, 1980, p. 21.

9. Gardner, quoted in Daniel Laskin, "Challenging the Literary Naysayers," *Horizon* 21, no. 7 (July 1978): 36.

10. Robert A. Morace, "Introduction," in Morace and Van Spanckeren, *John Gardner*, p. xix.

11. Greg Morris, "A Babylonian in Batavia: Mesopotamian Literature and Lore in *The Sunlight Dialogues*," in ibid., p. 37.

12. Gardner, quoted in Laskin, "Challenging the Literary Naysayers," 34.

13. Richard Chase, *The American Novel and Its Tradition* (Garden City: Doubleday, 1957), p. 201.

14. Ibid., pp. 201-2.

15. Ibid., p. 184.

16. Ibid., p. 5.

17. Judy Smith Murr, "John Gardner's Order and Disorder: *Grendel* and *The Sunlight Dialogues*," *Critique: Studies in Modern Fiction* 18, no. 2 (1976): 105.

18. Quoted in Stephen Singular, "The Sound and Fury over Fiction," *New York Times Magazine*, July 8, 1979, p. 15.

19. Quoted in Bellamy, *New Fiction*, p. 189.

20. Robert L. Caserio, *Plot, Story, and the Novel: From Dickens and Poe to the Modern Period* (Princeton: Princeton Univ. Press, 1979), p. 168.

21. Gardner, *Moral Fiction*, pp. 92, 60, 66, 125, 19, 37.

22. Conversation with John Gardner, March 31, 1979.

23. Robert A. Morace, "Playing the Middle against Both Ends: The Connected Vision of *Mickelsson's Ghost*," unpublished paper, Daemen College, Amherst, New York.

EIGHT: Joyce Carol Oates

1. Joyce Carol Oates, interviewed by Joe David Bellamy, *New Fiction*, pp. 21, 30.
2. Oates, quoted in Mary Kathryn Grant, R.S.M., *The Tragic Vision of Joyce Carol Oates* (Durham: Duke Univ. Press, 1978), p. 164.
3. G.F. Waller, *Dreaming America: Obsession and Transcendence in the Fiction of Joyce Carol Oates* (Baton Rouge: Louisiana State Univ. Press, 1979), p. 198.
4. Ibid., p. 28.
5. Oates, quoted in Ellen G. Friedman, *Joyce Carol Oates* (New York: Frederick Ungar, 1980), p. 6.
6. Oates, *Edge of Impossibility*, p. 6.
7. Ibid., p. 96.
8. Oates, "Visionary Art of Flannery O'Connor," p. 162.
9. Oates, *Edge of Impossibility*, p. 4.
10. Ibid., p. 7.
11. Joyce Carol Oates, "D.H. Lawrence: The Hostile Sun," in *New Heaven, New Earth*, pp. 67, 68.
12. Waller, *Dreaming America*, p. 40.
13. Oates, *Edge of Impossibility*, pp. 217-18.
14. Walter Sullivan, "The Artificial Demon: Joyce Carol Oates and the Dimensions of the Real," in Linda W. Wagner, *American Modern: Essays in Fiction and Poetry* (Port Washington, N.Y.: Kennikat Press, 1980), p. 85.
15. Oates, quoted in Waller, *Dreaming America*, p. 22.
16. Oates, *Edge of Impossibility*, p. 118.
17. Oates, quoted in Waller, *Dreaming America*, p. 5.
18. Oates, *Edge of Impossibility*, pp. 98, 112.
19. Ibid., p. 113.
20. Waller, *Dreaming America*, p. 71.
21. Oates, quoted in Wagner, *American Modern*, pp. xvii-xviii.
22. See Joan V. Creighton, *Joyce Carol Oates* (Boston: Twayne, 1979).
23. Oates, *Edge of Impossibility*, p. 92.
24. Bell, *American Romance*, p. 129.
25. Oates, *Edge of Impossibility*, p. 3.
26. Ibid., p. 73.
27. Ibid., p. 82.
28. Freidman, *Joyce Carol Oates*, p. 139.
29. Creighton, *Joyce Carol Oates*, p. 105.
30. See Wesley A. Kort, *Shriven Selves: Religious Problems in Recent American Fiction* (Philadelphia: Fortress, 1972).
31. Ibid., p. 145.
32. Oates, *Edge of Impossibility*, p. 89.

NINE: Joan Didion

1. Joan Didion, "On the Morning after the Sixties," in *The White Album* (New York: Pocket Books/Simon and Schuster, 1979), p. 204.
2. Ibid., p. 205.

3. Joan Didion, "I Can't Get That Monster Out of My Mind," in *Slouching Towards Bethlehem* (New York: Simon and Schuster, 1968), p. 3.

4. Joan Didion, "In the Islands," in *White Album*, pp. 134-35.

5. Didion, "The White Album," in ibid., p. 44.

6. Didion, "In Bed," in ibid., p. 169.

7. Didion, "In Bogota," in ibid., p. 192.

8. Didion, "White Album," p. 8.

9. Didion, "Holy Water," in *White Album*, p. 65.

10. Alfred Kazin, *Bright Book of Life: American Novelists and Storytellers from Hemingway to Mailer* (Boston: Little, Brown, 1973), p. 194.

11. Katherine Usher Henderson, *Joan Didion* (New York: Frederick Ungar, 1980), p. 143.

12. Didion, "The Women's Movement," in *White Album*, p. 112.

13. Didion, "Notes from a Native Daughter," in *Slouching Towards Bethlehem*, p. 172.

14. See Mark Rayden Winchell, *Joan Didion* (New York: Twayne, 1980).

15. Didion, "Women's Movement," pp. 116-17.

16. Winchell, *Joan Didion*, p. 166.

17. Mark Schorer, "Novels and Nothingness," *American Scholar* 40 (Winter 1970-71): 174.

18. Didion, quoted in Henderson, *Joan Didion*, pp. 5, 6.

19. Didion, "In Bed," p. 170.

20. Winchell, *Joan Didion*, pp. 31, 136.

21. Didion, "Slouching Towards Bethlehem," *Slouching Towards Bethlehem*, p. 123.

22. Didion, "Bureaucrats," in *White Album*, p. 79.

23. Didion, "Comrade Laski, C.P.U.S.A. (M.-L.)" *Slouching Towards Bethlehem*, p. 66.

24. Kazin, *Bright Book of Life*, p. 192.

25. Henderson, *Joan Didion*, p. 133.

26. Didion, quoted in ibid., p. 17.

27. Didion, "White Album," p. 43.

28. See Tony Tanner, *City of Words: American Fiction, 1950-1970* (New York: Harper and Row, 1971).

29. Henderson, *Joan Didion*, p. 47.

30. See Henderson's analysis in ibid., pp. 21-22.

31. See, for example, David L. Minter, *The Interpreted Design as Structural Principle in American Prose* (New Haven: Yale Univ. Press, 1969).

TEN: Hawthorne and the Sixties

1. See Jerome Klinkowitz, *Literary Disruptions: The Making of a Post-Contemporary American Fiction* (Urbana: Univ. of Illinois Press, 1975); and Samuel Coale, "The Cinematic Self of Jerzy Kosinski," *Modern Fiction Studies* 20, no. 3 (Autumn 1974): 359-70.

2. Raymond M. Olderman, *Beyond the Wasteland: The American Novel in the Nineteen-Sixties* (New Haven: Yale Univ. Press, 1972), pp. 5, 7, 23.

3. Ibid., p. 120.

4. Ihab Hassan, *Radical Innocence* (Princeton: Princeton Univ. Press, 1961), p. 43.

5. Nathaniel Hawthorne to J.T. Fields, Boston, Nov. 3, 1850, no. 453. Hawthorne Papers, Ohio State University Library, Columbus.

6. Nathaniel Hawthorne to Sophia Peabody, Boston, Dec. 22, 1841, no. 222.

7. Nathaniel Hawthorne to Sophia Peabody, Salem, Oct. 4, 1840, no. 173.

8. Nathaniel Hawthorne to Sophia Peabody, Boston, Feb. 7, 1840, no. 138.

9. Nathaniel Hawthorne to Sophia Peabody, Boston, May 19, 1840, no. 159.

10. Nathaniel Hawthorne to Sophia Peabody, Salem, Apr. 15, 1840, no. 151.

11. Nathaniel Hawthorne to Sophia Peabody, Brook Farm, Oct. 18, 1841, no. 216.

12. Nathaniel Hawthorne to Charles A. Putnam, Lenox, Sept. 16, 1851, no. 512.

13. Nathaniel Hawthorne to Sophia Peabody, Boston, June 11, 1840, no. 163.

14. Nathaniel Hawthorne to E.A. Duyckinck, Lenox, Apr. 27, 1851, no. 482.

15. Nathaniel Hawthorne to Horatio Bridge, Concord, May 3, 1843, no. 267.

16. Nathaniel Hawthorne to Sophia Peabody, Brook Farm, May 1, 1841, no. 194.

17. Ann Douglas, *The Feminization of American Culture* (New York: Avon, 1977), p. 317.

18. Norman Mailer, *The Armies of the Night* (New York: New American Library, 1968), p. 284.

19. Karl, *American Fictions*, pp. 520, 589.

20. R.P. Blackmur, "Afterward," *The Celestial Railroad and Other Stories* (New York: New American Library, 1963), p. 293.

PRIMARY SOURCES

JOHN CHEEVER

The Wapshot Chronicle. New York: Harper and Row, 1957.

The Wapshot Scandal. New York: Harper and Row, 1963.

Bullet Park. New York: Knopf, 1969.

Falconer. New York: Knopf, 1976.

The Stories of John Cheever. New York: Knopf, 1978.

Oh What A Paradise It Seems. New York: Knopf, 1982.

ROBERT COOVER

The Public Burning. New York: Viking, 1977.

JOAN DIDION

Run River. [1963] New York: Pocket Books, 1978.

Play It As It Lays. [1970] New York: Pocket Books, 1978.

A Book of Common Prayer. New York: Simon and Schuster, 1977.

Democracy. New York: Simon and Schuster, 1984.

WILLIAM FAULKNER

As I Lay Dying. [1930] New York: Vintage, 1964.

Light in August. [1932] London: Penguin, 1960.

Absalom, Absalom! [1936] New York: Modern Library, 1951.

HAROLD FREDERIC

The Damnation of Theron Ware. [1896] New York: Holt, Rinehart, and Winston, 1967.

JOHN GARDNER

The Resurrection. [1966] New York: Ballantine, 1974.

Grendel. [1971] New York: Ballantine, 1977.

Nickel Mountain. [1973] New York: Ballantine, 1975.

The Sunlight Dialogues. New York: Knopf, 1973.

The King's Indian. [1974] New York: Ballantine, 1976.

October Light. New York: Knopf, 1976.

The Art of Living. New York: Knopf, 1981.

Mickelsson's Ghosts. New York: Knopf, 1982.

JOHN HAWKES

Virginie: Her Two Lives. New York: Harper and Row, 1982.

NATHANIEL HAWTHORNE
  The Centenary Edition of the Works of Nathaniel Hawthorne, ed. William
    Charvat et al. Columbus: Ohio State Univ. Press, 1963-.
JOSEPH HELLER
  Something Happened. New York: Knopf, 1974.
NORMAN MAILER
  Barbary Shore. New York: New American Library, 1951.
  The Deer Park. New York: G.P. Putnam's, 1955.
  An American Dream. New York: Dial Press, 1965.
  Why Are We in Vietnam? New York: G.P. Putnam's, 1967.
  The Executioner's Song. [1979] New York: Warner, 1980.
  Ancient Evenings. Boston: Little, Brown, 1983.
CARSON McCULLERS
  Reflections in a Golden Eye. [1941] New York: Bantam, 1966.
  The Ballad of the Sad Café. [1951] New York: Bantam, 1964.
HERMAN MELVILLE
  Moby-Dick. [1851] New York: Houghton Mifflin, 1956.
  Pierre, or The Ambiguities. [1852] New York: Grove Press, 1957.
  The Confidence-Man: His Masquerade. [1857] New York: Norton, 1971.
  Billy Budd and Other Tales. New York: New American Library, 1961.
JOYCE CAROL OATES
  The Assassins. New York: Fawcett Crest, 1975.
  The Triumph of the Spider Monkey. New York: Fawcett Crest, 1976.
  Son of the Morning. New York: Fawcett Crest, 1978.
  Bellefleur. New York: E.P. Dutton, 1981.
FLANNERY O'CONNOR
  The Violent Bear It Away. [1955] New York: New American Library,
    1961.
THOMAS PYNCHON
  Gravity's Rainbow. New York: Viking, 1973.
PHILIP ROTH
  The Ghost Writer. [1979] New York: Fawcett Crest, 1980.
WILLIAM STYRON
  Lie Down in Darkness. New York: Random House, 1951.
  Set This House on Fire. New York: Random House, 1960.
  The Confessions of Nat Turner. New York: Random House, 1967.
  Sophie's Choice. New York: Random House, 1979.
PAUL THEROUX
  The Mosquito Coast. Boston: Houghton Mifflin, 1982.

JOHN UPDIKE
  Rabbit, Run. New York: Knopf, 1960.
  Of the Farm. [1965] New York: Fawcett Crest, 1965.
  Couples. New York: Knopf, 1968.
  Rabbit Redux. New York: Knopf, 1971.
  A Month of Sundays. [1974] New York: Fawcett Crest, 1976.
  Rabbit Is Rich. New York: Knopf, 1981.
  The Witches of Eastwick. New York: Knopf, 1984.
KURT VONNEGUT
  Slaughterhouse-Five or The Children's Crusade. New York: Delacorte Press, 1969.

BIBLIOGRAPHICAL ESSAY

HAVING studied and analyzed and delighted in Hawthorne and Hawthorne criticism for over fifteen years, I find it very difficult to determine which critics have had more effect upon me than others. Clearly the work and presence of Hyatt Waggoner at Brown University stands foremost in my mind, followed in no particular order by the pioneering work of such critics as F.O. Matthiessen, Charles Feidelson, Leslie Fiedler, Northrop Frye, Harry Levin, Daniel Hoffman, Richard Harter Fogle, Leo Marx, and R.W.B. Lewis. Particular works which I have turned to with persistent regularity include Richard Chase's *The American Novel and Its Tradition* (Garden City: Doubleday Anchor, 1957) for his exploration of the American romance; Lionel Trilling's famous essay, "Manners, Morals, and the Novel" in *The Liberal Imagination* (New York: Viking, 1950) for his Hawthornian distinction between the romance and the novel; Michael Davitt Bell's excellent *The Development of American Romance: The Sacrifice of Relation* (Chicago: Univ. of Chicago Press, 1980) for his thorough examination of the radical dualism at the heart of American romantic theory; Joel Porte's *The Romance in America: Studies in Cooper, Poe, Hawthorne, Melville, and James* (Middletown: Wesleyan Univ. Press, 1969) for his knowledge about romantic spells and hidden guilts, and for his clearly identifying Hawthorne as the first great theorist of the American romance; and John T. Irwin's *American Hieroglyphics* (New Haven: Yale Univ. Press, 1980) for his highly suggestive and fascinating look at the process of doubling in American romance and the essentially Manichean nature of its dark vision.

So many other commentators on the American romance have influenced me that it is possible here only to give them an appropriate nod for their investigations and conclusions. The list is long but not inclusive. These include Edgar Dryden, *Nathaniel Hawthorne: The Poetics of Enchantment* (Ithaca: Cornell Univ. Press, 1977), for his discussion of the dialectic between enchantment and disenchantment in Hawthorne's romances; Richard H. Brodhead, *Hawthorne, Melville, and the Novel* (Chicago: Univ.

of Chicago Press, 1976), for a decisive look at the uneasy alliance in
Hawthorne between brute actuality and imagination's shadows; Rita K.
Gollin, *Nathaniel Hawthorne and the Truth of Dreams* (Baton Rouge: Louisiana State Univ. Press, 1979), for her exploration of Hawthorne's mode
of daydreaming and of the multiple consciousness it produced; John F.
Lynen, *The Design of the Present: Essays on Time and Form in American
Literature* (New Haven: Yale Univ. Press, 1969), for his interpretation
of the interpenetration of the present moment and eternity in Puritan
consciousness, which suggests the form of episodic tableaux that make
up the best of American romances; and Richard Poirier, *A World Elsewhere:
The Place of Style in American Literature* (New York: Oxford Univ. Press,
1966), for his analysis of the American self in relation to the surrounding
world and that self's flowering in a particular literary style at the expense of a particular social environment.

The list continues. It includes Angus Fletcher, *Allegory: The Theory
of a Symbolic Mode* (Ithaca: Cornell Univ. Press, 1964), who carefully
explains the relationship between moral conflicts, allegorical signs, and
the compulsive psychology that attends them both; Edwin M. Eigner,
*The Metaphysical Novel in England and America: Dickens, Bulwer, Melville,
and Hawthorne* (Berkeley: Univ. of California Press, 1978), who revealed
the necessity of remoteness and distance for the romance and the tack
the romance often takes in observing the creative process itself; David
L. Minter, *The Interpreted Design as a Structural Principle in American Prose*
(New Haven: Yale Univ. Press, 1969), who placed the man of action
and the man of interpretation in a long-running American morality play;
Ursula Brumm, *American Thought and Religious Typology* (New Brunswick:
Rutgers Univ. Press, 1970), who spelled out the Puritans' sense of history
as a tale of redemption and who linked Calvinist predestination with certain psychological cycles; and Richard Swigg, *Lawrence, Hardy and American
Literature* (London: Oxford Univ. Press, 1972), who subtly explored the
moral petrifaction in Hawthorne's later romances and the dilemma of
artistic control the author experienced.

I could not conclude this inadequate list without paying homage to
a few more distinguished critics. These would include William H. Shurr,
Rappaccini's Children: American Writers in a Calvinist World (Lexington:
Univ. Press of Kentucky, 1981) for his perceptive overview of Hawthorne's
shadow and its consequences; Gary Lindberg, *The Confidence Man in
American Literature* (New York: Oxford Univ. Press, 1982), for his ex-

ploration of American paradoxes and the strange and uneasy relationships between outward action and inward brooding; Sharon Cameron, *The Corporeal Self: Allegories of the Body in Melville and Hawthorne* (Baltimore: Johns Hopkins Univ. Press, 1981), for her meticulous examination of the split between body and soul in those two writers and in allegory's formalizing that essential split between the individual self and the world at large; Donald A. Ringe, *American Gothic: Imagination and Reason in Nineteenth-Century Fiction* (Lexington: Univ. Press of Kentucky, 1982), for his careful compilation of the gothic devices and techniques of many American romancers; and Robert D. Richardson, Jr., *Myth and Literature in the American Renaissance* (Bloomington: Indiana Univ. Press, 1978), for his astute conclusions about the use of particular myths and essential archetypes in the literature of Hawthorne's day. I am certain I have left out many valuable critical analyses and can only apologize for my present state of mind if I have done so.

The number of critics who have assisted me in their work by discussing contemporary writers would again be staggering. Those that come immediately to mind include Tony Tanner, *City of Words: American Fiction, 1950-1970* (New York: Harper and Row, 1971); Raymond M. Olderman, *Beyond the Wasteland: The American Novel in the Nineteen-Sixties* (New Haven: Yale Univ. Press, 1972); Wesley A. Kort, *Shriven Selves: Religious Problems in Recent American Fiction* (Philadelphia: Fortress Press, 1972); Frederick R. Karl, *American Fictions, 1940-1980* (New York: Harper and Row, 1983); Alfred Kazin, *Bright Book of Life: American Novelists and Storytellers from Hemingway to Mailer* (Boston: Atlantic-Little, Brown, 1973); Larzer Ziff, *Literary Democracy: The Declaration of Cultural Independence in America* (New York: Viking, 1981); Warner Berthoff, *A Literature without Qualities: American Writing since 1945* (Berkeley: Univ. of California Press, 1979) and Jerome Klinkowitz, *Literary Disruptions: The Making of a Post-Contemporary American Fiction* (Urbana: Univ. of Illinois Press, 1975).

Critics I have admired on individual American writers include George W. Hunt on John Cheever and John Updike; Robert Solotaroff, Richard Poirier and Robert Begiebing on Norman Mailer; Katherine Usher Henderson on Joan Didion; G.F. Waller on Joyce Carol Oates; Edward P. Vargo on John Updike; R.G. Collins and Lynne Waldeland on John Cheever; and Robert A. Morace, Gregory Morris, and David Cowart on John Gardner.

Two recent books on Hawthorne which I have read but which came out too late to be used in this study are Gloria C. Erlich's *Family Themes and Hawthorne's Fiction: The Tenacious Web* (New Brunswick: Rutgers Univ. Press, 1984) and Philip Young's *Hawthorne's Secret: An Un-Told Tale* (Boston: David R. Godine Publisher, 1984). Both deal suggestively with incest in Hawthorne's ancestry and in his relationship with his sister Ebe.

INDEX

Abbott, Jack, 34
Absalom, Absalom! (Faulkner), 9, 15, 69, 72-74, 176, 179
Adams, Henry, 1; *Democracy,* 200; *The Education of Henry Adams,* 200
Advertisements for Myself (Mailer), 34
"Alice Doane's Appeal" (Hawthorne), 7-8, 9-12
alienation. *See* isolation
allegory: in Hawthorne, 2, 6-7, 9, 19, 20, 23, 87; romantic, 12-13, 14, 26, 46, 80, 129, 134-35, 136, 137, 138, 206; contradictions in, 16; Michael Bell on, 20; in Melville, 27; history of, 32; Christian sense of, 32; political, 35; gnostic, 39; of American character, 49; in Frederic, 60; method of, 67; O'Connor on, 85; sexual, 145; in Sixties, 203, 214. *See also* symbolism
ambiguity: Manichean, 31, 32, 90-91, 93, 96, 142, 180; and evil, 94; of fiction, 101, 182; and form, 185
An American Dream (Mailer). *See Moby Dick, An American Dream*
Ancient Evenings (Mailer), 9, 19, 23-24, 42-45
"Angel of the Bridge" (Cheever), 120
Angels of Light (Oates), 165, 170
Armies of the Night, The (Mailer), 26, 34, 200
Arnold, Matthew, 155
art, 121, 147, 151-52
"Art of Living, The" (Gardner), 150
Asals, Frederick, 86, 87
As I Lay Dying (Faulkner), 70
Assassins, The (Oates), 163, 164, 165, 170-71, 174, 176
Auschwitz, 93, 99

Ballad of the Sad Cafe, The (McCullers), 83
Balzac, Honoré de, 168
Barbary Shore (Mailer), 35
Barrett, William, 2, 25
Barth, John, 203, 205
Barthelme, Donald, 203, 205
Bell, Michael, 4, 20
Bellefleur (Oates), 9, 165, 171, 176-79, 209
Bellow, Saul, 148, 211
"Benito Cereno" (Melville), 24, 33
Bergson, Henri-Louis, 64
Bierce, Ambrose, 205
Black House, The (Theroux), 212
Blackmur, R.P., 216
Blithedale Romance, The (Hawthorne), 20, 32, 58, 100, 207; Manicheism in, 6, 7, 18; subversion in, 19; compared with *Barbary Shore,* 35; style of, 67; compared with Updike, 123, 124, 137
Bloom, Harold, 2
Book of Common Prayer, A (Didion), 184, 186, 191-97, 201
Bosquet, Alain, 23-24
Braudy, Leo, 39
Brodhead, Richard, 14
Brooks, Peter, 39
"Brothers, The" (Cheever), 108-9
Brothers Karamazov, The (Dostoevski), 174
Brown, Charles Brockden, 15
Bullet Park (Cheever), 113-14, 115, 119, 209, 210, 227

Cady, Edwin H., 46-47
Calvinism: in Hawthorne, 1, 85, 216; in Melville, 24, 25; in Faulkner, 69,